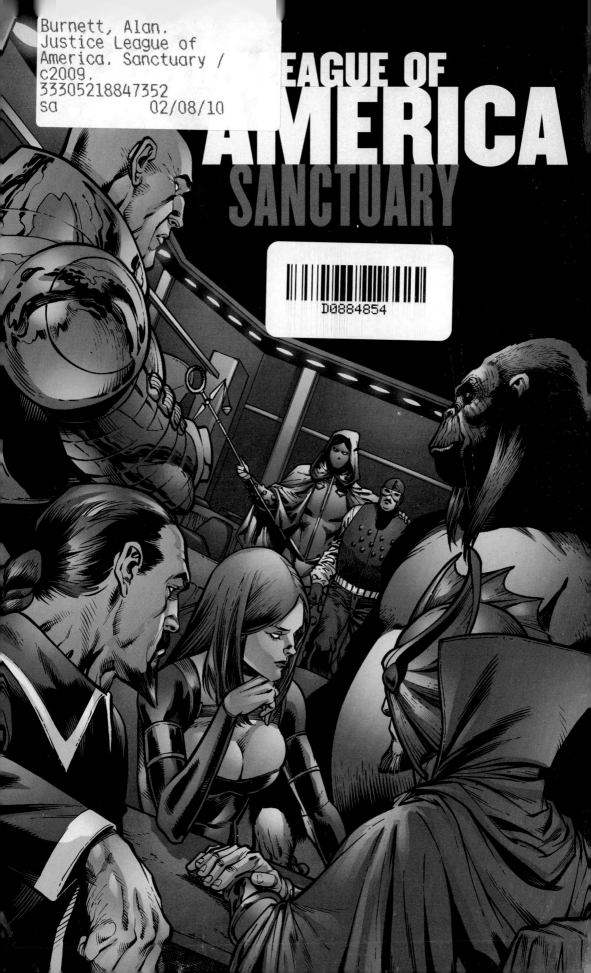

EAGUE OF
AMERICA
SANCTUARY

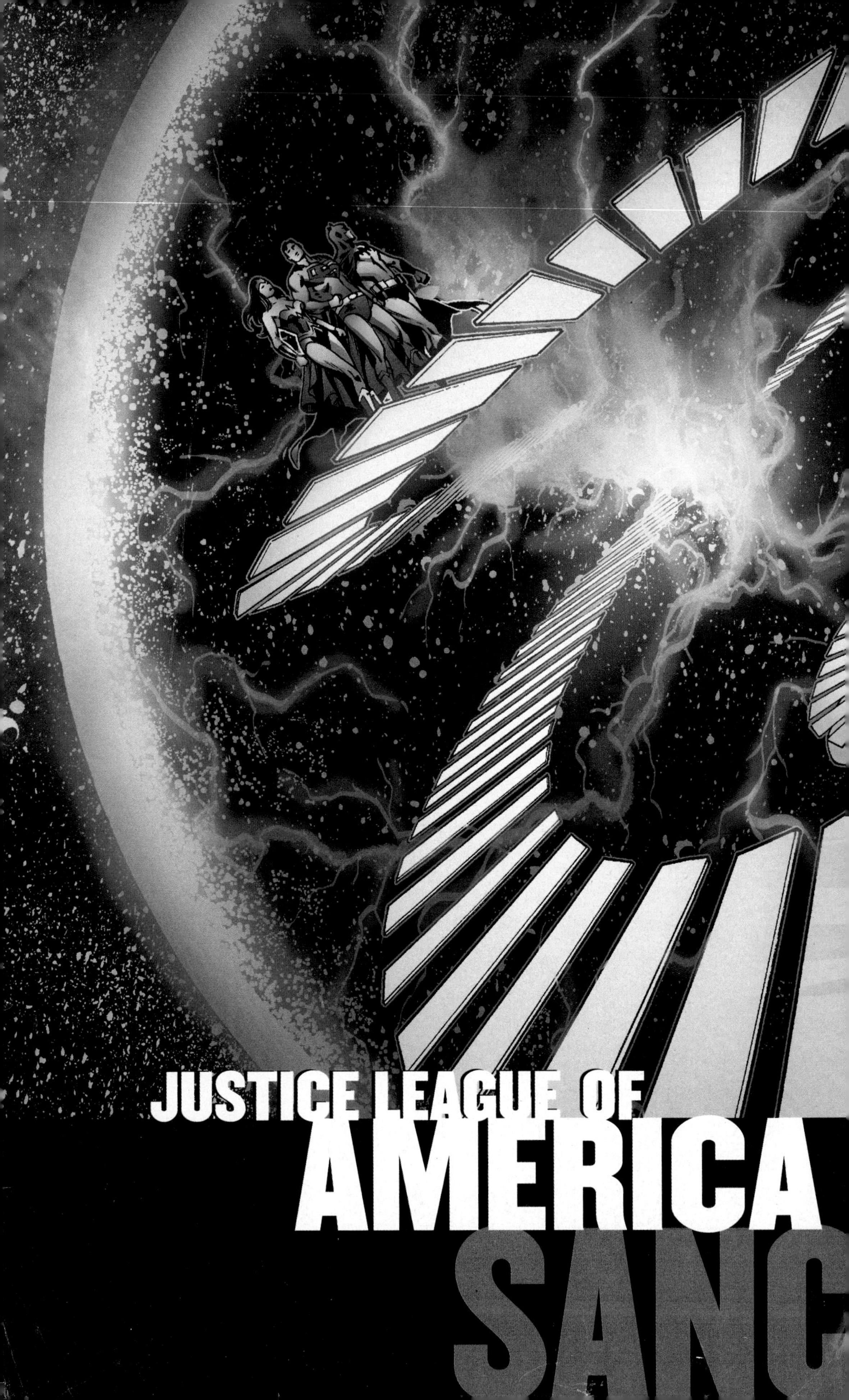
JUSTICE LEAGUE OF
AMERICA
SANC

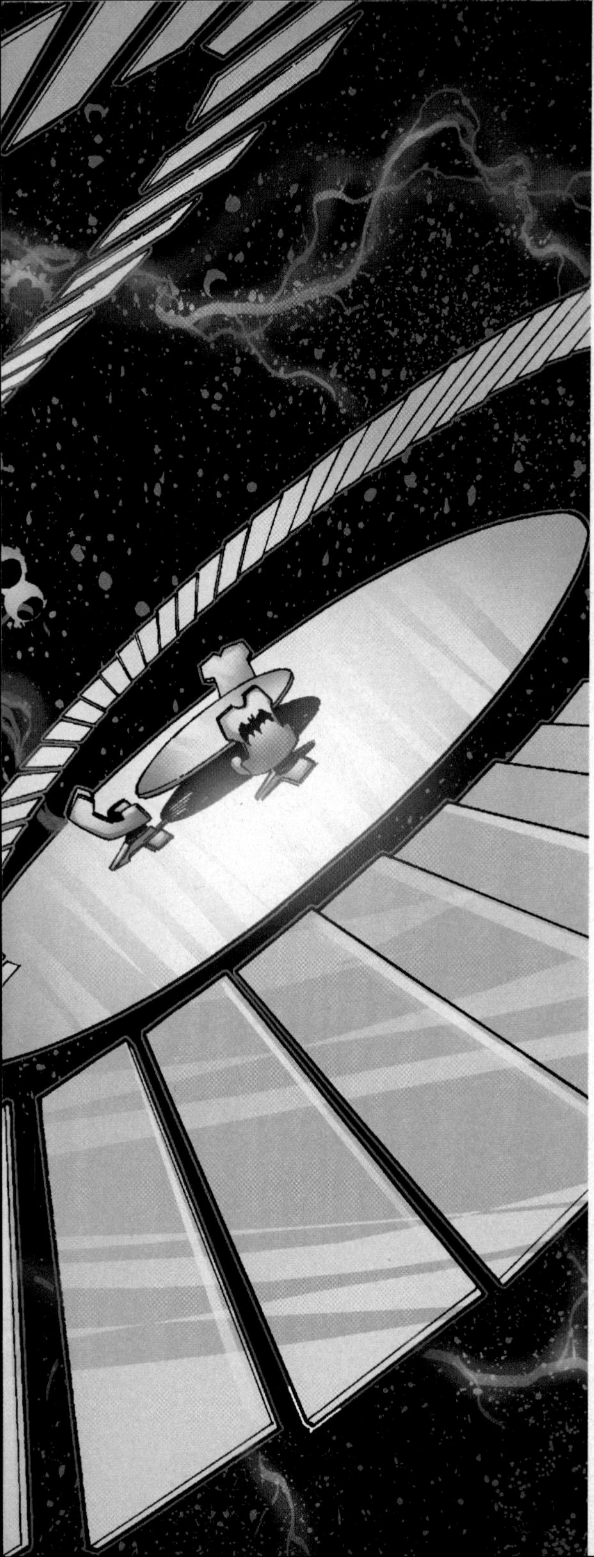

Sanctuary

Alan Burnett Writer
Ed Benes Penciller
Sandra Hope
Mariah Benes
Ed Benes
Ruy José Inkers

"Meanwhile, Back in the Kitchen..."

Dwayne McDuffie Writer
Jon Boy Meyers Penciller
Serge LaPointe Inker

"Meanwhile, Back at Owl Creek Bridge..."

Dwayne McDuffie Writer
Jon Boy Meyers Penciller
Mark Irwin Inker

Back Up to Speed

Dwayne McDuffie Writer
Ethan Van Sciver Artist

The Gathering Crisis

Dwayne McDuffie Writer
Carlos Pacheco Penciller
Jesus Merino Inker

Rob Leigh Letterer
Pete Pantazis
Rod Reis
Brian Miller (Hi-Fi) Colorists

TUARY

Dan DiDio Senior VP-Executive Editor
Eddie Berganza Editor-original series
Adam Schlagman Assistant Editor-original series
Sean Mackiewicz Editor-collected edition
Robbin Brosterman Senior Art Director
Paul Levitz President & Publisher
Georg Brewer VP-Design & DC Direct Creative
Richard Bruning Senior VP-Creative Director
Patrick Caldon Executive VP-Finance & Operations
Chris Caramalis VP-Finance
John Cunningham VP-Marketing
Terri Cunningham VP-Managing Editor
Amy Genkins Senior VP-Business & Legal Affairs
Alison Gill VP-Manufacturing
David Hyde VP-Publicity
Hank Kanalz VP-General Manager, WildStorm
Jim Lee Editorial Director-WildStorm
Gregory Noveck Senior VP-Creative Affairs
Sue Pohja VP-Book Trade Sales
Steve Rotterdam Senior VP-Sales & Marketing
Cheryl Rubin Senior VP-Brand Management
Alysse Soll VP-Advertising & Custom Publishing
Jeff Trojan VP-Business Development, DC Direct
Bob Wayne VP-Sales

Cover by **Ed Benes**
with **Alex Sinclair**

Justice League of America: Sanctuary

Published by DC Comics. Cover, text and compilation
Copyright © 2009 DC Comics. All Rights Reserved.

Originally published in single magazine form in
JUSTICE LEAGUE OF AMERICA 17-21. Copyright © 2008
DC Comics. All Rights Reserved. All characters, their
distinctive likenesses and related elements featured in this
publication are trademarks of DC Comics. The stories,
characters and incidents featured in this publication
are entirely fictional. DC Comics does not read or accept
unsolicited submissions of ideas, stories or artwork.

DC Comics, 1700 Broadway, New York, NY 10019
A Warner Bros. Entertainment Company
Printed in USA. First Printing.
HC ISBN: 978-1-4012-1992-5
SC ISBN: 978-1-4012-2010-5

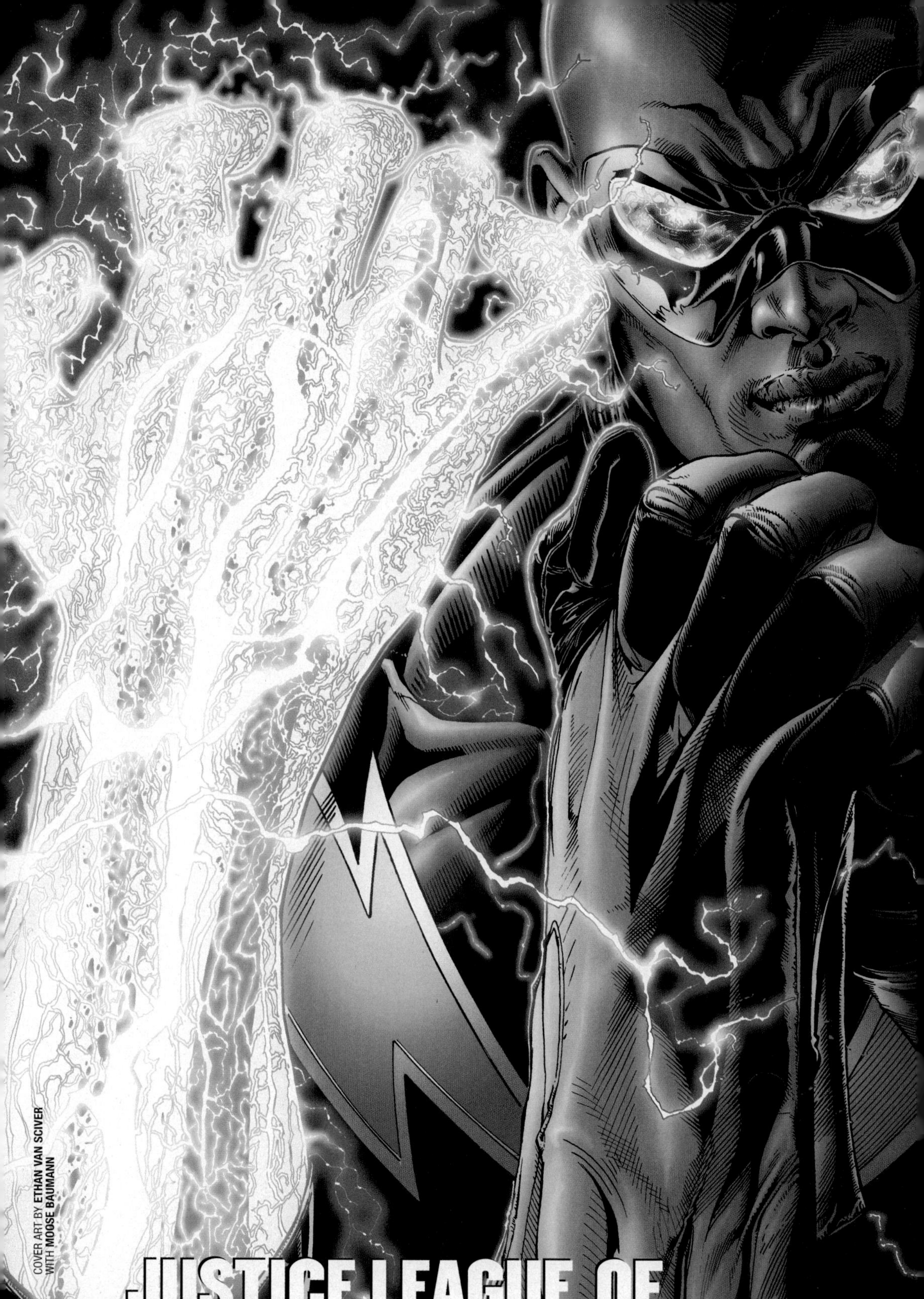
COVER ART BY ETHAN VAN SCIVER
WITH MOOSE BAUMANN

JUSTICE LEAGUE OF AMERICA

SANCTUARY PART ONE
"MEANWHILE, BACK IN THE KITCHEN..."

Sanctuary Part One

Alan Burnett
Writer

Ed Benes
Penciller

Sandra Hope
Mariah Benes
Ed Benes
Inkers

Rob Leigh
Letterer

Rod Reis
Colorist

"Meanwhile, Back in the Kitchen..."

Dwayne McDuffie
Writer

Jon Boy Meyers
Penciller

Serge LaPointe
Inker

Rob Leigh
Letterer

Pete Pantazis
Colorist

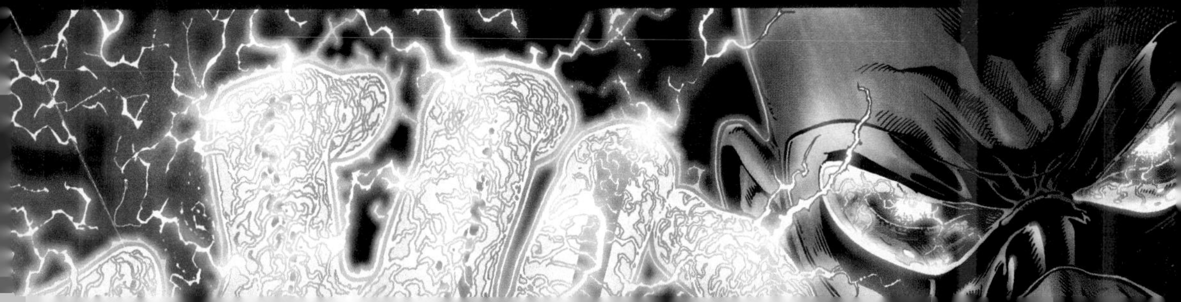

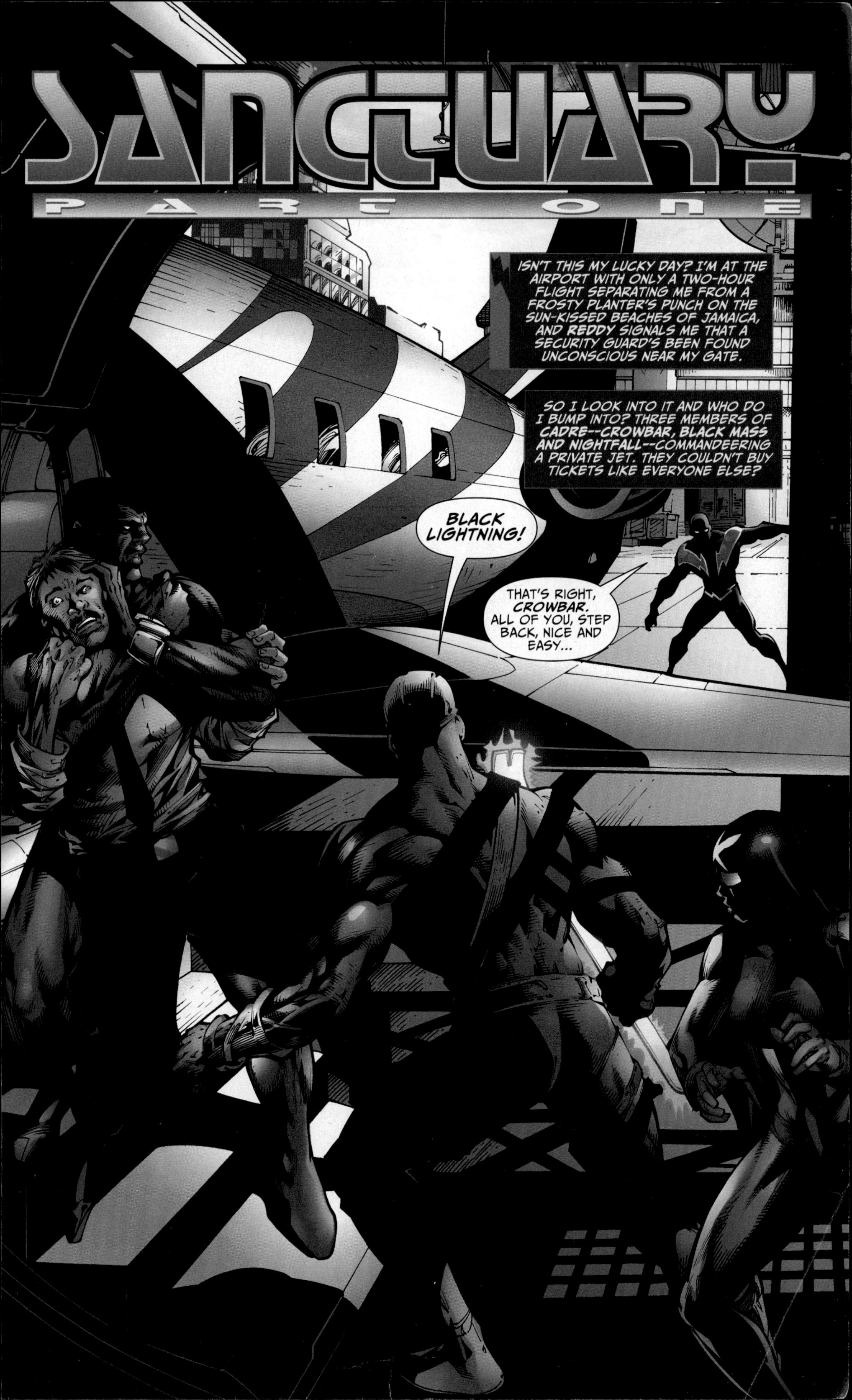
SANCTUARY
PART ONE
ISN'T THIS MY LUCKY DAY? I'M AT THE AIRPORT WITH ONLY A TWO-HOUR FLIGHT SEPARATING ME FROM A FROSTY PLANTER'S PUNCH ON THE SUN-KISSED BEACHES OF JAMAICA, AND REDDY SIGNALS ME THAT A SECURITY GUARD'S BEEN FOUND UNCONSCIOUS NEAR MY GATE.
SO I LOOK INTO IT AND WHO DO I BUMP INTO? THREE MEMBERS OF CADRE--CROWBAR, BLACK MASS AND NIGHTFALL--COMMANDEERING A PRIVATE JET. THEY COULDN'T BUY TICKETS LIKE EVERYONE ELSE?
BLACK LIGHTNING!
THAT'S RIGHT, CROWBAR. ALL OF YOU, STEP BACK, NICE AND EASY...

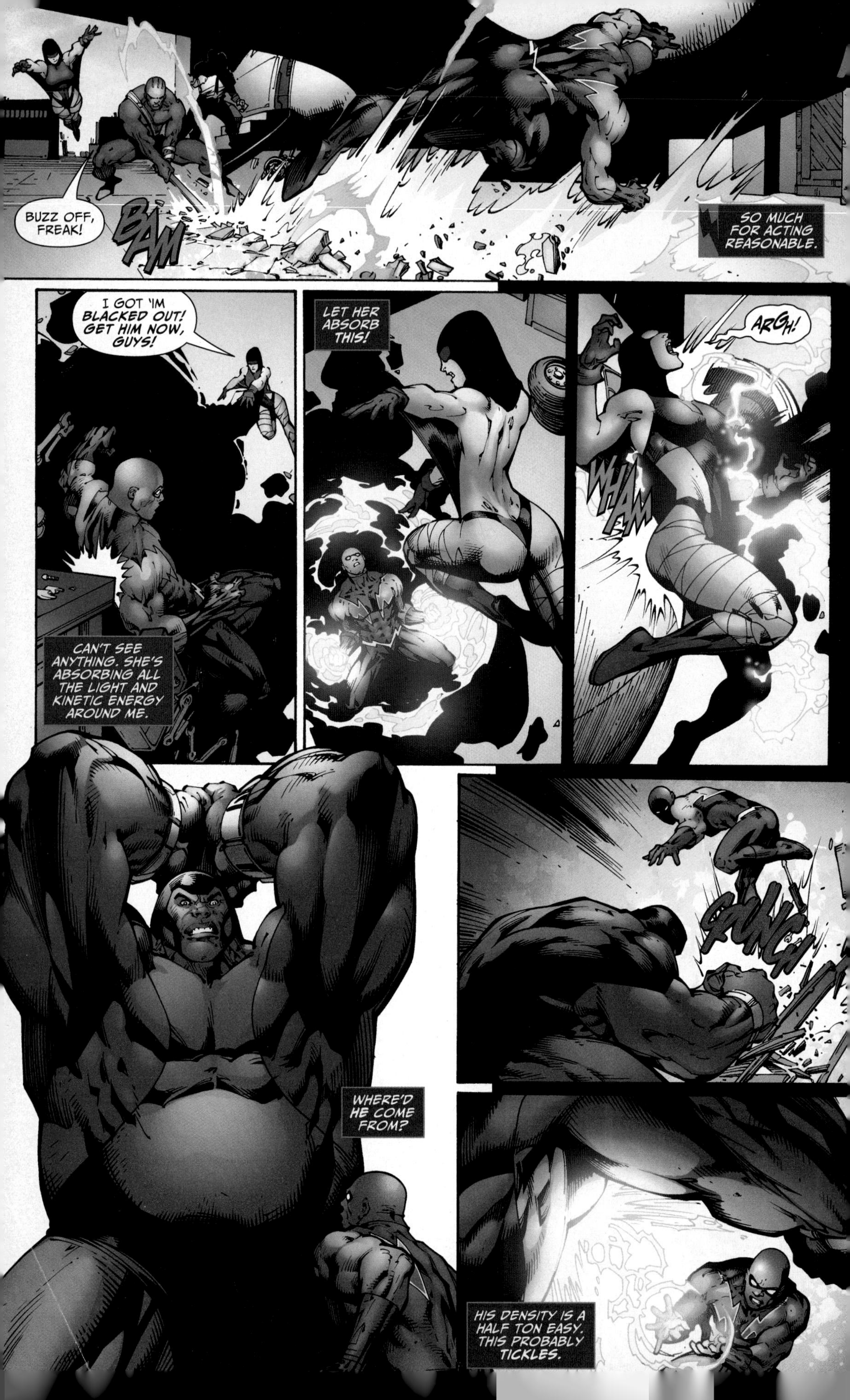
BUZZ OFF, FREAK!
BAM
SO MUCH FOR ACTING REASONABLE.
I GOT 'IM BLACKED OUT! GET HIM NOW, GUYS!
CAN'T SEE ANYTHING. SHE'S ABSORBING ALL THE LIGHT AND KINETIC ENERGY AROUND ME.
LET HER ABSORB THIS!
ARGH!
WHAM
SPUNCH
WHERE'D HE COME FROM?
HIS DENSITY IS A HALF TON EASY. THIS PROBABLY TICKLES.

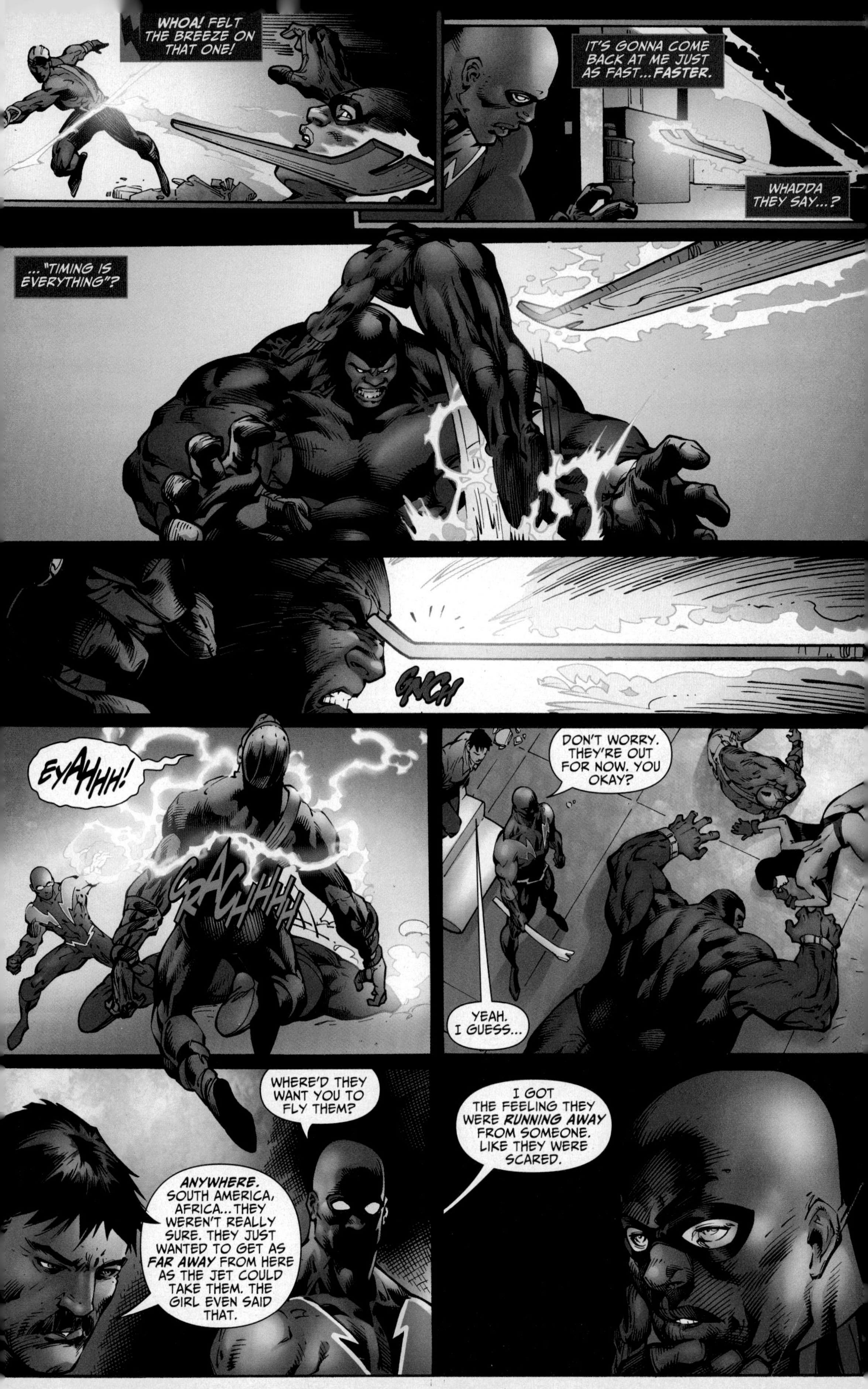
WHOA! FELT THE BREEZE ON THAT ONE!
IT'S GONNA COME BACK AT ME JUST AS FAST... FASTER.
WHADDA THEY SAY...?
..."TIMING IS EVERYTHING"?
GNCH
EyAHHH!
GRACHHHH
DON'T WORRY. THEY'RE OUT FOR NOW. YOU OKAY?
YEAH. I GUESS...
WHERE'D THEY WANT YOU TO FLY THEM?
ANYWHERE. SOUTH AMERICA, AFRICA... THEY WEREN'T REALLY SURE. THEY JUST WANTED TO GET AS FAR AWAY FROM HERE AS THE JET COULD TAKE THEM. THE GIRL EVEN SAID THAT.
I GOT THE FEELING THEY WERE RUNNING AWAY FROM SOMEONE. LIKE THEY WERE SCARED.

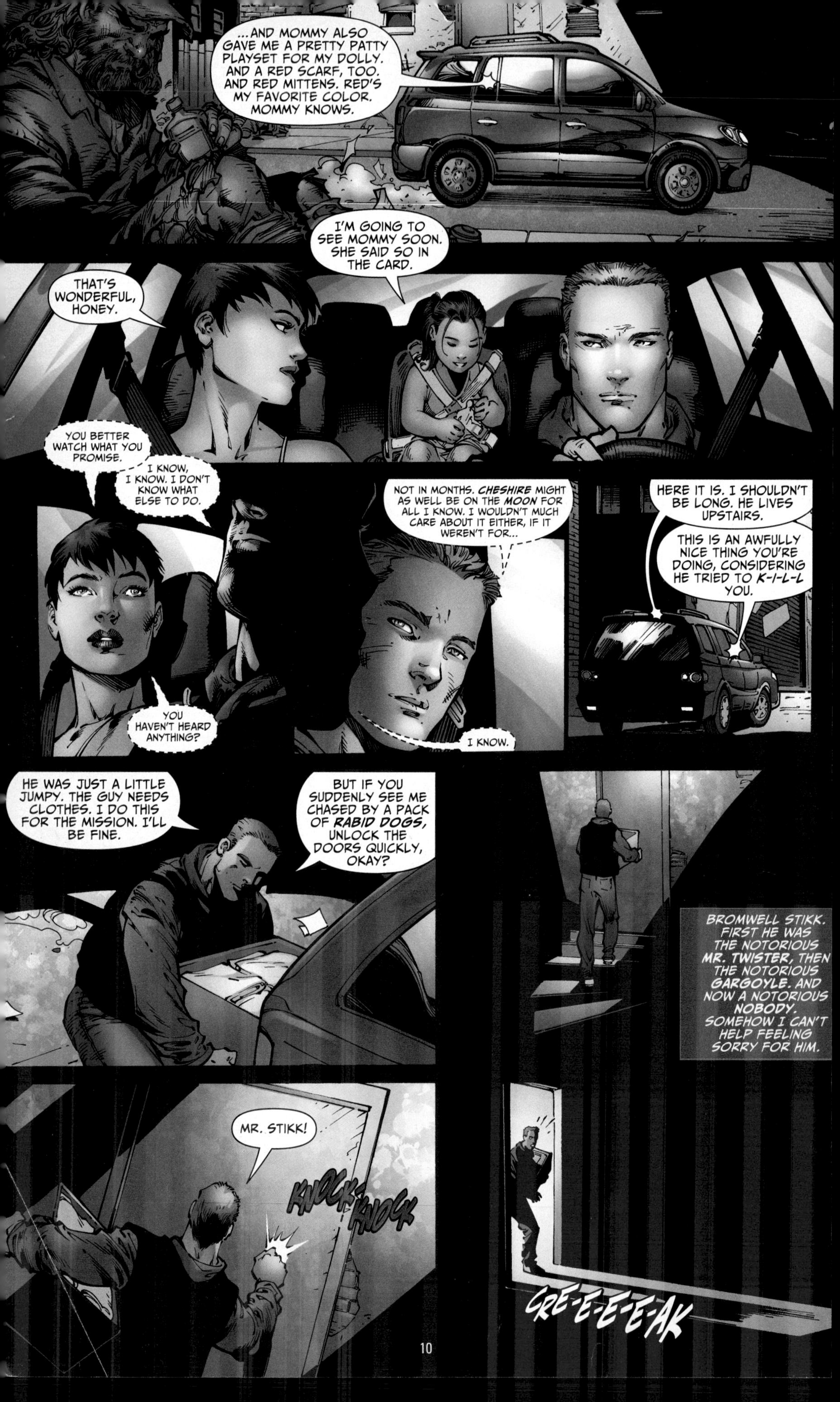

...AND MOMMY ALSO GAVE ME A PRETTY PATTY PLAYSET FOR MY DOLLY. AND A RED SCARF, TOO. AND RED MITTENS. RED'S MY FAVORITE COLOR. MOMMY KNOWS.
I'M GOING TO SEE MOMMY SOON. SHE SAID SO IN THE CARD.
THAT'S WONDERFUL, HONEY.
YOU BETTER WATCH WHAT YOU PROMISE.
I KNOW, I KNOW. I DON'T KNOW WHAT ELSE TO DO.
YOU HAVEN'T HEARD ANYTHING?
NOT IN MONTHS. CHESHIRE MIGHT AS WELL BE ON THE MOON FOR ALL I KNOW. I WOULDN'T MUCH CARE ABOUT IT EITHER, IF IT WEREN'T FOR...
I KNOW.
HERE IT IS. I SHOULDN'T BE LONG. HE LIVES UPSTAIRS.
THIS IS AN AWFULLY NICE THING YOU'RE DOING, CONSIDERING HE TRIED TO K-I-L-L YOU.
HE WAS JUST A LITTLE JUMPY. THE GUY NEEDS CLOTHES. I DO THIS FOR THE MISSION. I'LL BE FINE.
BUT IF YOU SUDDENLY SEE ME CHASED BY A PACK OF RABID DOGS, UNLOCK THE DOORS QUICKLY, OKAY?
BROMWELL STIKK. FIRST HE WAS THE NOTORIOUS MR. TWISTER, THEN THE NOTORIOUS GARGOYLE. AND NOW A NOTORIOUS NOBODY. SOMEHOW I CAN'T HELP FEELING SORRY FOR HIM.
MR. STIKK!
KNOCK-KNOCK
CRE-E-E-E-AK

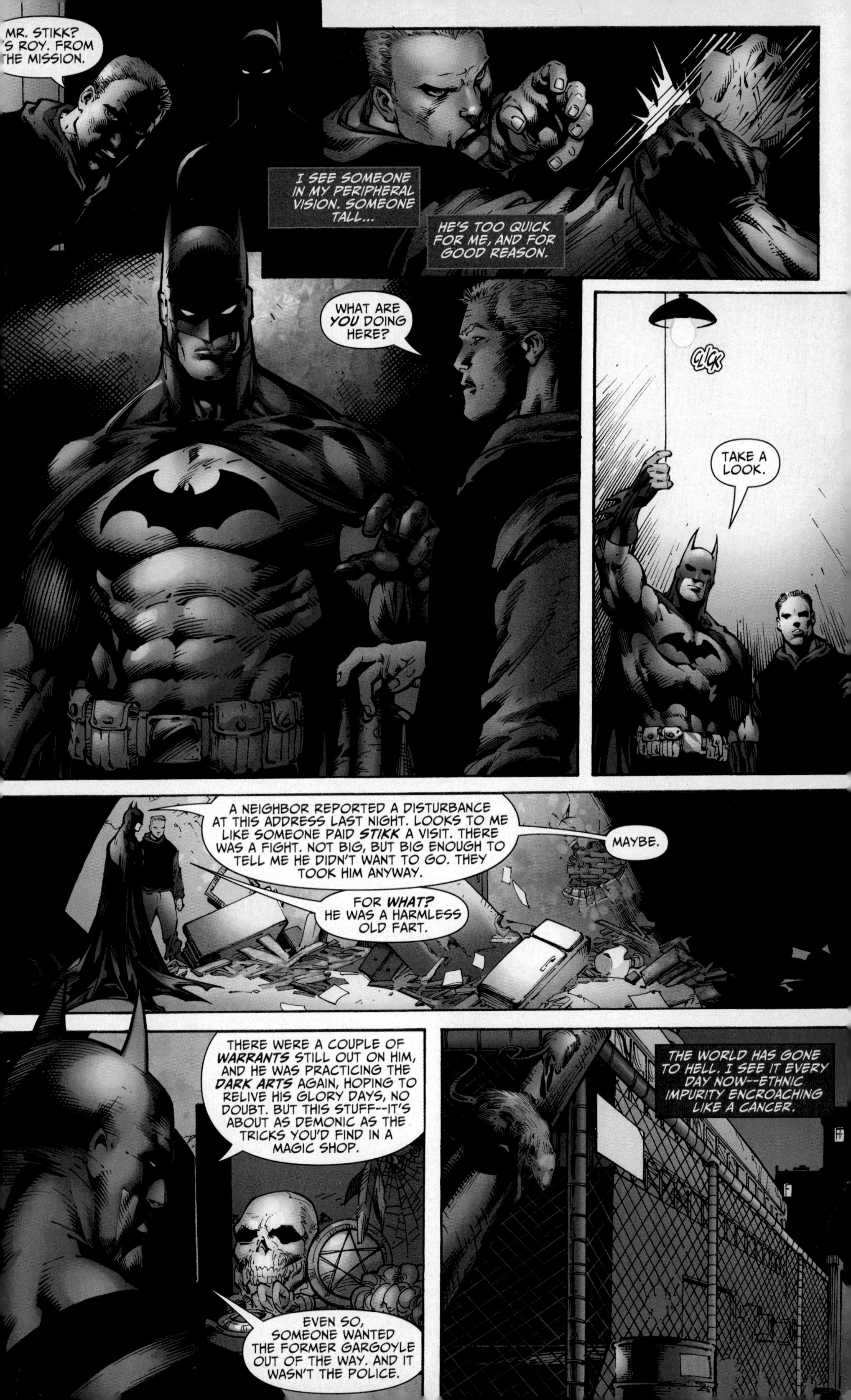
MR. STIKK? 'S ROY. FROM THE MISSION.
I SEE SOMEONE IN MY PERIPHERAL VISION. SOMEONE TALL...
HE'S TOO QUICK FOR ME, AND FOR GOOD REASON.
WHAT ARE YOU DOING HERE?
CLICK
TAKE A LOOK.
A NEIGHBOR REPORTED A DISTURBANCE AT THIS ADDRESS LAST NIGHT. LOOKS TO ME LIKE SOMEONE PAID STIKK A VISIT. THERE WAS A FIGHT. NOT BIG, BUT BIG ENOUGH TO TELL ME HE DIDN'T WANT TO GO. THEY TOOK HIM ANYWAY.
MAYBE.
FOR WHAT? HE WAS A HARMLESS OLD FART.
THERE WERE A COUPLE OF WARRANTS STILL OUT ON HIM, AND HE WAS PRACTICING THE DARK ARTS AGAIN, HOPING TO RELIVE HIS GLORY DAYS, NO DOUBT. BUT THIS STUFF--IT'S ABOUT AS DEMONIC AS THE TRICKS YOU'D FIND IN A MAGIC SHOP.
EVEN SO, SOMEONE WANTED THE FORMER GARGOYLE OUT OF THE WAY. AND IT WASN'T THE POLICE.
THE WORLD HAS GONE TO HELL. I SEE IT EVERY DAY NOW--ETHNIC IMPURITY ENCROACHING LIKE A CANCER.

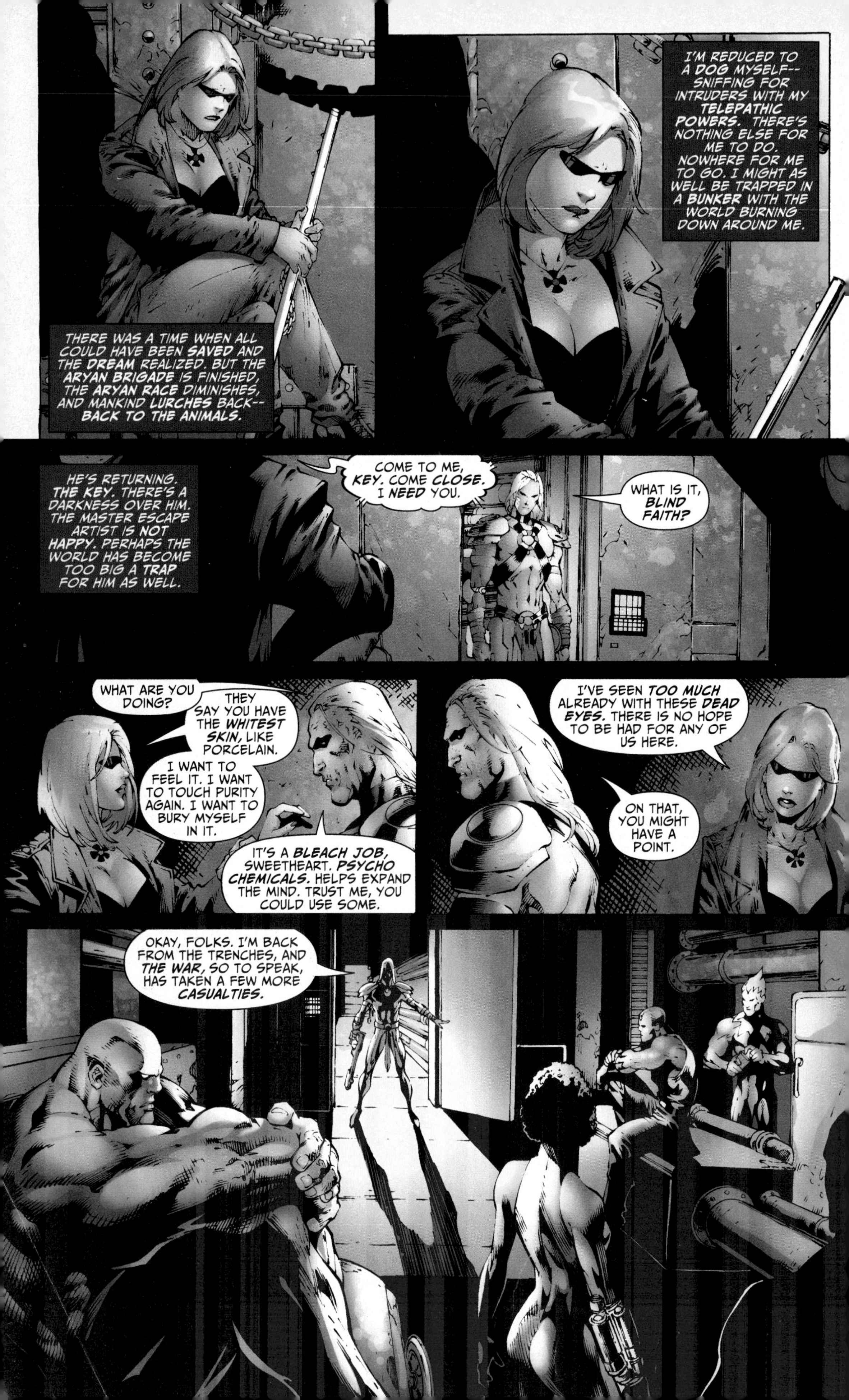
THERE WAS A TIME WHEN ALL COULD HAVE BEEN SAVED AND THE DREAM REALIZED. BUT THE ARYAN BRIGADE IS FINISHED, THE ARYAN RACE DIMINISHES, AND MANKIND LURCHES BACK-- BACK TO THE ANIMALS.
I'M REDUCED TO A DOG MYSELF-- SNIFFING FOR INTRUDERS WITH MY TELEPATHIC POWERS. THERE'S NOTHING ELSE FOR ME TO DO. NOWHERE FOR ME TO GO. I MIGHT AS WELL BE TRAPPED IN A BUNKER WITH THE WORLD BURNING DOWN AROUND ME.
HE'S RETURNING. THE KEY. THERE'S A DARKNESS OVER HIM. THE MASTER ESCAPE ARTIST IS NOT HAPPY. PERHAPS THE WORLD HAS BECOME TOO BIG A TRAP FOR HIM AS WELL.
COME TO ME, KEY. COME CLOSE. I NEED YOU.
WHAT IS IT, BLIND FAITH?
WHAT ARE YOU DOING?
THEY SAY YOU HAVE THE WHITEST SKIN, LIKE PORCELAIN.
I WANT TO FEEL IT. I WANT TO TOUCH PURITY AGAIN. I WANT TO BURY MYSELF IN IT.
IT'S A BLEACH JOB, SWEETHEART. PSYCHO CHEMICALS. HELPS EXPAND THE MIND. TRUST ME, YOU COULD USE SOME.
I'VE SEEN TOO MUCH ALREADY WITH THESE DEAD EYES. THERE IS NO HOPE TO BE HAD FOR ANY OF US HERE.
ON THAT, YOU MIGHT HAVE A POINT.
OKAY, FOLKS. I'M BACK FROM THE TRENCHES, AND THE WAR, SO TO SPEAK, HAS TAKEN A FEW MORE CASUALTIES.

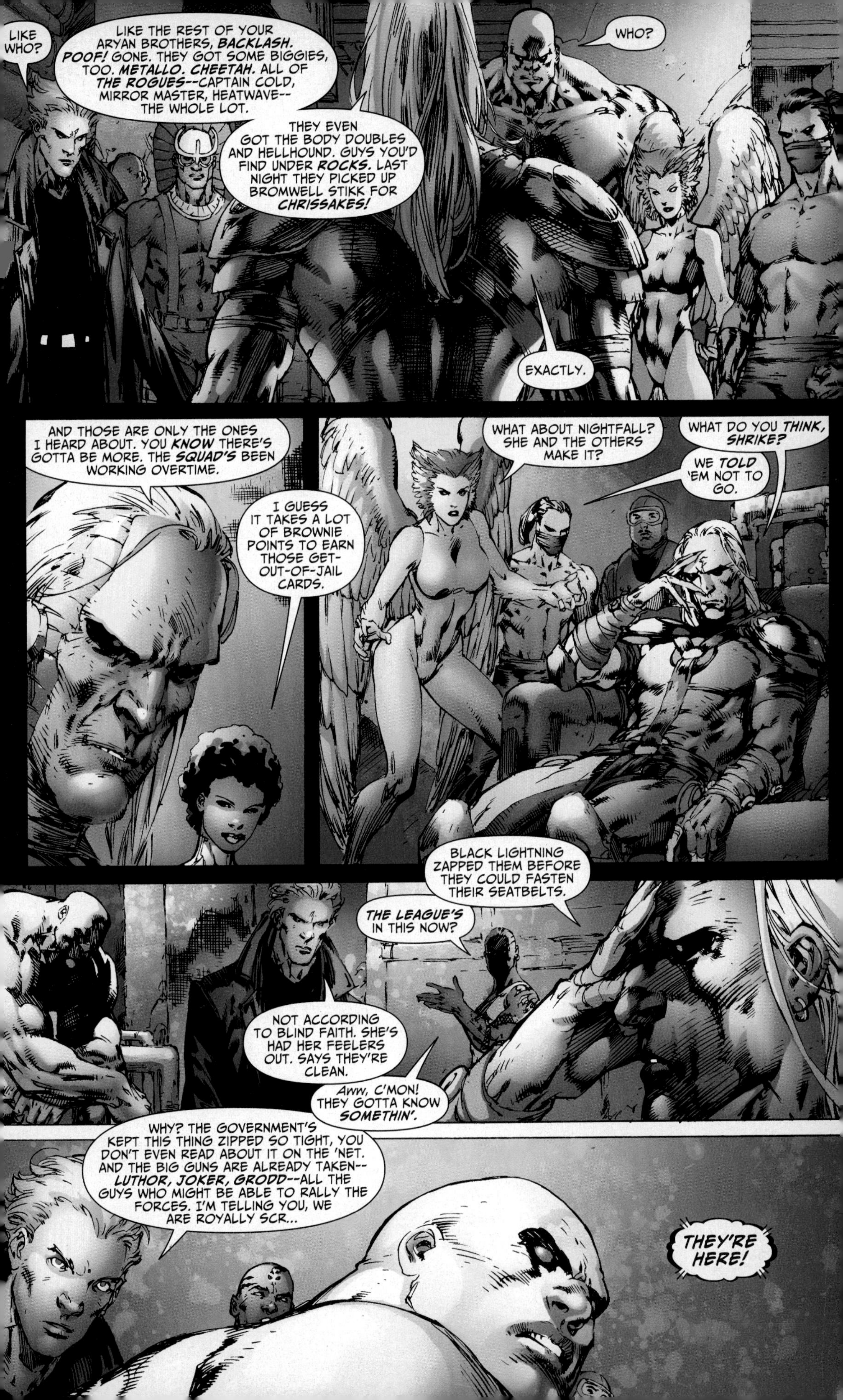
LIKE THE REST OF YOUR ARYAN BROTHERS, BACKLASH. POOF! GONE. THEY GOT SOME BIGGIES, TOO. METALLO. CHEETAH. ALL OF THE ROGUES--CAPTAIN COLD, MIRROR MASTER, HEATWAVE--THE WHOLE LOT.
LIKE WHO?
THEY EVEN GOT THE BODY DOUBLES AND HELLHOUND. GUYS YOU'D FIND UNDER ROCKS. LAST NIGHT THEY PICKED UP BROMWELL STIKK FOR CHRISSAKES!
WHO?
EXACTLY.
AND THOSE ARE ONLY THE ONES I HEARD ABOUT. YOU KNOW THERE'S GOTTA BE MORE. THE SQUAD'S BEEN WORKING OVERTIME.
I GUESS IT TAKES A LOT OF BROWNIE POINTS TO EARN THOSE GET-OUT-OF-JAIL CARDS.
WHAT ABOUT NIGHTFALL? SHE AND THE OTHERS MAKE IT?
WHAT DO YOU THINK, SHRIKE?
WE TOLD 'EM NOT TO GO.
BLACK LIGHTNING ZAPPED THEM BEFORE THEY COULD FASTEN THEIR SEATBELTS.
THE LEAGUE'S IN THIS NOW?
NOT ACCORDING TO BLIND FAITH. SHE'S HAD HER FEELERS OUT. SAYS THEY'RE CLEAN.
Aww, C'MON! THEY GOTTA KNOW SOMETHIN'.
WHY? THE GOVERNMENT'S KEPT THIS THING ZIPPED SO TIGHT, YOU DON'T EVEN READ ABOUT IT ON THE 'NET. AND THE BIG GUNS ARE ALREADY TAKEN--LUTHOR, JOKER, GRODD--ALL THE GUYS WHO MIGHT BE ABLE TO RALLY THE FORCES. I'M TELLING YOU, WE ARE ROYALLY SCR...
THEY'RE HERE!

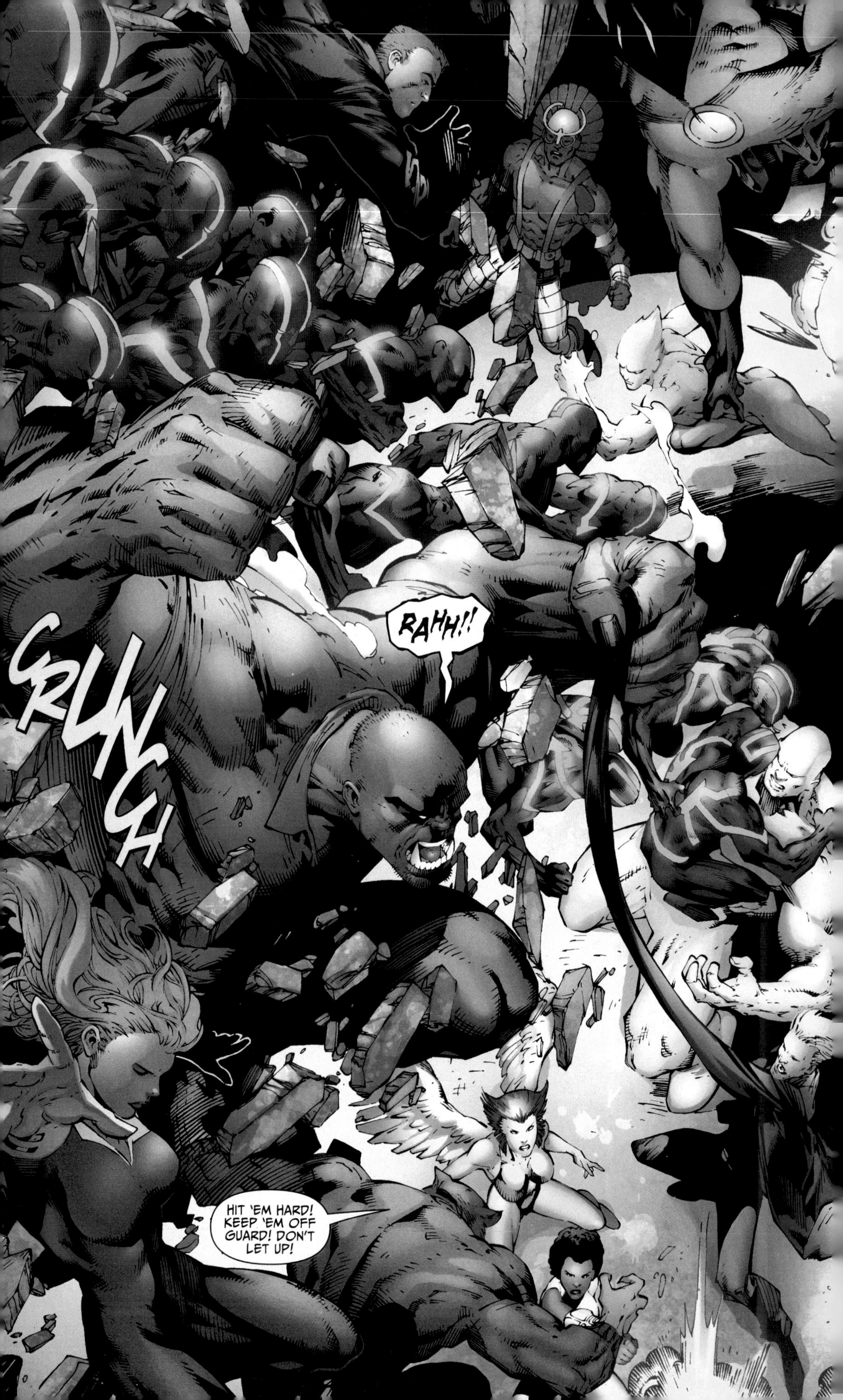
RAHH!!
CRUNCH
HIT 'EM HARD! KEEP 'EM OFF GUARD! DON'T LET UP!

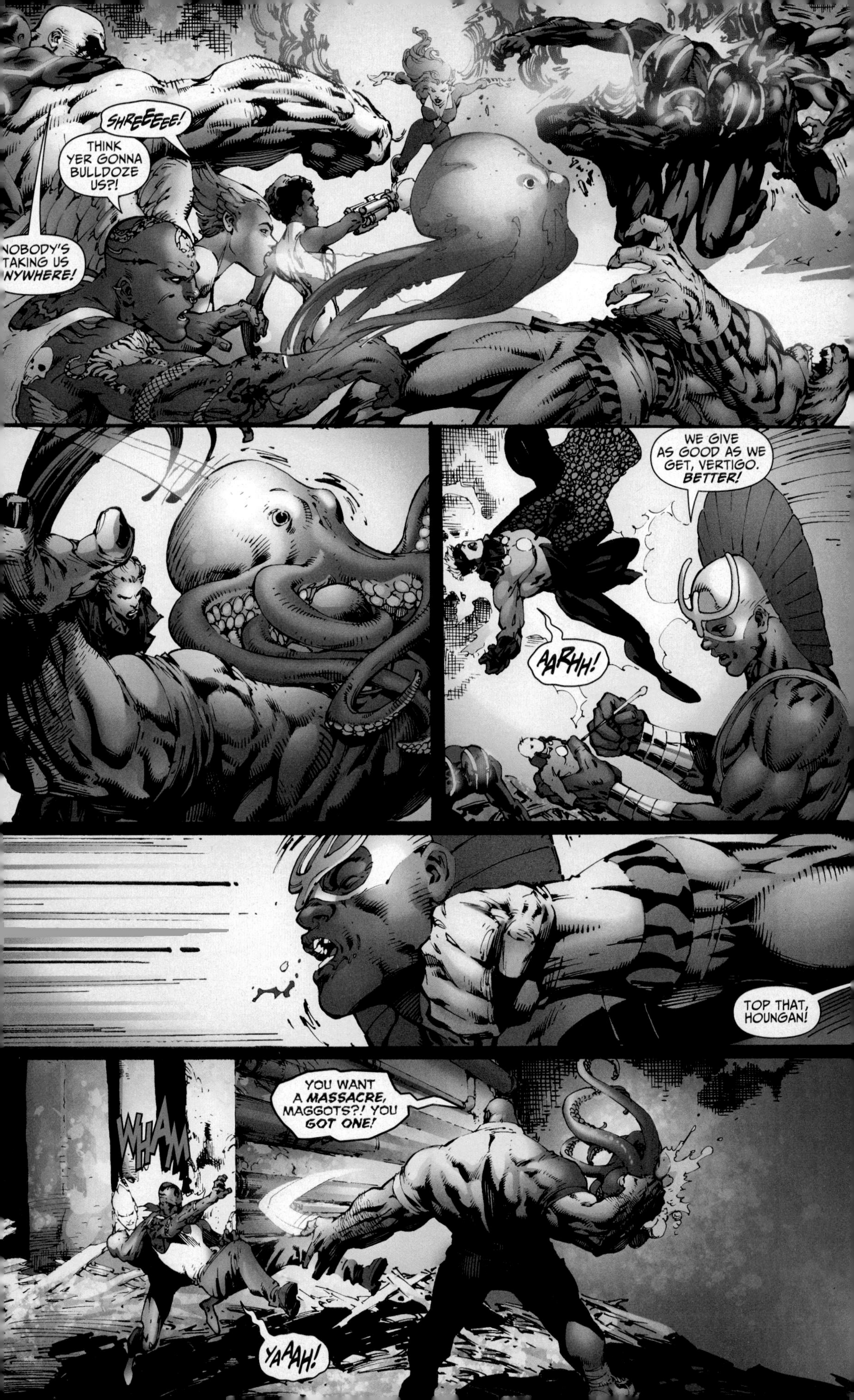
SHREEEEEE!
THINK YER GONNA BULLDOZE US?!
NOBODY'S TAKING US ANYWHERE!
WE GIVE AS GOOD AS WE GET, VERTIGO. BETTER!
AARHH!
TOP THAT, HOUNGAN!
WHAM
YOU WANT A MASSACRE, MAGGOTS?! YOU GOT ONE!
YAAAH!

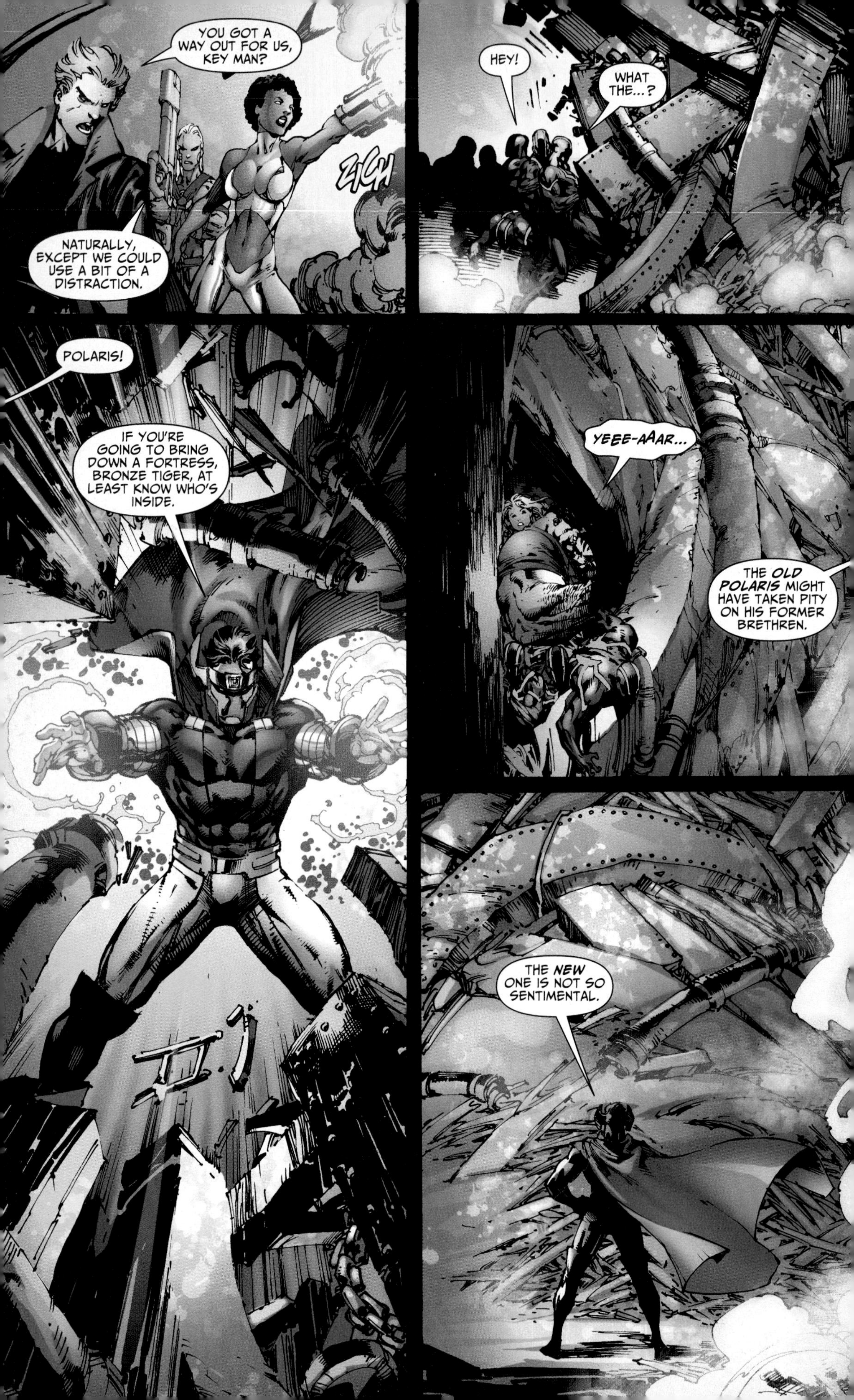
YOU GOT A WAY OUT FOR US, KEY MAN?
NATURALLY, EXCEPT WE COULD USE A BIT OF A DISTRACTION.
ZZCH
HEY!
WHAT THE...?
POLARIS!
IF YOU'RE GOING TO BRING DOWN A FORTRESS, BRONZE TIGER, AT LEAST KNOW WHO'S INSIDE.
YEEE-AAAR...
THE OLD POLARIS MIGHT HAVE TAKEN PITY ON HIS FORMER BRETHREN.
THE NEW ONE IS NOT SO SENTIMENTAL.

KRAAAAACH

RAAAARR!

EVERYONE'S LEFT! WE'VE GOT CHASE AFTER THEM.

YOU WON'T FIND THEM OUTSIDE. THE KEY HAD AN ESCAPE PLAN. BY THE TIME WE FIND OUT HOW HE DID IT, THEY'LL BE HALF A WORLD AWAY.

NOT ALL OF 'EM.

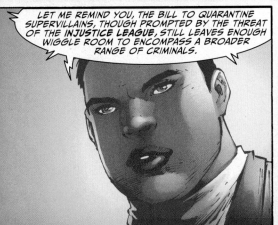

WE GOT "TOOTHLESS" HERE...

...AND POLLYANNA.

OH, YEAH. TWO OUT OF ELEVEN. THE WALL'S GONNA BE THRILLED.

LET ME REMIND YOU, THE BILL TO QUARANTINE SUPERVILLAINS, THOUGH PROMPTED BY THE THREAT OF THE INJUSTICE LEAGUE, STILL LEAVES ENOUGH WIGGLE ROOM TO ENCOMPASS A BROADER RANGE OF CRIMINALS.

SO YOU HAVE BEEN COLLECTING OTHER SUPERVILLAINS.

I DIDN'T SAY THAT.

WELL, HAVE YOU?

IF WE HAVE, IT WOULD CERTAINLY BE WITHIN THE LETTER AS WELL AS THE SPIRIT OF THE LAW.

AND YOU STILL REFUSE TO IDENTIFY THE PRISON PLANET?

MY DEAR DARK KNIGHT, YOU KNOW AS WELL AS I THAT I CAN'T DIVULGE THAT INFORMATION, NO MORE THAN I CAN PROVIDE A MAP OF C.I.A. SAFE HOUSES. ALL I CAN TELL YOU IS THAT EVERY MOVE WE MAKE IS PERFECTLY LEGAL.

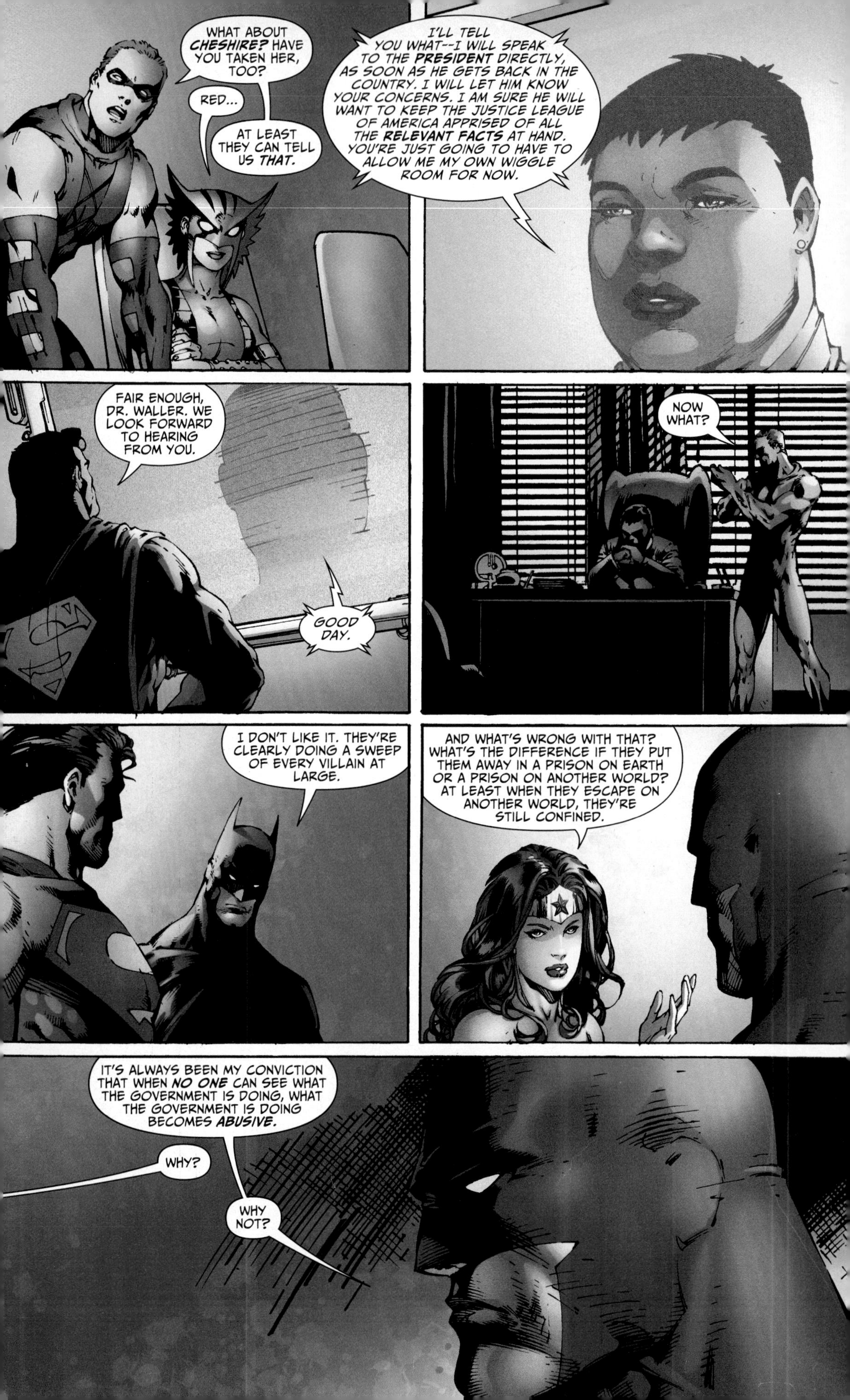
WHAT ABOUT CHESHIRE? HAVE YOU TAKEN HER, TOO?
RED...
AT LEAST THEY CAN TELL US THAT.
I'LL TELL YOU WHAT--I WILL SPEAK TO THE PRESIDENT DIRECTLY, AS SOON AS HE GETS BACK IN THE COUNTRY. I WILL LET HIM KNOW YOUR CONCERNS. I AM SURE HE WILL WANT TO KEEP THE JUSTICE LEAGUE OF AMERICA APPRISED OF ALL THE RELEVANT FACTS AT HAND. YOU'RE JUST GOING TO HAVE TO ALLOW ME MY OWN WIGGLE ROOM FOR NOW.
FAIR ENOUGH, DR. WALLER. WE LOOK FORWARD TO HEARING FROM YOU.
GOOD DAY.
NOW WHAT?
I DON'T LIKE IT. THEY'RE CLEARLY DOING A SWEEP OF EVERY VILLAIN AT LARGE.
AND WHAT'S WRONG WITH THAT? WHAT'S THE DIFFERENCE IF THEY PUT THEM AWAY IN A PRISON ON EARTH OR A PRISON ON ANOTHER WORLD? AT LEAST WHEN THEY ESCAPE ON ANOTHER WORLD, THEY'RE STILL CONFINED.
IT'S ALWAYS BEEN MY CONVICTION THAT WHEN NO ONE CAN SEE WHAT THE GOVERNMENT IS DOING, WHAT THE GOVERNMENT IS DOING BECOMES ABUSIVE.
WHY?
WHY NOT?

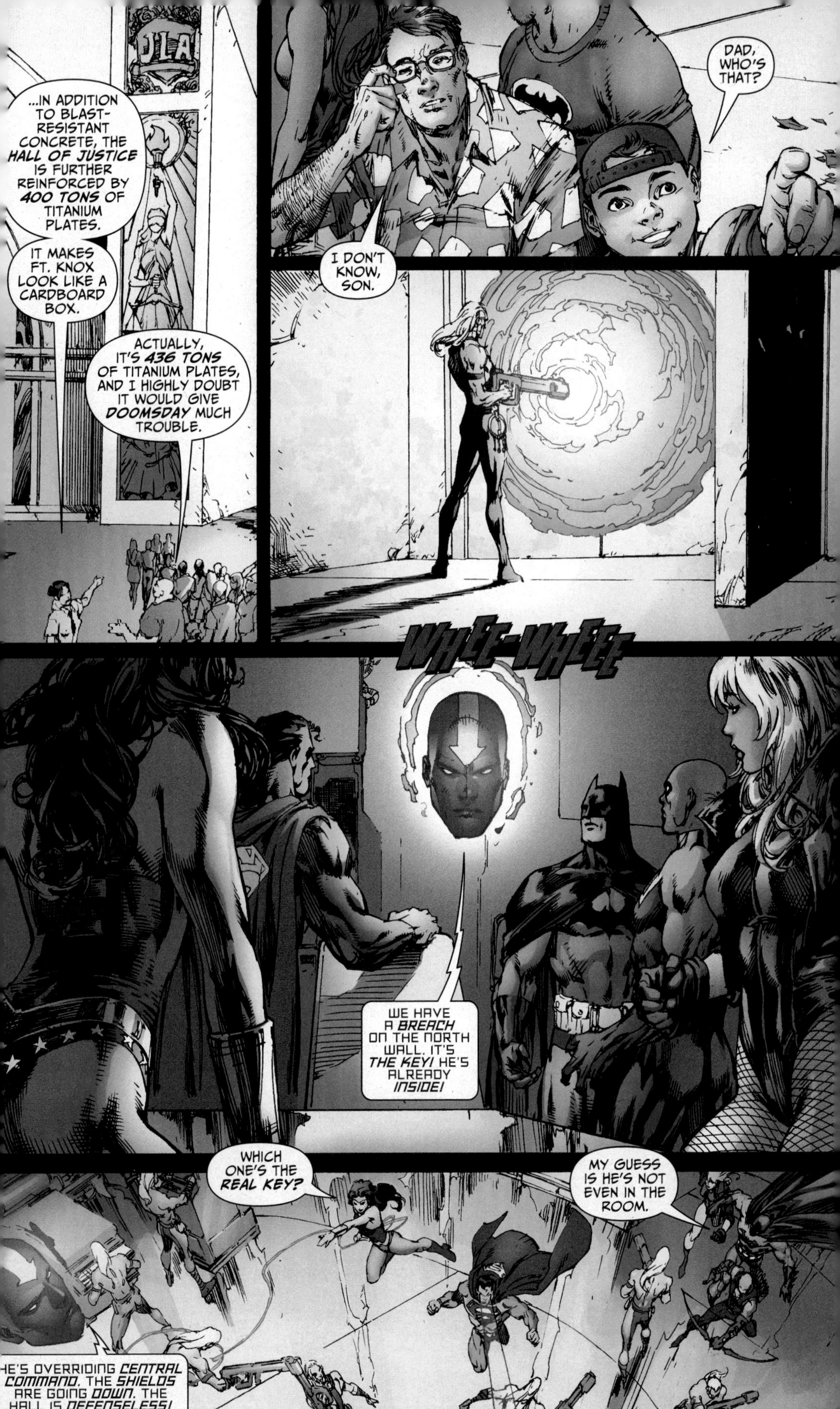

...IN ADDITION TO BLAST-RESISTANT CONCRETE, THE HALL OF JUSTICE IS FURTHER REINFORCED BY 400 TONS OF TITANIUM PLATES.
IT MAKES FT. KNOX LOOK LIKE A CARDBOARD BOX.
ACTUALLY, IT'S 436 TONS OF TITANIUM PLATES, AND I HIGHLY DOUBT IT WOULD GIVE DOOMSDAY MUCH TROUBLE.
DAD, WHO'S THAT?
I DON'T KNOW, SON.
WHEE-WHEEE
WE HAVE A BREACH ON THE NORTH WALL. IT'S THE KEY! HE'S ALREADY INSIDE!
WHICH ONE'S THE REAL KEY?
MY GUESS IS HE'S NOT EVEN IN THE ROOM.
HE'S OVERRIDING CENTRAL COMMAND. THE SHIELDS ARE GOING DOWN. THE HALL IS DEFENSELESS! I'VE LOST CONTR...

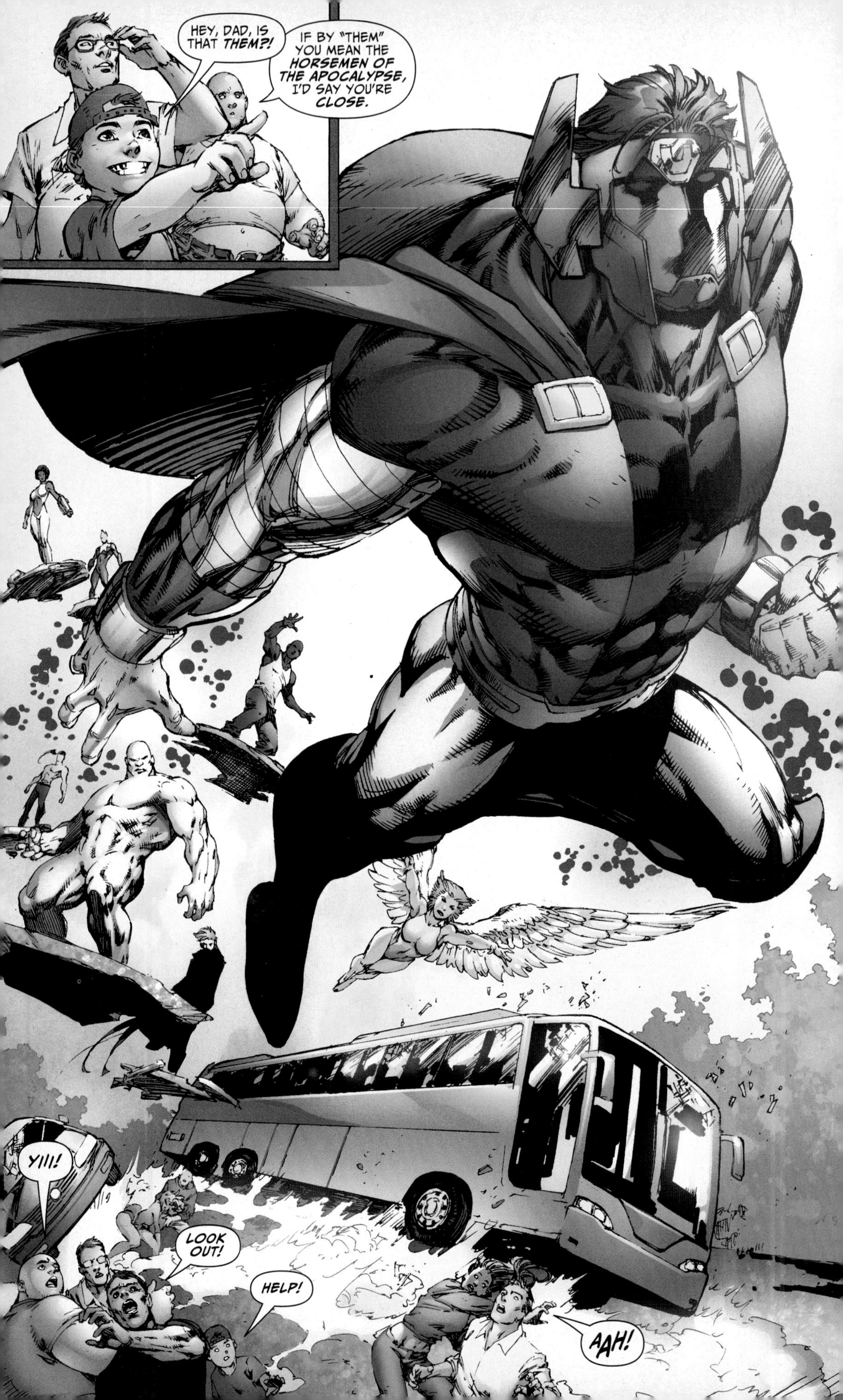
HEY, DAD, IS THAT THEM?!
IF BY "THEM" YOU MEAN THE HORSEMEN OF THE APOCALYPSE, I'D SAY YOU'RE CLOSE.
YIII!
LOOK OUT!
HELP!
AAH!

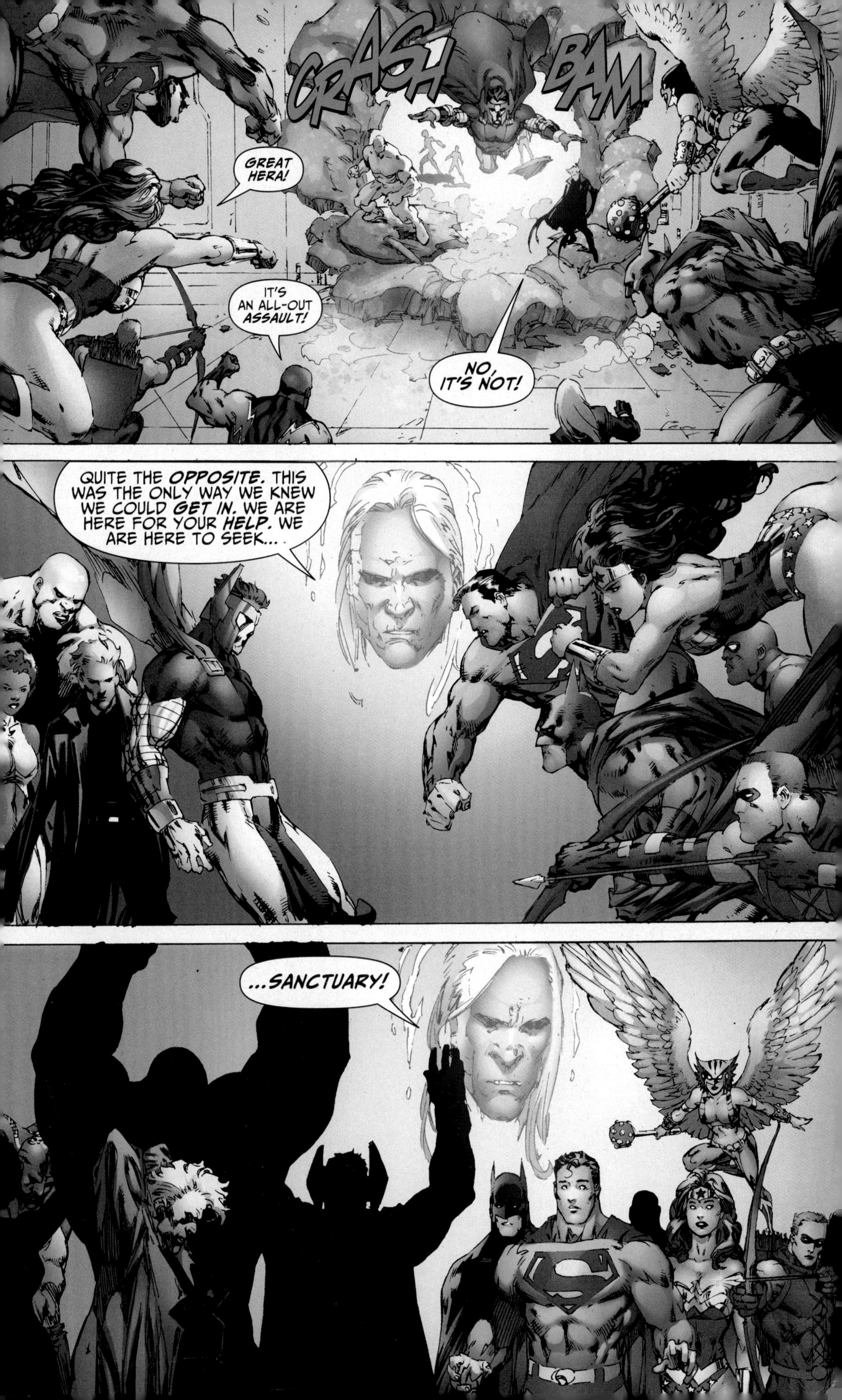
CRASH
BAM
GREAT HERA!
IT'S AN ALL-OUT ASSAULT!
NO, IT'S NOT!
QUITE THE OPPOSITE. THIS WAS THE ONLY WAY WE KNEW WE COULD GET IN. WE ARE HERE FOR YOUR HELP. WE ARE HERE TO SEEK...
...SANCTUARY!

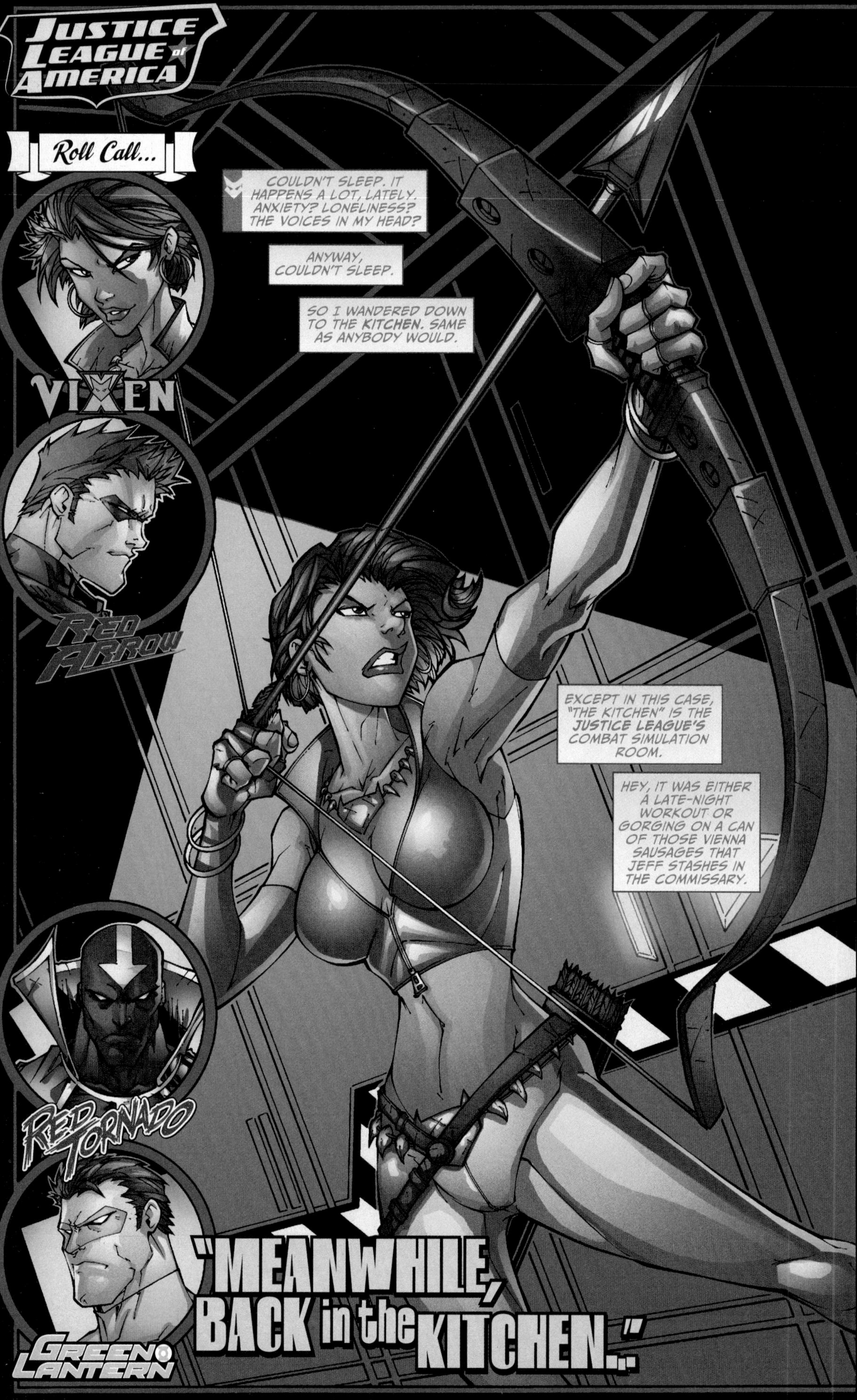

JUSTICE LEAGUE of AMERICA
Roll Call...
VIXEN
RED ARROW
RED TORNADO
GREEN LANTERN
COULDN'T SLEEP. IT HAPPENS A LOT, LATELY. ANXIETY? LONELINESS? THE VOICES IN MY HEAD?
ANYWAY, COULDN'T SLEEP.
SO I WANDERED DOWN TO THE KITCHEN. SAME AS ANYBODY WOULD.
EXCEPT IN THIS CASE, "THE KITCHEN" IS THE JUSTICE LEAGUE'S COMBAT SIMULATION ROOM.
HEY, IT WAS EITHER A LATE-NIGHT WORKOUT OR GORGING ON A CAN OF THOSE VIENNA SAUSAGES THAT JEFF STASHES IN THE COMMISSARY.
"MEANWHILE, BACK in the KITCHEN..."

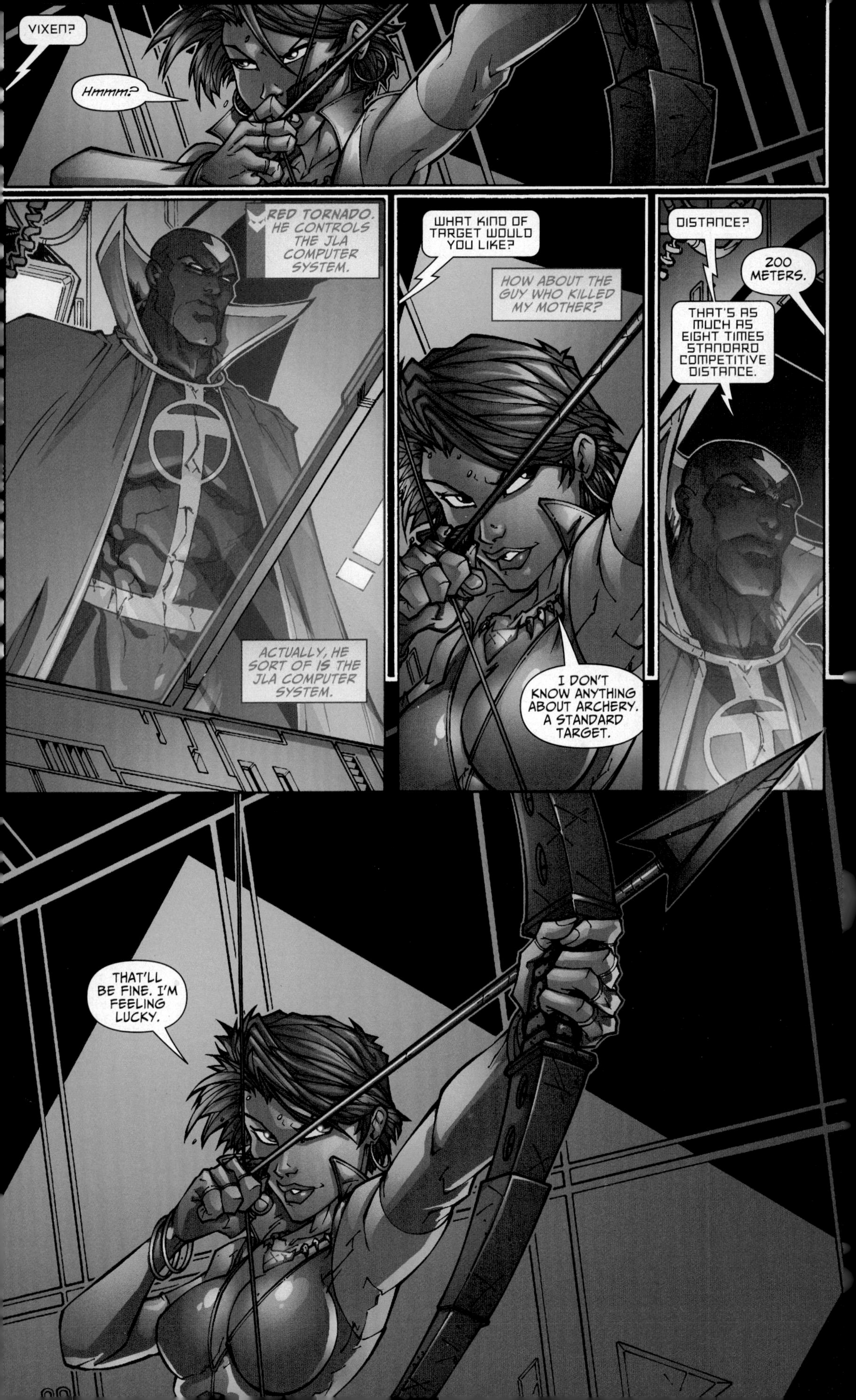
VIXEN?
Hmmm?
RED TORNADO. HE CONTROLS THE JLA COMPUTER SYSTEM.
ACTUALLY, HE SORT OF IS THE JLA COMPUTER SYSTEM.
WHAT KIND OF TARGET WOULD YOU LIKE?
HOW ABOUT THE GUY WHO KILLED MY MOTHER?
I DON'T KNOW ANYTHING ABOUT ARCHERY. A STANDARD TARGET.
DISTANCE?
200 METERS.
THAT'S AS MUCH AS EIGHT TIMES STANDARD COMPETITIVE DISTANCE.
THAT'LL BE FINE. I'M FEELING LUCKY.

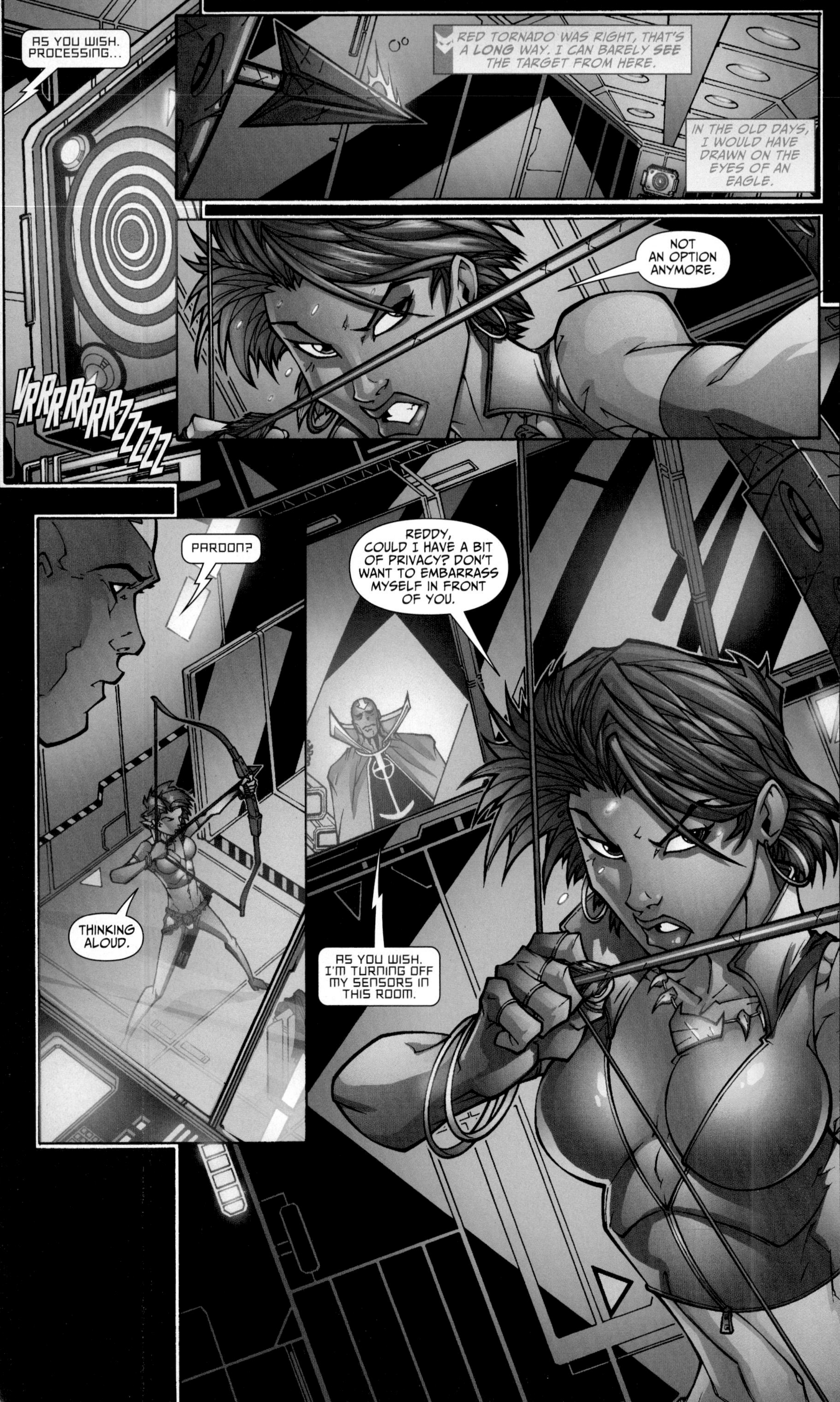
AS YOU WISH. PROCESSING...
RED TORNADO WAS RIGHT, THAT'S A LONG WAY. I CAN BARELY SEE THE TARGET FROM HERE.
IN THE OLD DAYS, I WOULD HAVE DRAWN ON THE EYES OF AN EAGLE.
NOT AN OPTION ANYMORE.
VRRRRRRRZZZZZ
PARDON?
THINKING ALOUD.
REDDY, COULD I HAVE A BIT OF PRIVACY? DON'T WANT TO EMBARRASS MYSELF IN FRONT OF YOU.
AS YOU WISH. I'M TURNING OFF MY SENSORS IN THIS ROOM.

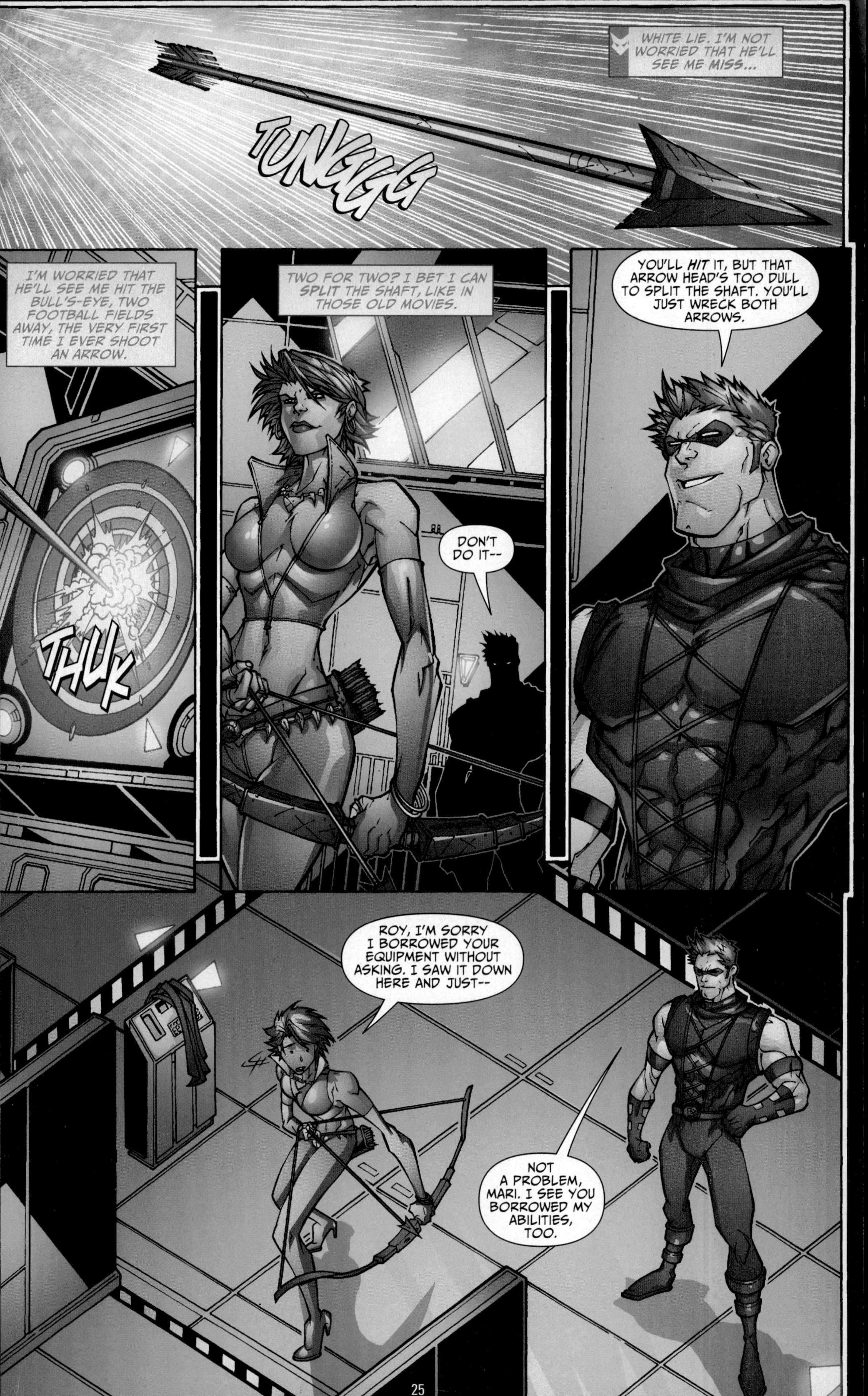
WHITE LIE. I'M NOT WORRIED THAT HE'LL SEE ME MISS...
TUNGGG
I'M WORRIED THAT HE'LL SEE ME HIT THE BULL'S-EYE, TWO FOOTBALL FIELDS AWAY, THE VERY FIRST TIME I EVER SHOOT AN ARROW.
THUK
TWO FOR TWO? I BET I CAN SPLIT THE SHAFT, LIKE IN THOSE OLD MOVIES.
DON'T DO IT--
YOU'LL HIT IT, BUT THAT ARROW HEAD'S TOO DULL TO SPLIT THE SHAFT. YOU'LL JUST WRECK BOTH ARROWS.
ROY, I'M SORRY I BORROWED YOUR EQUIPMENT WITHOUT ASKING. I SAW IT DOWN HERE AND JUST--
NOT A PROBLEM, MARI. I SEE YOU BORROWED MY ABILITIES, TOO.

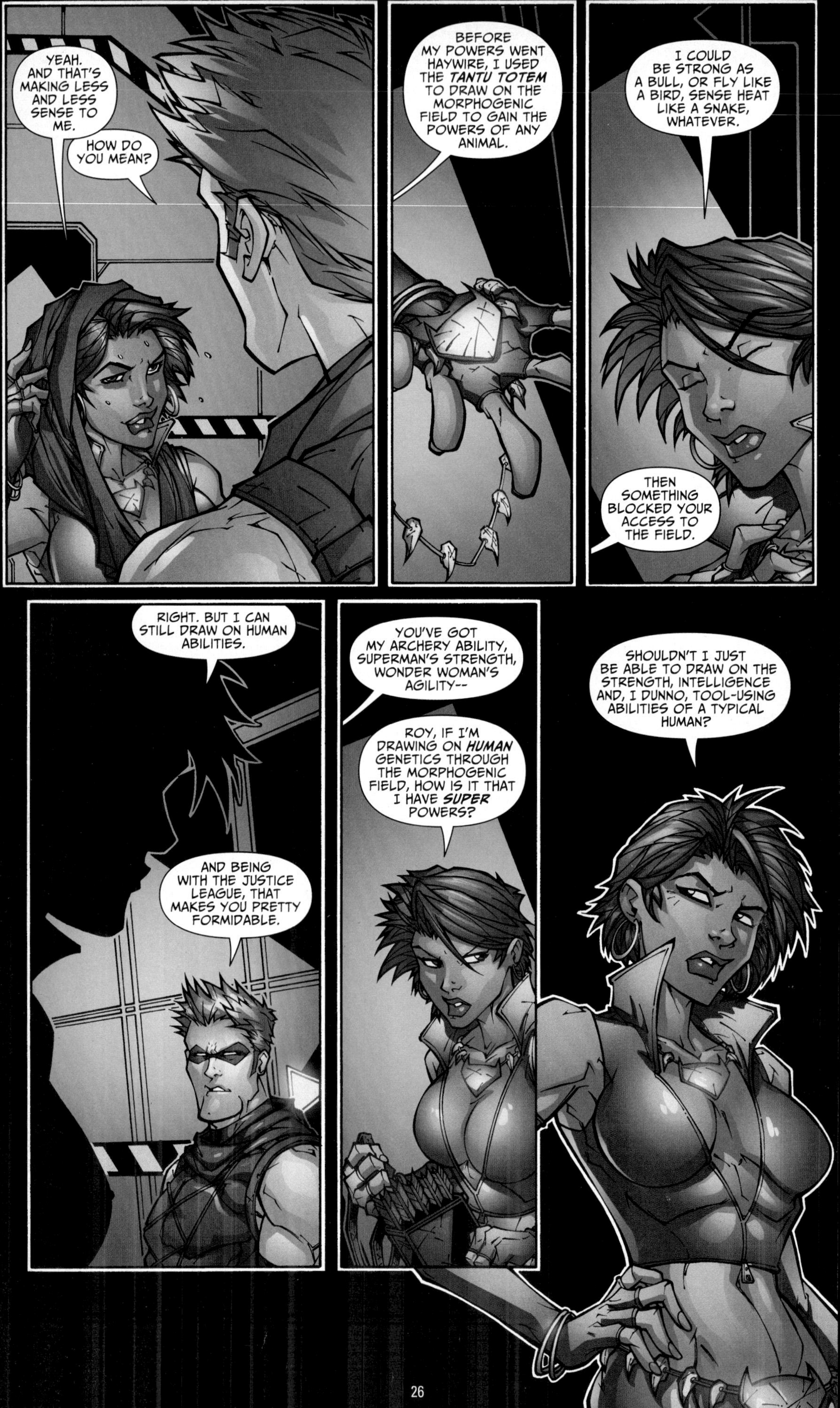
YEAH. AND THAT'S MAKING LESS AND LESS SENSE TO ME.
HOW DO YOU MEAN?
BEFORE MY POWERS WENT HAYWIRE, I USED THE TANTU TOTEM TO DRAW ON THE MORPHOGENIC FIELD TO GAIN THE POWERS OF ANY ANIMAL.
I COULD BE STRONG AS A BULL, OR FLY LIKE A BIRD, SENSE HEAT LIKE A SNAKE, WHATEVER.
THEN SOMETHING BLOCKED YOUR ACCESS TO THE FIELD.
RIGHT. BUT I CAN STILL DRAW ON HUMAN ABILITIES.
AND BEING WITH THE JUSTICE LEAGUE, THAT MAKES YOU PRETTY FORMIDABLE.
YOU'VE GOT MY ARCHERY ABILITY, SUPERMAN'S STRENGTH, WONDER WOMAN'S AGILITY--
ROY, IF I'M DRAWING ON HUMAN GENETICS THROUGH THE MORPHOGENIC FIELD, HOW IS IT THAT I HAVE SUPER POWERS?
SHOULDN'T I JUST BE ABLE TO DRAW ON THE STRENGTH, INTELLIGENCE AND, I DUNNO, TOOL-USING ABILITIES OF A TYPICAL HUMAN?

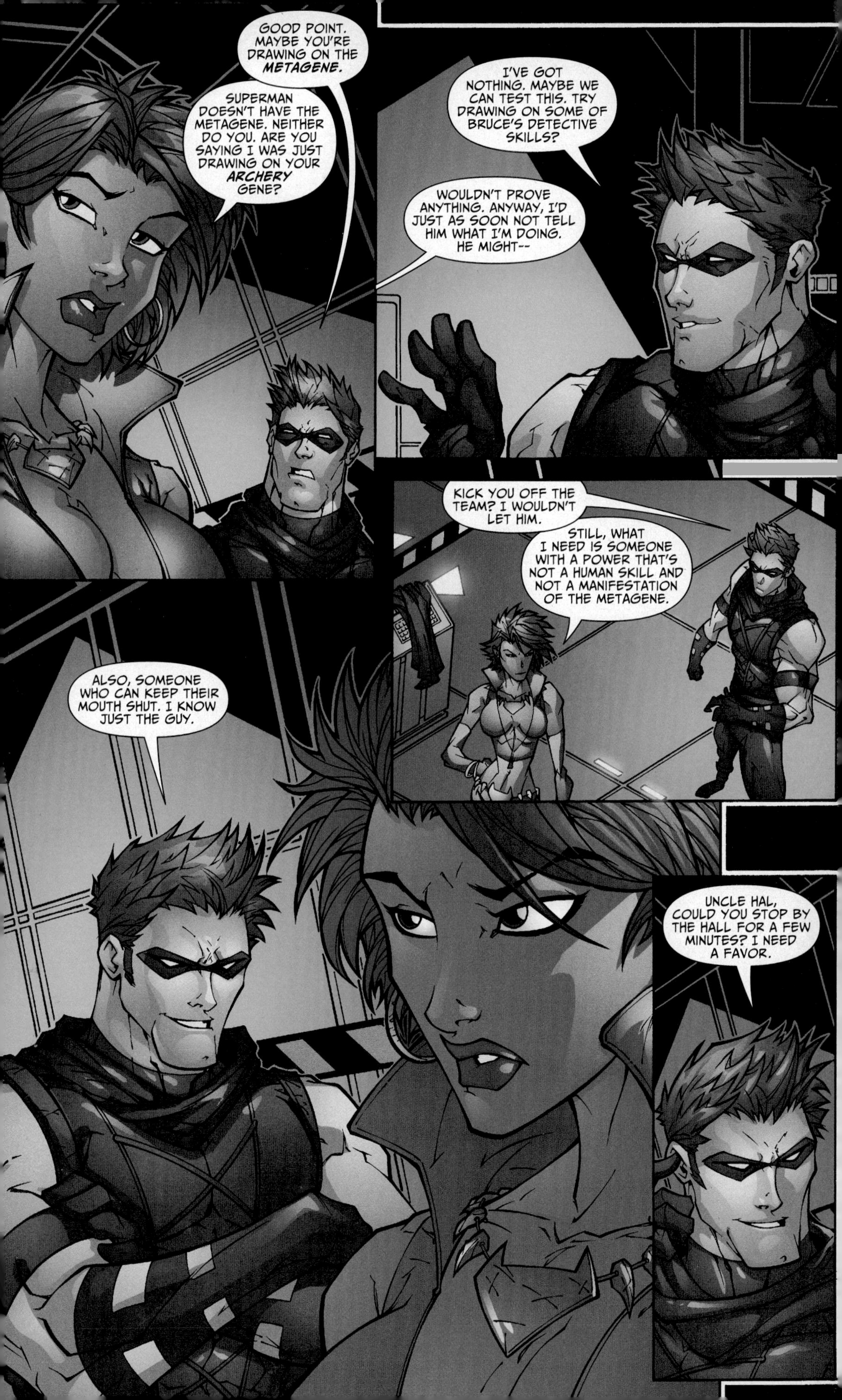
GOOD POINT. MAYBE YOU'RE DRAWING ON THE *METAGENE.*
SUPERMAN DOESN'T HAVE THE METAGENE. NEITHER DO YOU. ARE YOU SAYING I WAS JUST DRAWING ON YOUR *ARCHERY* GENE?
I'VE GOT NOTHING. MAYBE WE CAN TEST THIS. TRY DRAWING ON SOME OF BRUCE'S DETECTIVE SKILLS?
WOULDN'T PROVE ANYTHING. ANYWAY, I'D JUST AS SOON NOT TELL HIM WHAT I'M DOING. HE MIGHT--
KICK YOU OFF THE TEAM? I WOULDN'T LET HIM.
STILL, WHAT I NEED IS SOMEONE WITH A POWER THAT'S NOT A HUMAN SKILL AND NOT A MANIFESTATION OF THE METAGENE.
ALSO, SOMEONE WHO CAN KEEP THEIR MOUTH SHUT. I KNOW JUST THE GUY.
UNCLE HAL, COULD YOU STOP BY THE HALL FOR A FEW MINUTES? I NEED A FAVOR.

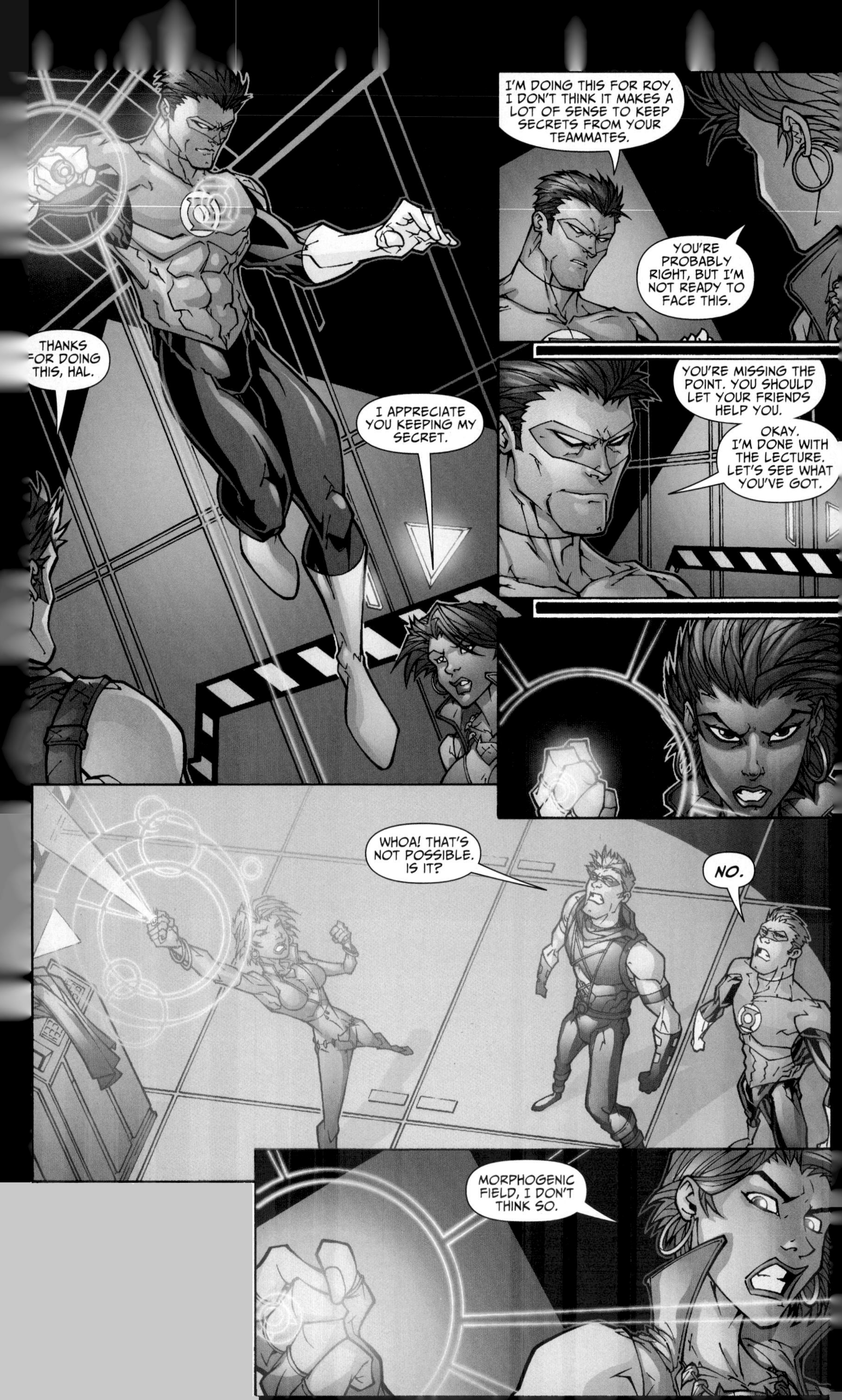
THANKS FOR DOING THIS, HAL.
I APPRECIATE YOU KEEPING MY SECRET.
I'M DOING THIS FOR ROY. I DON'T THINK IT MAKES A LOT OF SENSE TO KEEP SECRETS FROM YOUR TEAMMATES.
YOU'RE PROBABLY RIGHT, BUT I'M NOT READY TO FACE THIS.
YOU'RE MISSING THE POINT. YOU SHOULD LET YOUR FRIENDS HELP YOU.
OKAY. I'M DONE WITH THE LECTURE. LET'S SEE WHAT YOU'VE GOT.
WHOA! THAT'S NOT POSSIBLE. IS IT?
NO.
MORPHOGENIC FIELD, I DON'T THINK SO.

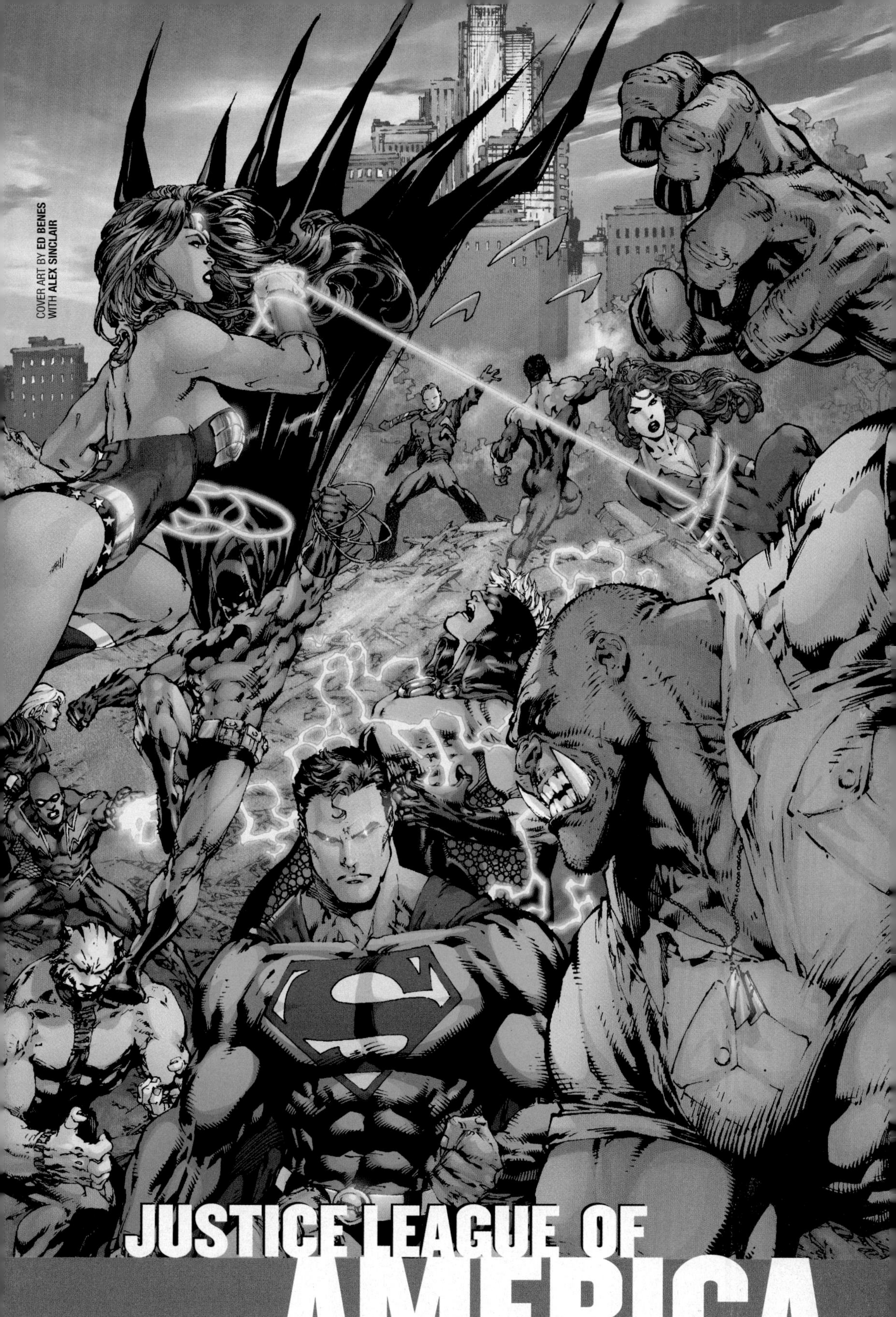

COVER ART BY **ED BENES**
WITH **ALEX SINCLAIR**

JUSTICE LEAGUE OF AMERICA

SANCTUARY PART TWO
"MEANWHILE, BACK AT OWL CREEK BRIDGE..."

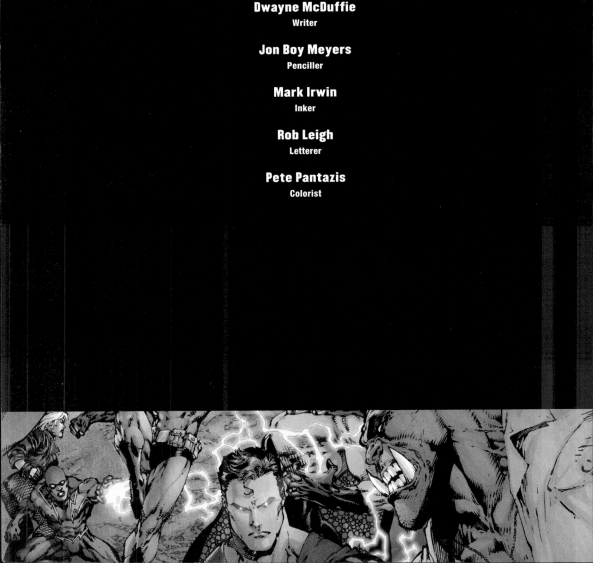

Dwayne McDuffie
Writer

Jon Boy Meyers
Penciller

Mark Irwin
Inker

Rob Leigh
Letterer

Pete Pantazis
Colorist

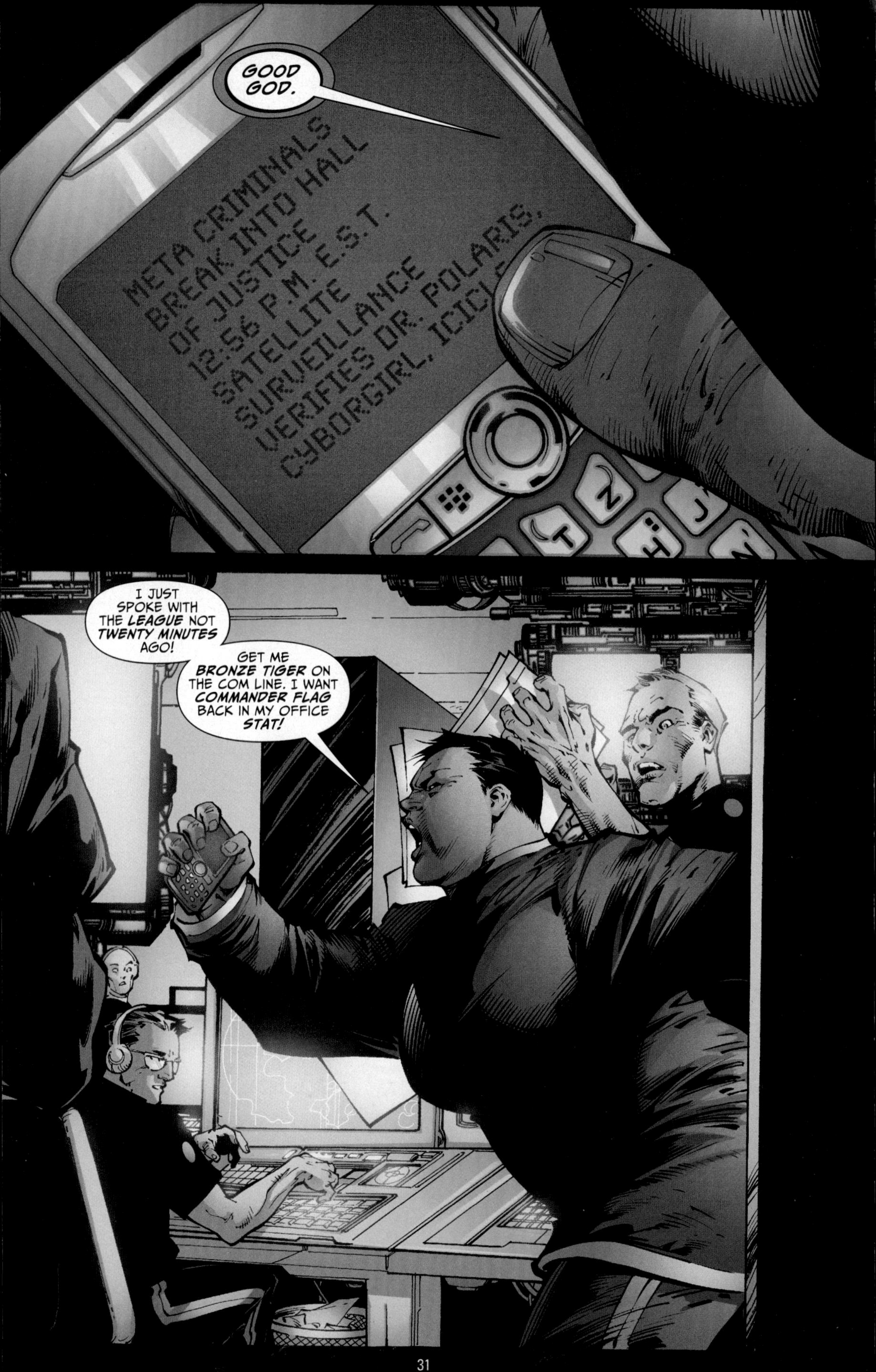
GOOD GOD.
META CRIMINALS BREAK INTO HALL OF JUSTICE 12:56 P.M. E.S.T. SATELLITE SURVEILLANCE VERIFIES DR. POLARIS, CYBORGIRL, ICICLE
I JUST SPOKE WITH THE *LEAGUE* NOT *TWENTY MINUTES* AGO!
GET ME *BRONZE TIGER* ON THE COM LINE. I WANT *COMMANDER FLAG* BACK IN MY OFFICE *STAT!*

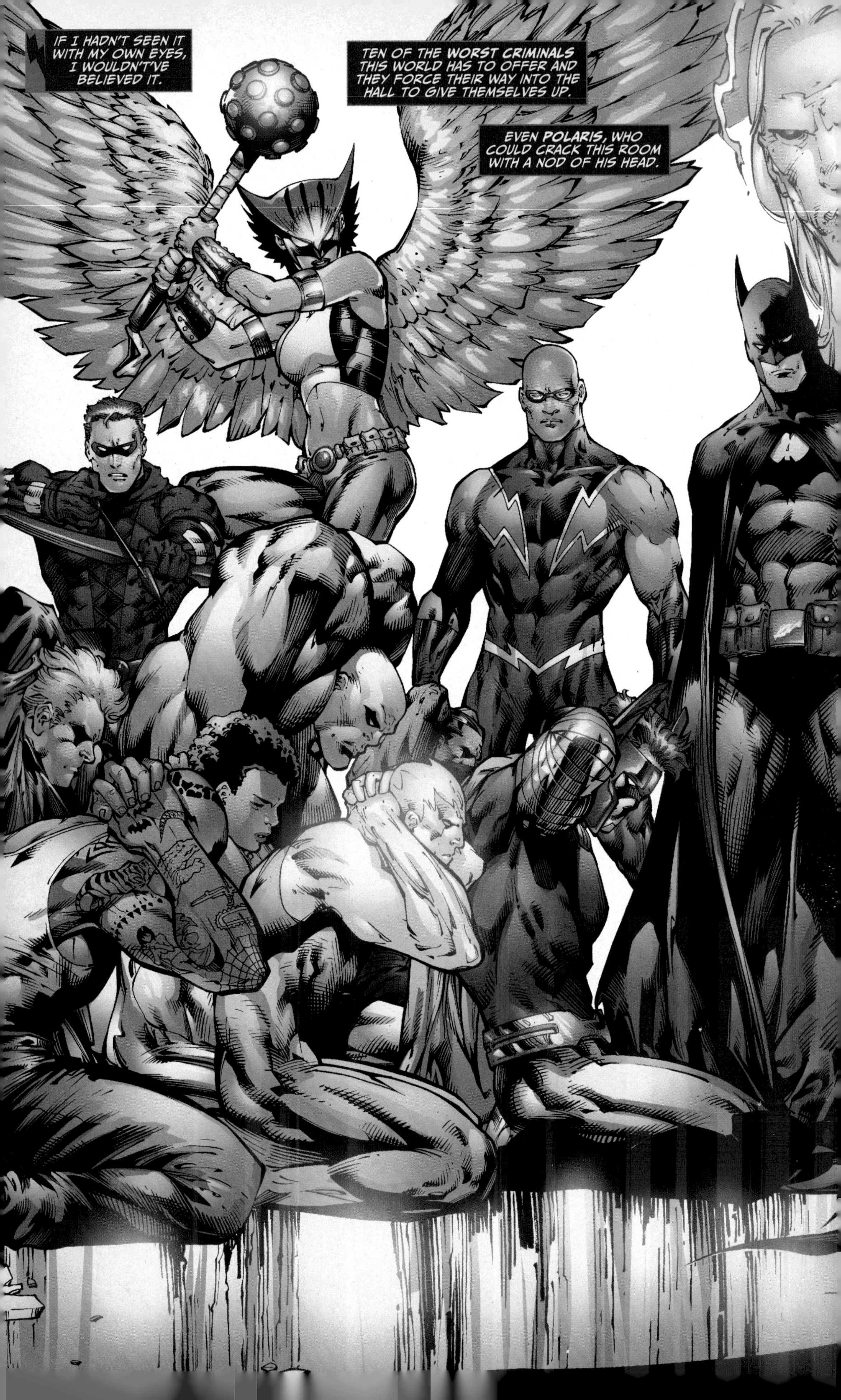
IF I HADN'T SEEN IT WITH MY OWN EYES, I WOULDN'T'VE BELIEVED IT.
TEN OF THE WORST CRIMINALS THIS WORLD HAS TO OFFER AND THEY FORCE THEIR WAY INTO THE HALL TO GIVE THEMSELVES UP.
EVEN POLARIS, WHO COULD CRACK THIS ROOM WITH A NOD OF HIS HEAD.

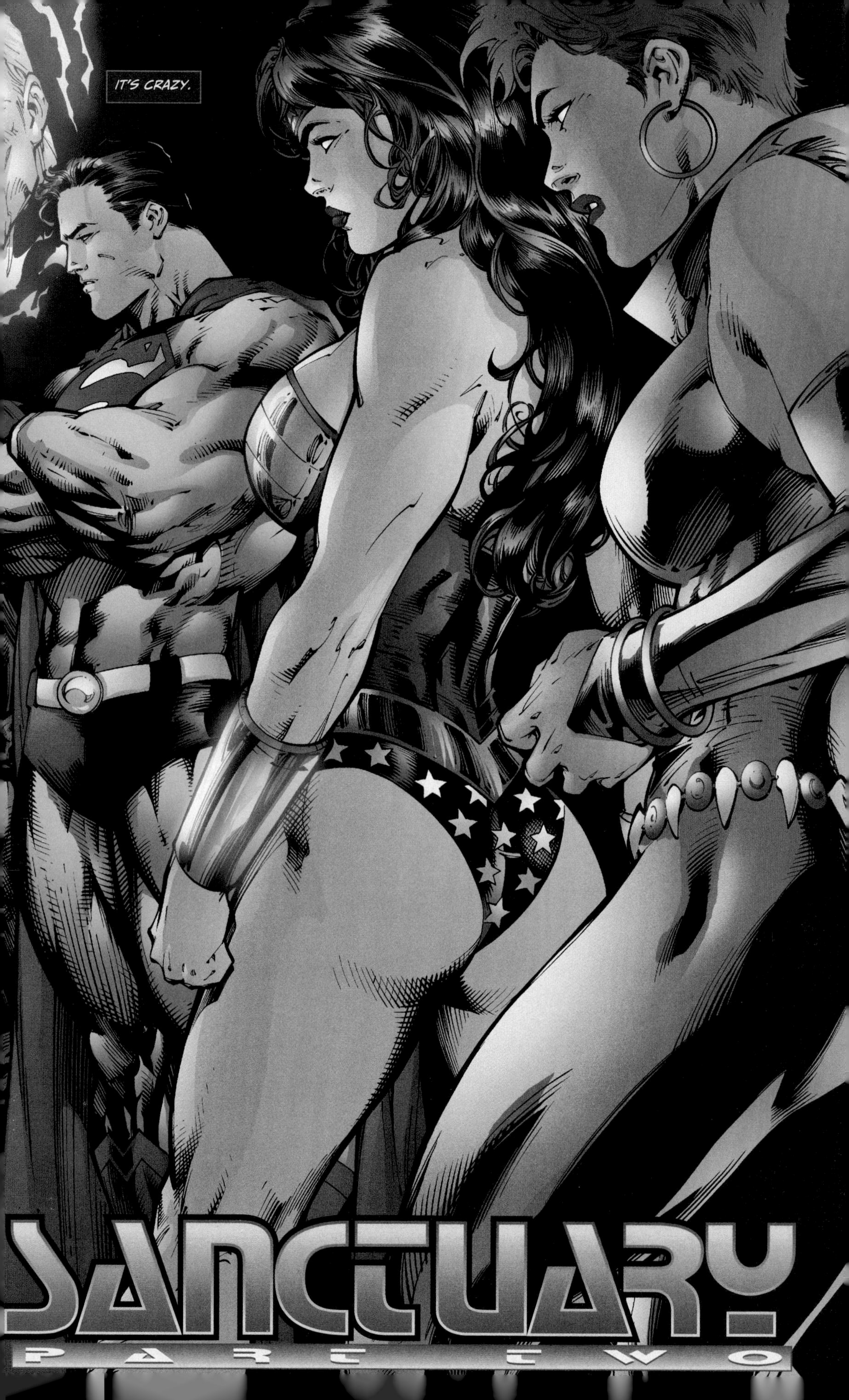
IT'S CRAZY.
SANCTUARY
PART TWO

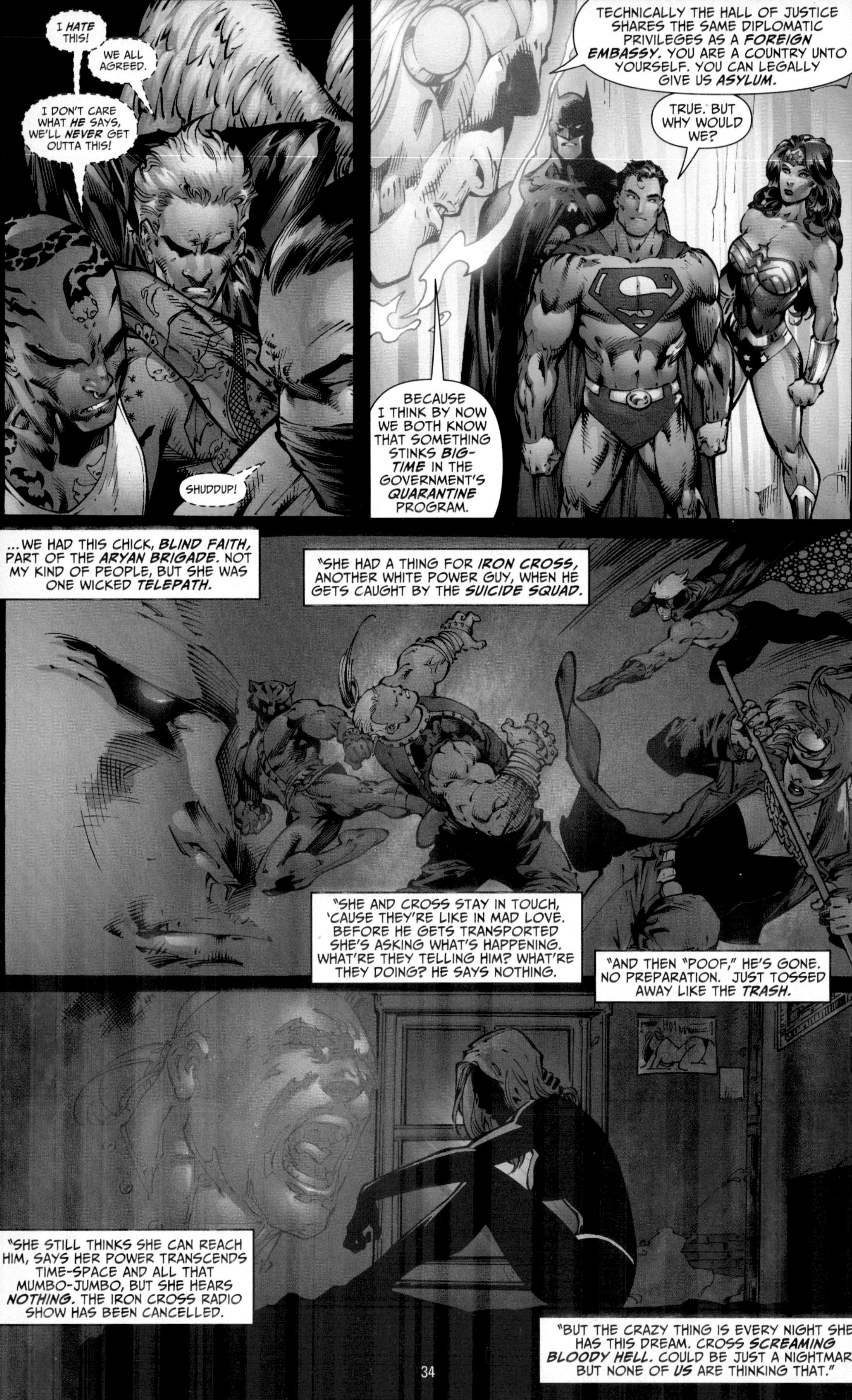
I HATE THIS!
WE ALL AGREED.
I DON'T CARE WHAT HE SAYS, WE'LL NEVER GET OUTTA THIS!
SHUDDUP!
TECHNICALLY THE HALL OF JUSTICE SHARES THE SAME DIPLOMATIC PRIVILEGES AS A FOREIGN EMBASSY. YOU ARE A COUNTRY UNTO YOURSELF. YOU CAN LEGALLY GIVE US ASYLUM.
TRUE. BUT WHY WOULD WE?
BECAUSE I THINK BY NOW WE BOTH KNOW THAT SOMETHING STINKS BIG-TIME IN THE GOVERNMENT'S QUARANTINE PROGRAM.
...WE HAD THIS CHICK, BLIND FAITH, PART OF THE ARYAN BRIGADE. NOT MY KIND OF PEOPLE, BUT SHE WAS ONE WICKED TELEPATH.
"SHE HAD A THING FOR IRON CROSS, ANOTHER WHITE POWER GUY, WHEN HE GETS CAUGHT BY THE SUICIDE SQUAD.
"SHE AND CROSS STAY IN TOUCH, 'CAUSE THEY'RE LIKE IN MAD LOVE. BEFORE HE GETS TRANSPORTED SHE'S ASKING WHAT'S HAPPENING. WHAT'RE THEY TELLING HIM? WHAT'RE THEY DOING? HE SAYS NOTHING.
"AND THEN "POOF," HE'S GONE. NO PREPARATION. JUST TOSSED AWAY LIKE THE TRASH.
"SHE STILL THINKS SHE CAN REACH HIM, SAYS HER POWER TRANSCENDS TIME-SPACE AND ALL THAT MUMBO-JUMBO, BUT SHE HEARS NOTHING. THE IRON CROSS RADIO SHOW HAS BEEN CANCELLED.
"BUT THE CRAZY THING IS EVERY NIGHT SHE HAS THIS DREAM. CROSS SCREAMING BLOODY HELL. COULD BE JUST A NIGHTMAR BUT NONE OF US ARE THINKING THAT."

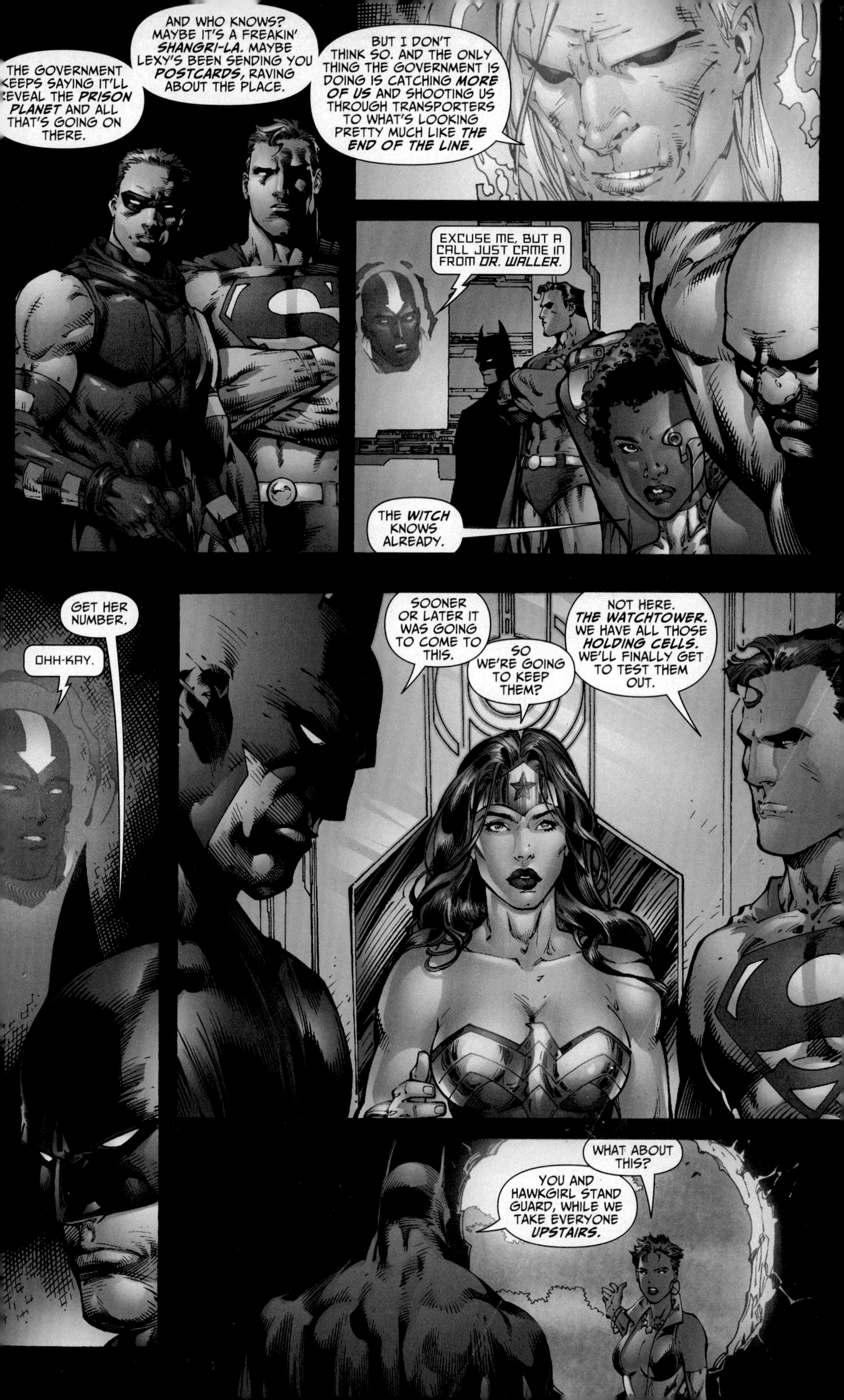
THE GOVERNMENT KEEPS SAYING IT'LL REVEAL THE PRISON PLANET AND ALL THAT'S GOING ON THERE.
AND WHO KNOWS? MAYBE IT'S A FREAKIN' SHANGRI-LA. MAYBE LEXY'S BEEN SENDING YOU POSTCARDS, RAVING ABOUT THE PLACE.
BUT I DON'T THINK SO. AND THE ONLY THING THE GOVERNMENT IS DOING IS CATCHING MORE OF US AND SHOOTING US THROUGH TRANSPORTERS TO WHAT'S LOOKING PRETTY MUCH LIKE THE END OF THE LINE.
EXCUSE ME, BUT A CALL JUST CAME IN FROM DR. WALLER.
THE WITCH KNOWS ALREADY.
GET HER NUMBER.
OHH-KAY.
SOONER OR LATER IT WAS GOING TO COME TO THIS.
SO WE'RE GOING TO KEEP THEM?
NOT HERE. THE WATCHTOWER. WE HAVE ALL THOSE HOLDING CELLS. WE'LL FINALLY GET TO TEST THEM OUT.
WHAT ABOUT THIS?
YOU AND HAWKGIRL STAND GUARD, WHILE WE TAKE EVERYONE UPSTAIRS.

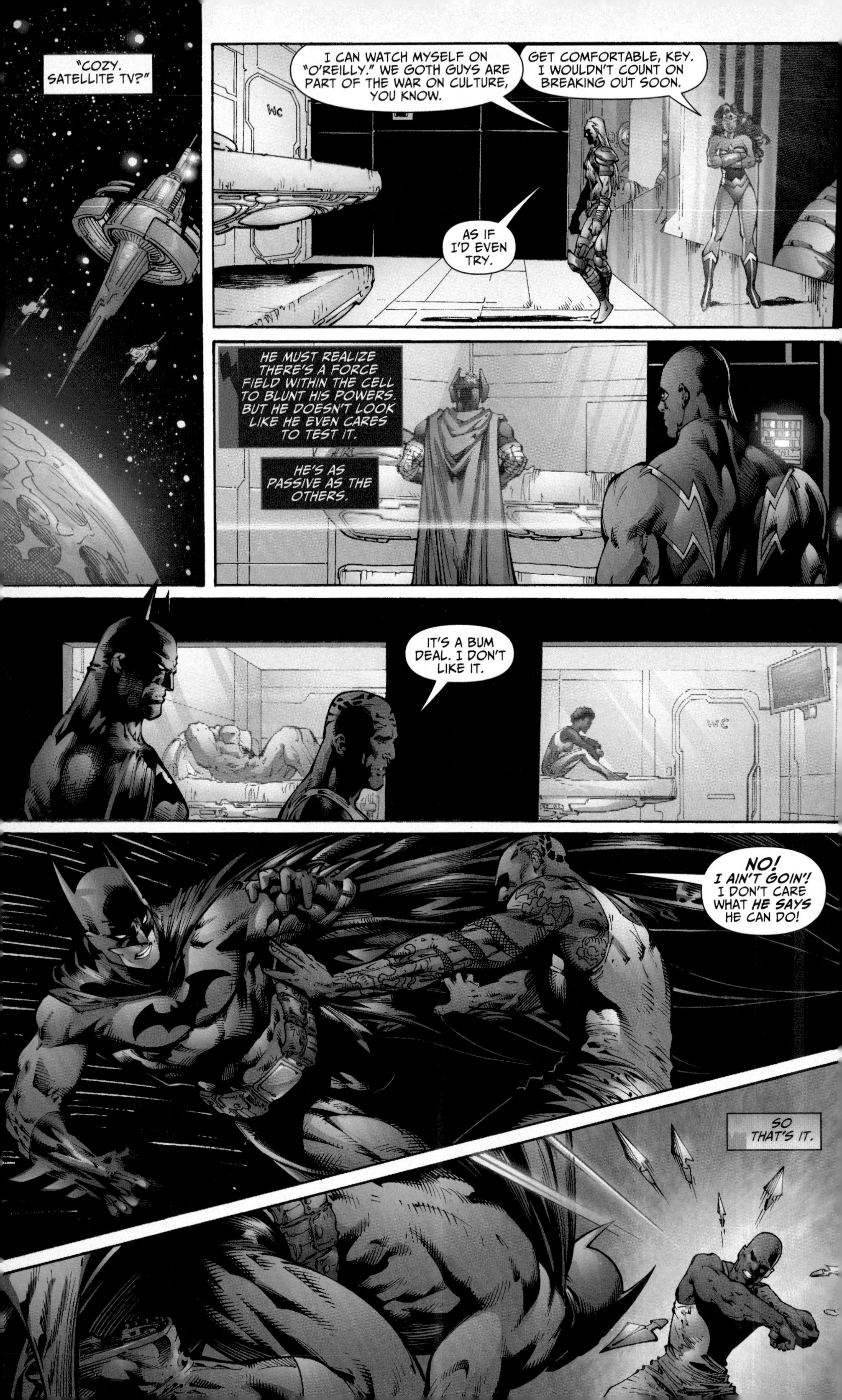
"COZY. SATELLITE TV?"
I CAN WATCH MYSELF ON "O'REILLY." WE GOTH GUYS ARE PART OF THE WAR ON CULTURE, YOU KNOW.
GET COMFORTABLE, KEY. I WOULDN'T COUNT ON BREAKING OUT SOON.
AS IF I'D EVEN TRY.
HE MUST REALIZE THERE'S A FORCE FIELD WITHIN THE CELL TO BLUNT HIS POWERS. BUT HE DOESN'T LOOK LIKE HE EVEN CARES TO TEST IT.
HE'S AS PASSIVE AS THE OTHERS.
IT'S A BUM DEAL. I DON'T LIKE IT.
NO! I AIN'T GOIN'! I DON'T CARE WHAT HE SAYS HE CAN DO!
SO THAT'S IT.

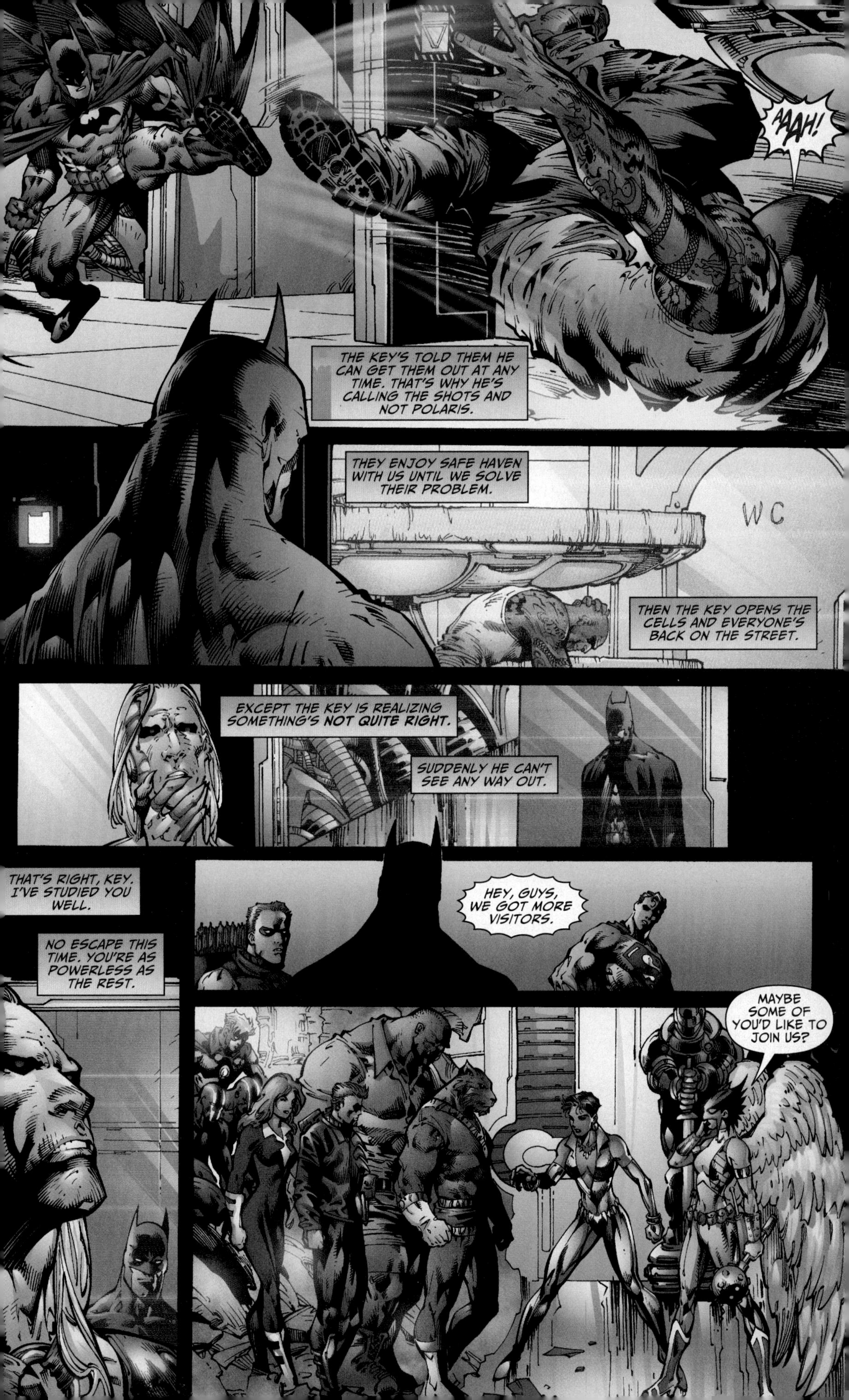
AAAH!
THE KEY'S TOLD THEM HE CAN GET THEM OUT AT ANY TIME. THAT'S WHY HE'S CALLING THE SHOTS AND NOT POLARIS.
THEY ENJOY SAFE HAVEN WITH US UNTIL WE SOLVE THEIR PROBLEM.
WC
THEN THE KEY OPENS THE CELLS AND EVERYONE'S BACK ON THE STREET.
EXCEPT THE KEY IS REALIZING SOMETHING'S NOT QUITE RIGHT.
SUDDENLY HE CAN'T SEE ANY WAY OUT.
THAT'S RIGHT, KEY. I'VE STUDIED YOU WELL.
NO ESCAPE THIS TIME. YOU'RE AS POWERLESS AS THE REST.
HEY, GUYS, WE GOT MORE VISITORS.
MAYBE SOME OF YOU'D LIKE TO JOIN US?

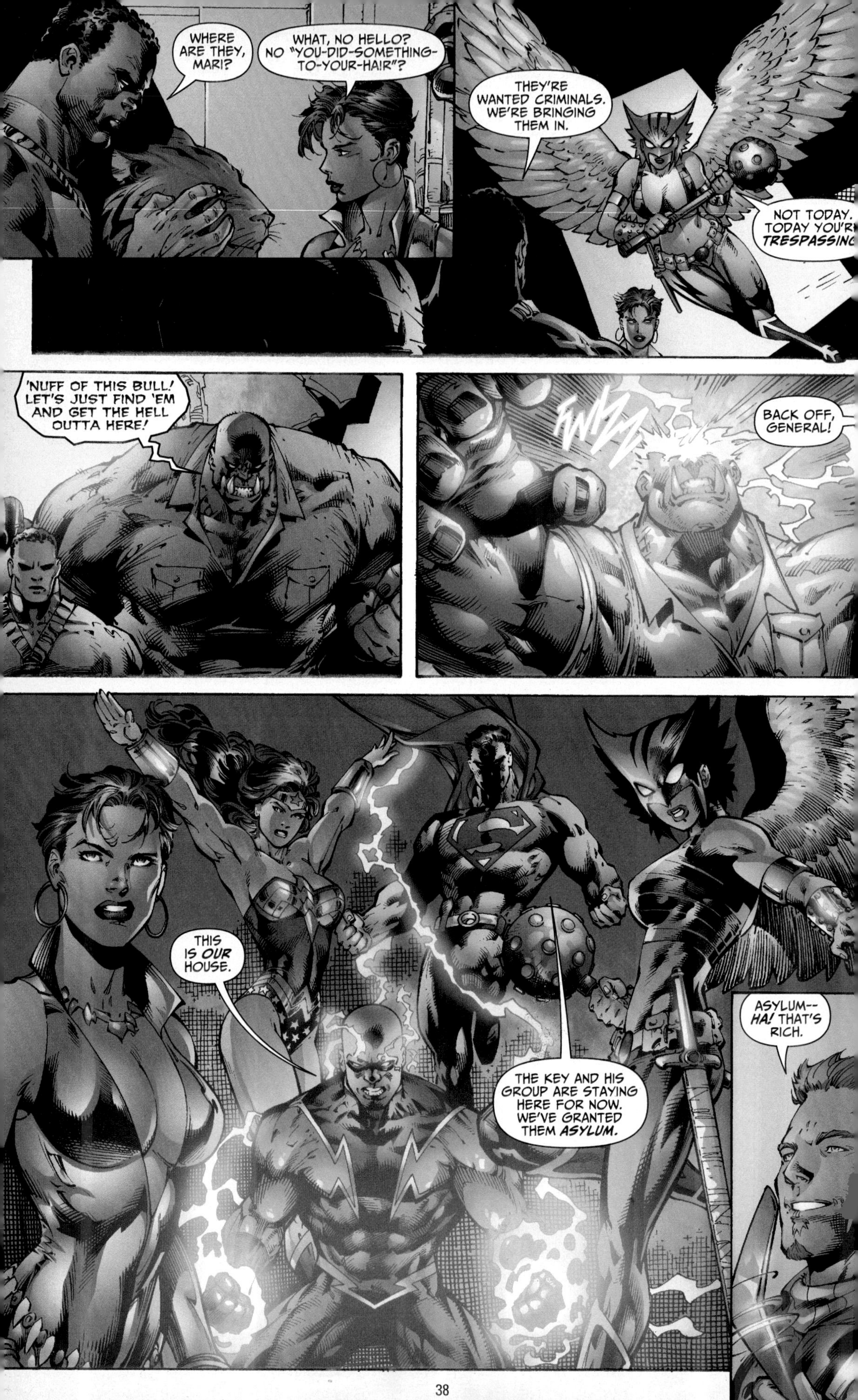

WHERE ARE THEY, MARI?
WHAT, NO HELLO? NO "YOU-DID-SOMETHING-TO-YOUR-HAIR"?
THEY'RE WANTED CRIMINALS. WE'RE BRINGING THEM IN.
NOT TODAY. TODAY YOU'RE TRESPASSING
'NUFF OF THIS BULL! LET'S JUST FIND 'EM AND GET THE HELL OUTTA HERE!
FWIZZ
BACK OFF, GENERAL!
THIS IS OUR HOUSE.
THE KEY AND HIS GROUP ARE STAYING HERE FOR NOW. WE'VE GRANTED THEM ASYLUM.
ASYLUM-- HA! THAT'S RICH.

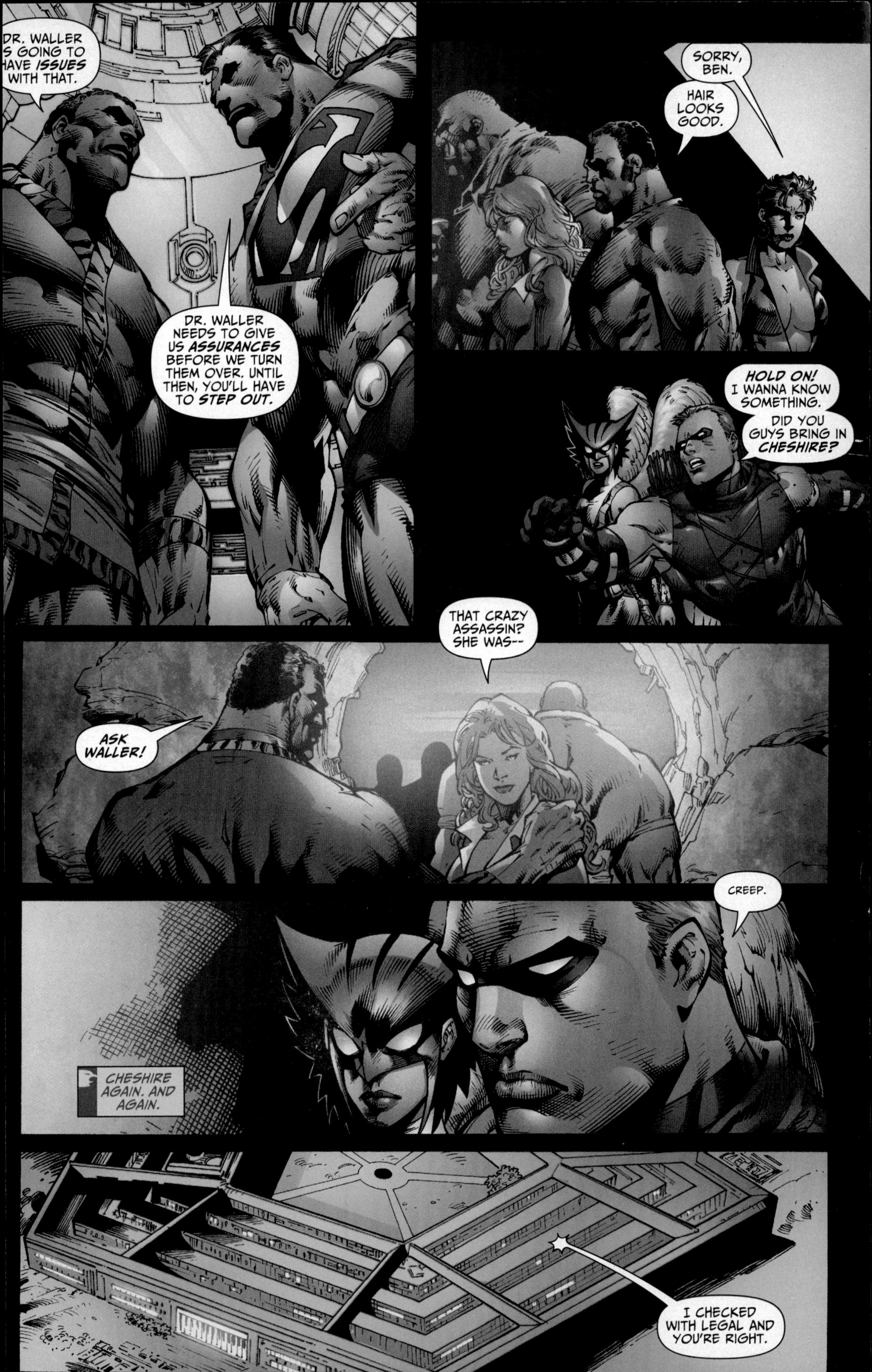
DR. WALLER IS GOING TO HAVE ISSUES WITH THAT.
DR. WALLER NEEDS TO GIVE US ASSURANCES BEFORE WE TURN THEM OVER. UNTIL THEN, YOU'LL HAVE TO STEP OUT.
SORRY, BEN.
HAIR LOOKS GOOD.
HOLD ON! I WANNA KNOW SOMETHING.
DID YOU GUYS BRING IN CHESHIRE?
THAT CRAZY ASSASSIN? SHE WAS--
ASK WALLER!
CREEP.
CHESHIRE AGAIN. AND AGAIN.
I CHECKED WITH LEGAL AND YOU'RE RIGHT.

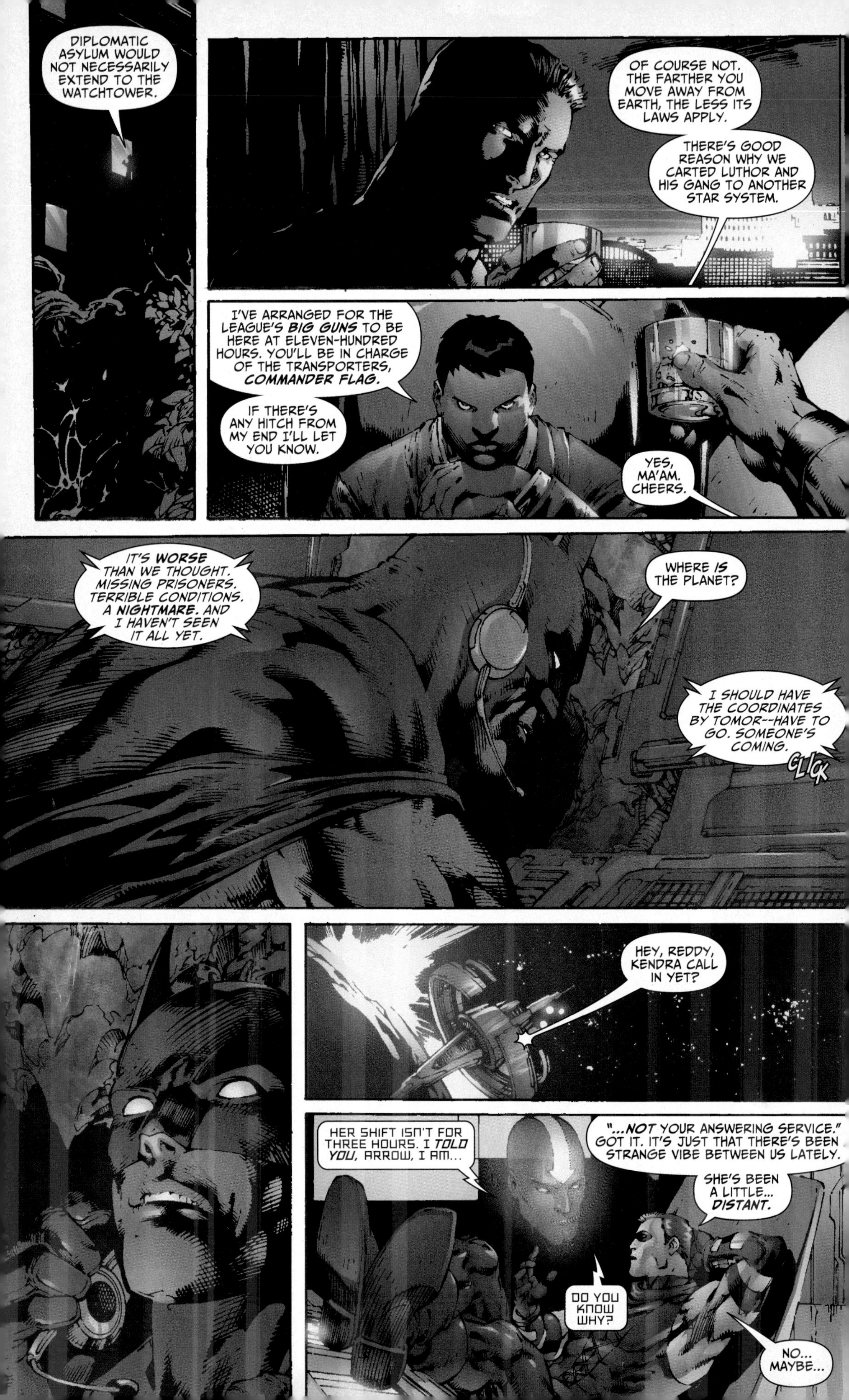
DIPLOMATIC ASYLUM WOULD NOT NECESSARILY EXTEND TO THE WATCHTOWER.
OF COURSE NOT. THE FARTHER YOU MOVE AWAY FROM EARTH, THE LESS ITS LAWS APPLY.
THERE'S GOOD REASON WHY WE CARTED LUTHOR AND HIS GANG TO ANOTHER STAR SYSTEM.
I'VE ARRANGED FOR THE LEAGUE'S BIG GUNS TO BE HERE AT ELEVEN-HUNDRED HOURS. YOU'LL BE IN CHARGE OF THE TRANSPORTERS, COMMANDER FLAG.
IF THERE'S ANY HITCH FROM MY END I'LL LET YOU KNOW.
YES, MA'AM. CHEERS.
IT'S WORSE THAN WE THOUGHT. MISSING PRISONERS. TERRIBLE CONDITIONS. A NIGHTMARE. AND I HAVEN'T SEEN IT ALL YET.
WHERE IS THE PLANET?
I SHOULD HAVE THE COORDINATES BY TOMOR--HAVE TO GO. SOMEONE'S COMING.
CLICK
HEY, REDDY, KENDRA CALL IN YET?
HER SHIFT ISN'T FOR THREE HOURS. I TOLD YOU, ARROW, I AM...
"...NOT YOUR ANSWERING SERVICE." GOT IT. IT'S JUST THAT THERE'S BEEN STRANGE VIBE BETWEEN US LATELY.
SHE'S BEEN A LITTLE... DISTANT.
DO YOU KNOW WHY?
NO... MAYBE...

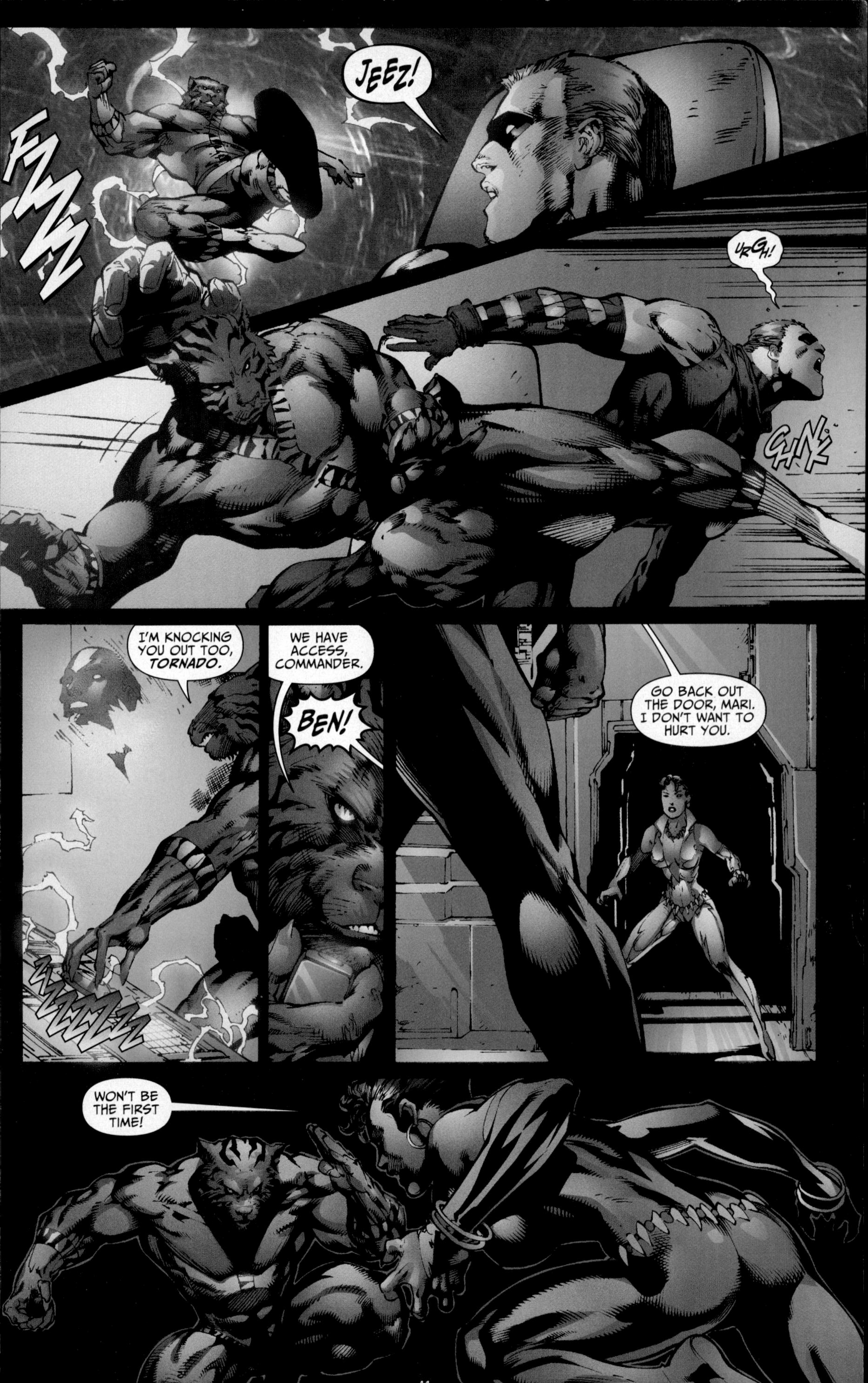
FZZZZ
JEEZ!
URGH!
CHNK
I'M KNOCKING YOU OUT TOO, TORNADO.
ZZZZZ
WE HAVE ACCESS, COMMANDER.
BEN!
GO BACK OUT THE DOOR, MARI. I DON'T WANT TO HURT YOU.
WON'T BE THE FIRST TIME!

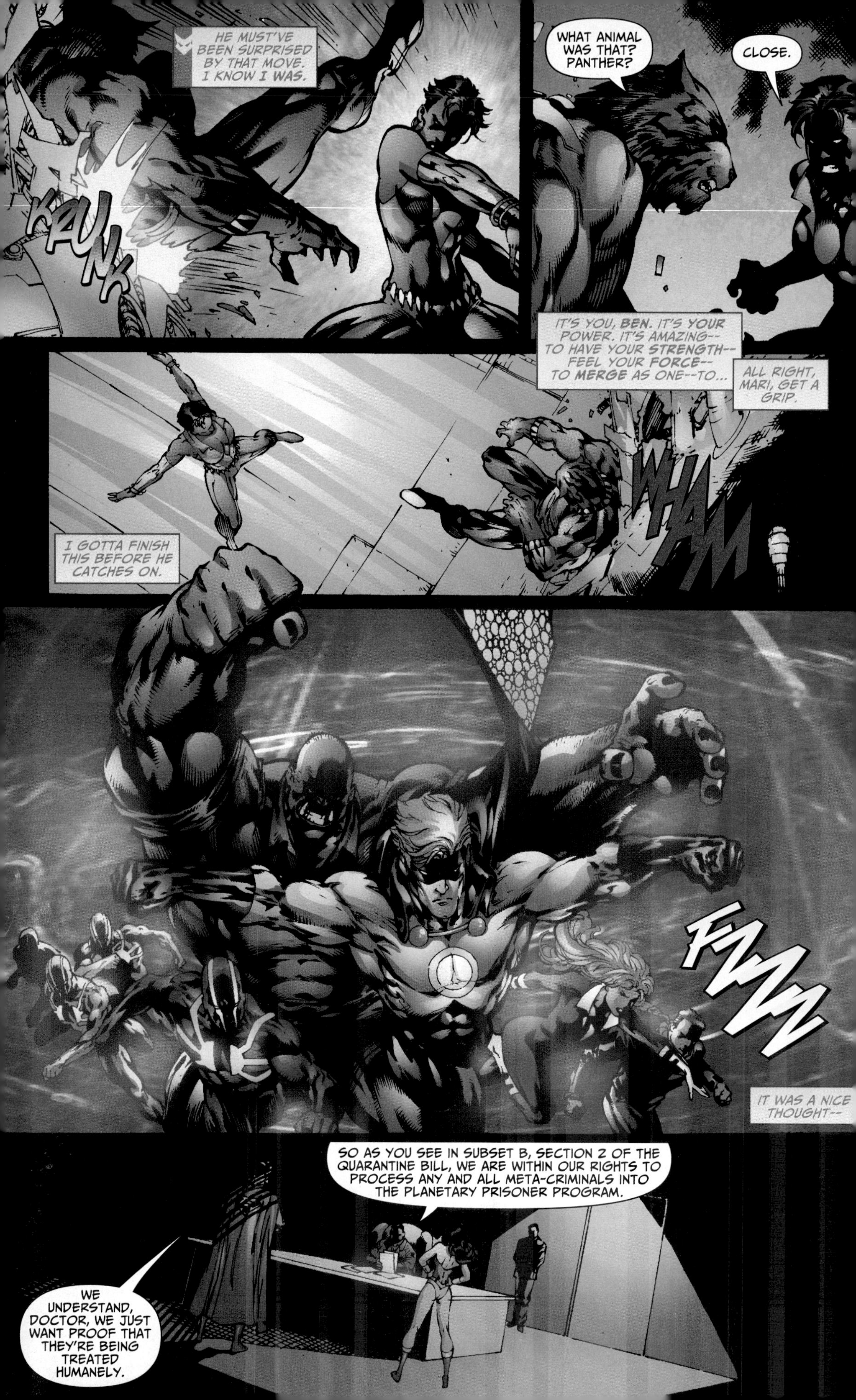
HE MUST'VE BEEN SURPRISED BY THAT MOVE. I KNOW I WAS.
KRUNK
WHAT ANIMAL WAS THAT? PANTHER?
CLOSE.
IT'S YOU, BEN. IT'S YOUR POWER. IT'S AMAZING-- TO HAVE YOUR STRENGTH-- FEEL YOUR FORCE-- TO MERGE AS ONE--TO...
ALL RIGHT, MARI, GET A GRIP.
I GOTTA FINISH THIS BEFORE HE CATCHES ON.
WHAM
FWM
IT WAS A NICE THOUGHT--
SO AS YOU SEE IN SUBSET B, SECTION 2 OF THE QUARANTINE BILL, WE ARE WITHIN OUR RIGHTS TO PROCESS ANY AND ALL META-CRIMINALS INTO THE PLANETARY PRISONER PROGRAM.
WE UNDERSTAND, DOCTOR, WE JUST WANT PROOF THAT THEY'RE BEING TREATED HUMANELY.

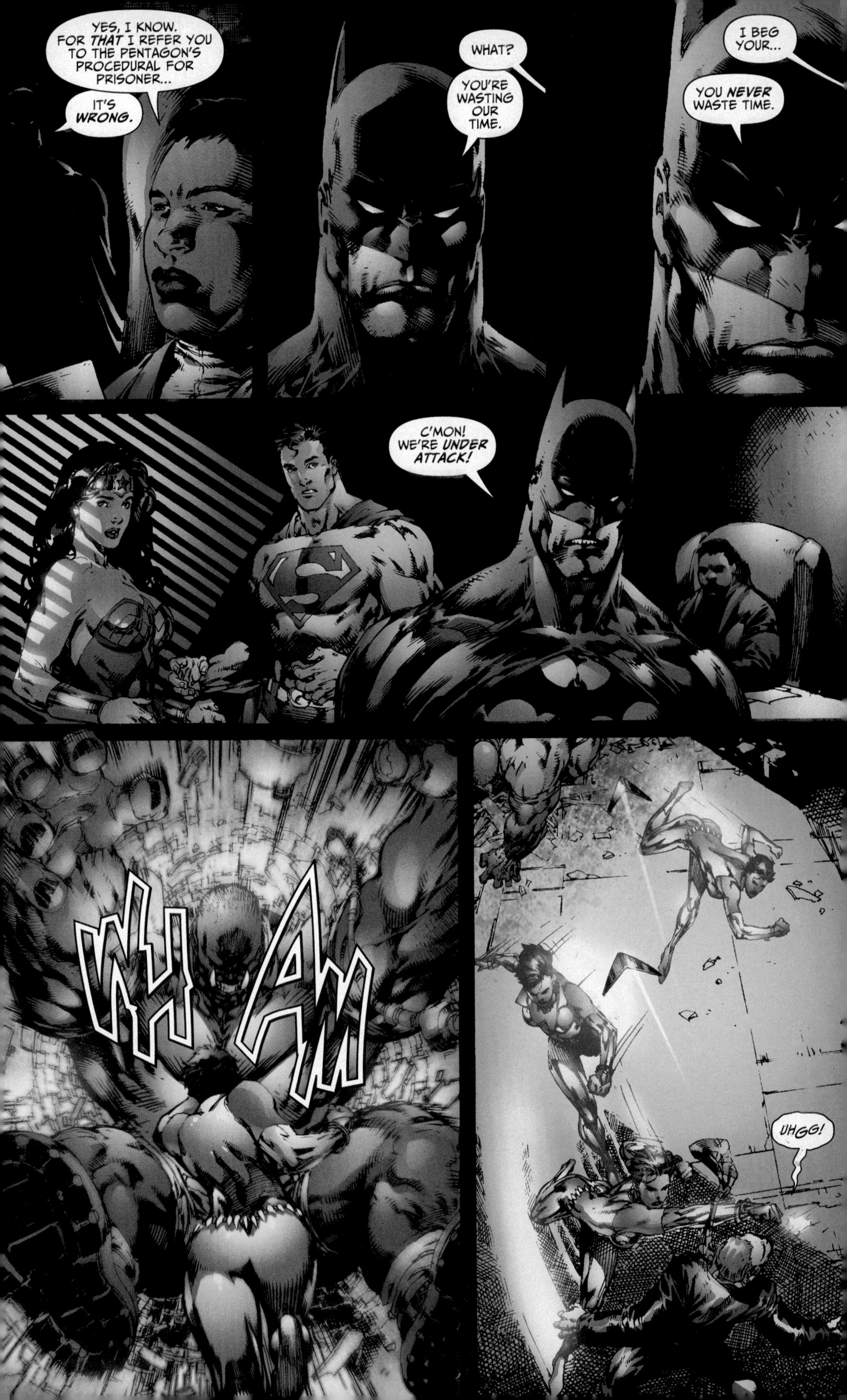
YES, I KNOW. FOR THAT I REFER YOU TO THE PENTAGON'S PROCEDURAL FOR PRISONER...
IT'S WRONG.
WHAT?
YOU'RE WASTING OUR TIME.
I BEG YOUR...
YOU NEVER WASTE TIME.
C'MON! WE'RE UNDER ATTACK!
WHAM
UHGG!

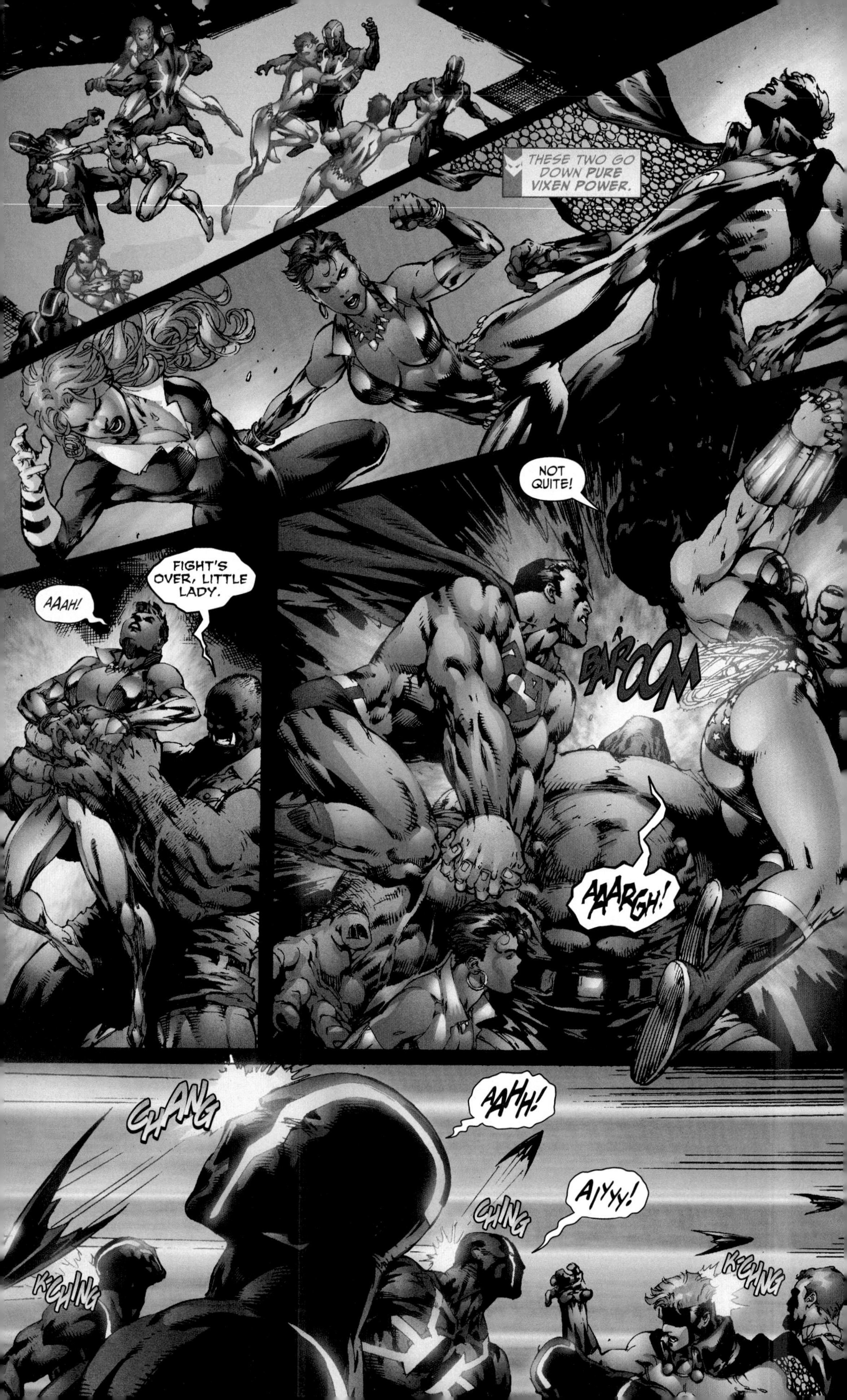
THESE TWO GO DOWN PURE VIXEN POWER.
NOT QUITE!
AAAH!
FIGHT'S OVER, LITTLE LADY.
BAROOM
AAARGH!
CHANG
AAHH!
AIYYY!
CHING
K-CHING
K-CHING

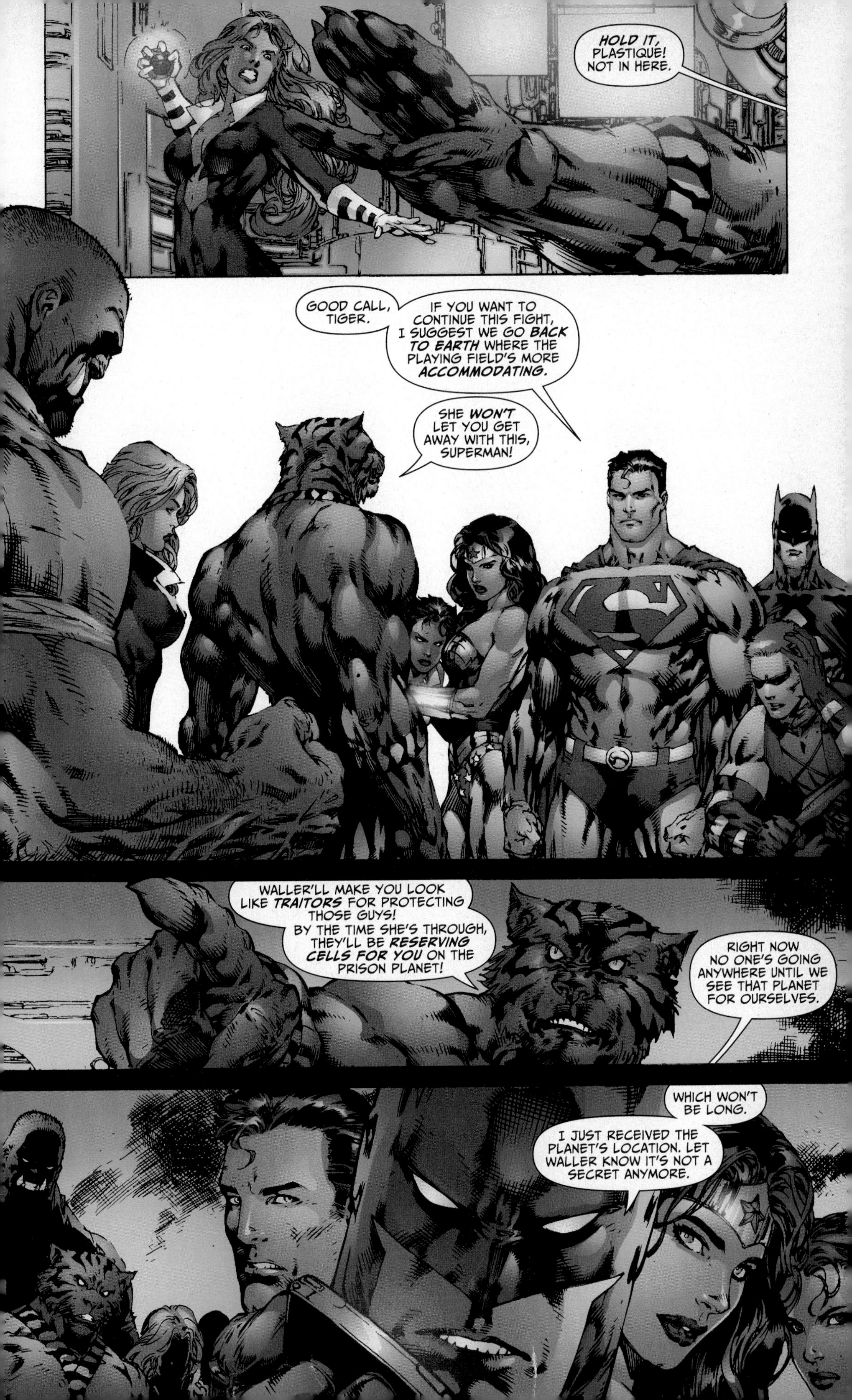
HOLD IT, PLASTIQUE! NOT IN HERE.
GOOD CALL, TIGER.
IF YOU WANT TO CONTINUE THIS FIGHT, I SUGGEST WE GO BACK TO EARTH WHERE THE PLAYING FIELD'S MORE ACCOMMODATING.
SHE WON'T LET YOU GET AWAY WITH THIS, SUPERMAN!
WALLER'LL MAKE YOU LOOK LIKE TRAITORS FOR PROTECTING THOSE GUYS!
BY THE TIME SHE'S THROUGH, THEY'LL BE RESERVING CELLS FOR YOU ON THE PRISON PLANET!
RIGHT NOW NO ONE'S GOING ANYWHERE UNTIL WE SEE THAT PLANET FOR OURSELVES.
WHICH WON'T BE LONG.
I JUST RECEIVED THE PLANET'S LOCATION. LET WALLER KNOW IT'S NOT A SECRET ANYMORE.

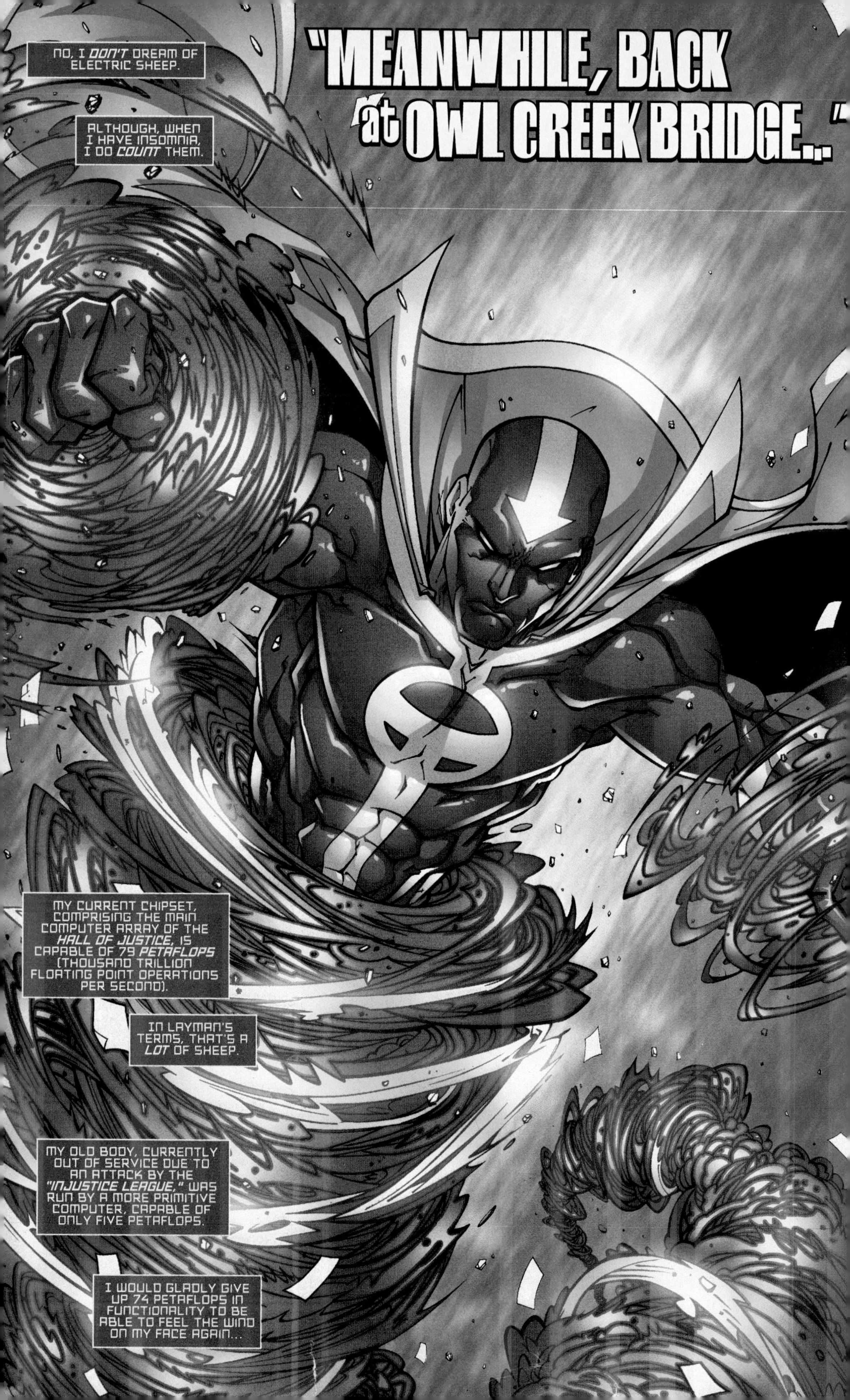
"MEANWHILE, BACK at OWL CREEK BRIDGE..."
NO, I DON'T DREAM OF ELECTRIC SHEEP.
ALTHOUGH, WHEN I HAVE INSOMNIA, I DO COUNT THEM.
MY CURRENT CHIPSET, COMPRISING THE MAIN COMPUTER ARRAY OF THE HALL OF JUSTICE, IS CAPABLE OF 79 PETAFLOPS (THOUSAND TRILLION FLOATING POINT OPERATIONS PER SECOND).
IN LAYMAN'S TERMS, THAT'S A LOT OF SHEEP.
MY OLD BODY, CURRENTLY OUT OF SERVICE DUE TO AN ATTACK BY THE "INJUSTICE LEAGUE," WAS RUN BY A MORE PRIMITIVE COMPUTER, CAPABLE OF ONLY FIVE PETAFLOPS.
I WOULD GLADLY GIVE UP 74 PETAFLOPS IN FUNCTIONALITY TO BE ABLE TO FEEL THE WIND ON MY FACE AGAIN...

...TO HOLD MY BEAUTIFUL WIFE IN MY ARMS...

...TO TAKE MY DAUGHTER'S HAND IN MINE.

BUT I *CAN'T.* NOT REALLY.

MY WIFE, *KATHY,* AND MY DAUGHTER, *TRAYA,* AREN'T REALLY HERE.

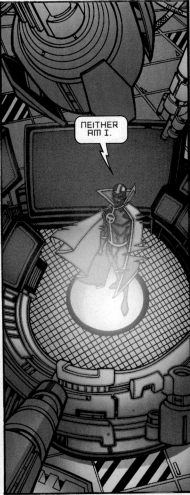

NEITHER AM I.

UNIQUE AMONG THE 140 ROOMS IN THE HALL OF JUSTICE, THE JLA BATTLE SIMULATION CHAMBER. "THE KITCHEN," IS DESIGNED TO CREATE REALISTIC SCENARIOS FOR TRAINING PURPOSES.

THESE IMAGES CAN ALSO BE MODIFIED TO CREATE AN UNREAL WORLD, WHERE I STILL HAVE THE POWER TO TOUCH THE PEOPLE I LOVE.

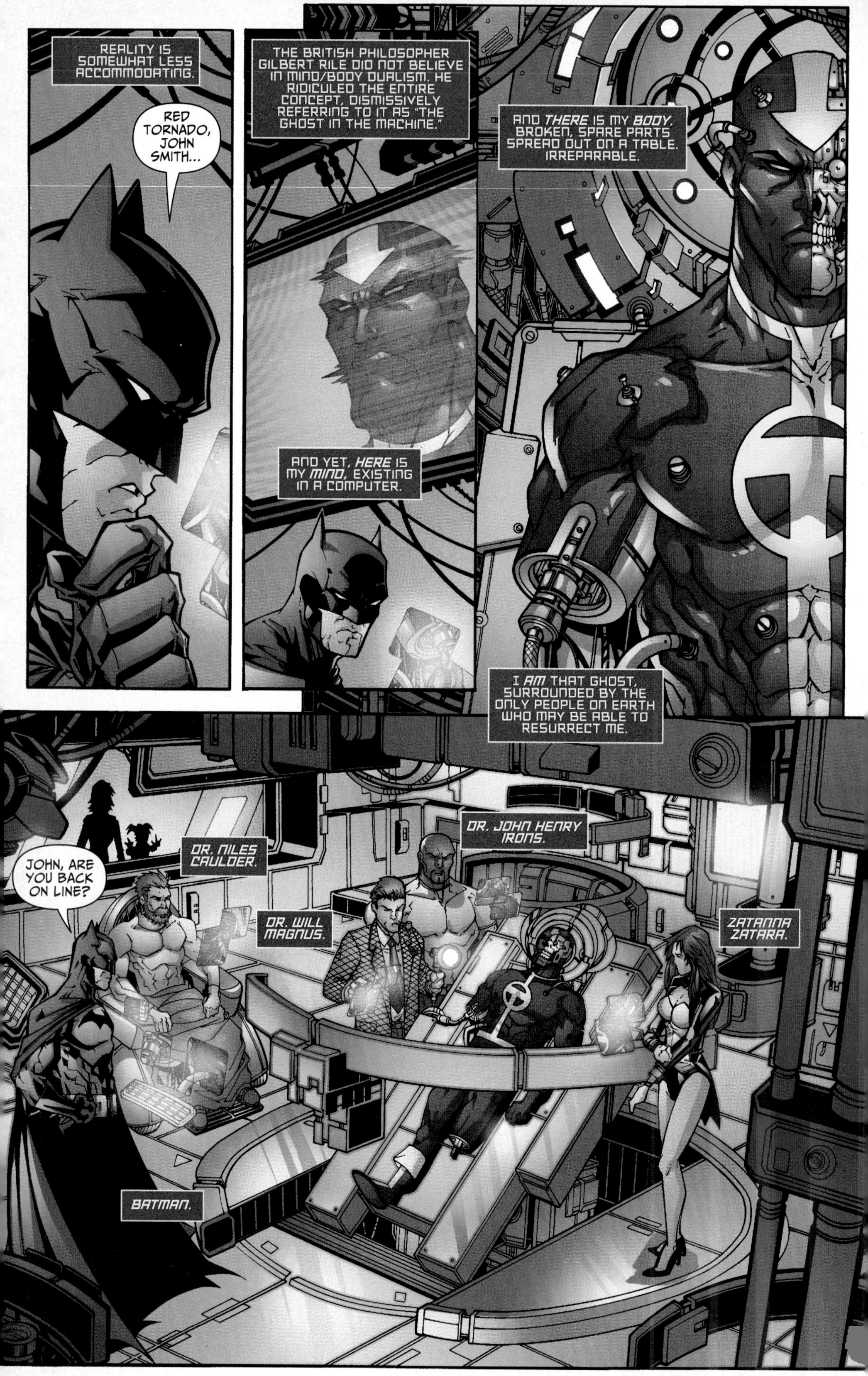

REALITY IS SOMEWHAT LESS ACCOMMODATING.
RED TORNADO, JOHN SMITH...
THE BRITISH PHILOSOPHER GILBERT RILE DID NOT BELIEVE IN MIND/BODY DUALISM. HE RIDICULED THE ENTIRE CONCEPT, DISMISSIVELY REFERRING TO IT AS "THE GHOST IN THE MACHINE."
AND YET, *HERE* IS MY *MIND*, EXISTING IN A COMPUTER.
AND *THERE* IS MY *BODY*. BROKEN, SPARE PARTS SPREAD OUT ON A TABLE. IRREPARABLE.
I *AM* THAT GHOST, SURROUNDED BY THE ONLY PEOPLE ON EARTH WHO MAY BE ABLE TO RESURRECT ME.
JOHN, ARE YOU BACK ON LINE?
DR. NILES CAULDER.
DR. JOHN HENRY IRONS.
DR. WILL MAGNUS.
ZATANNA ZATARA.
BATMAN.

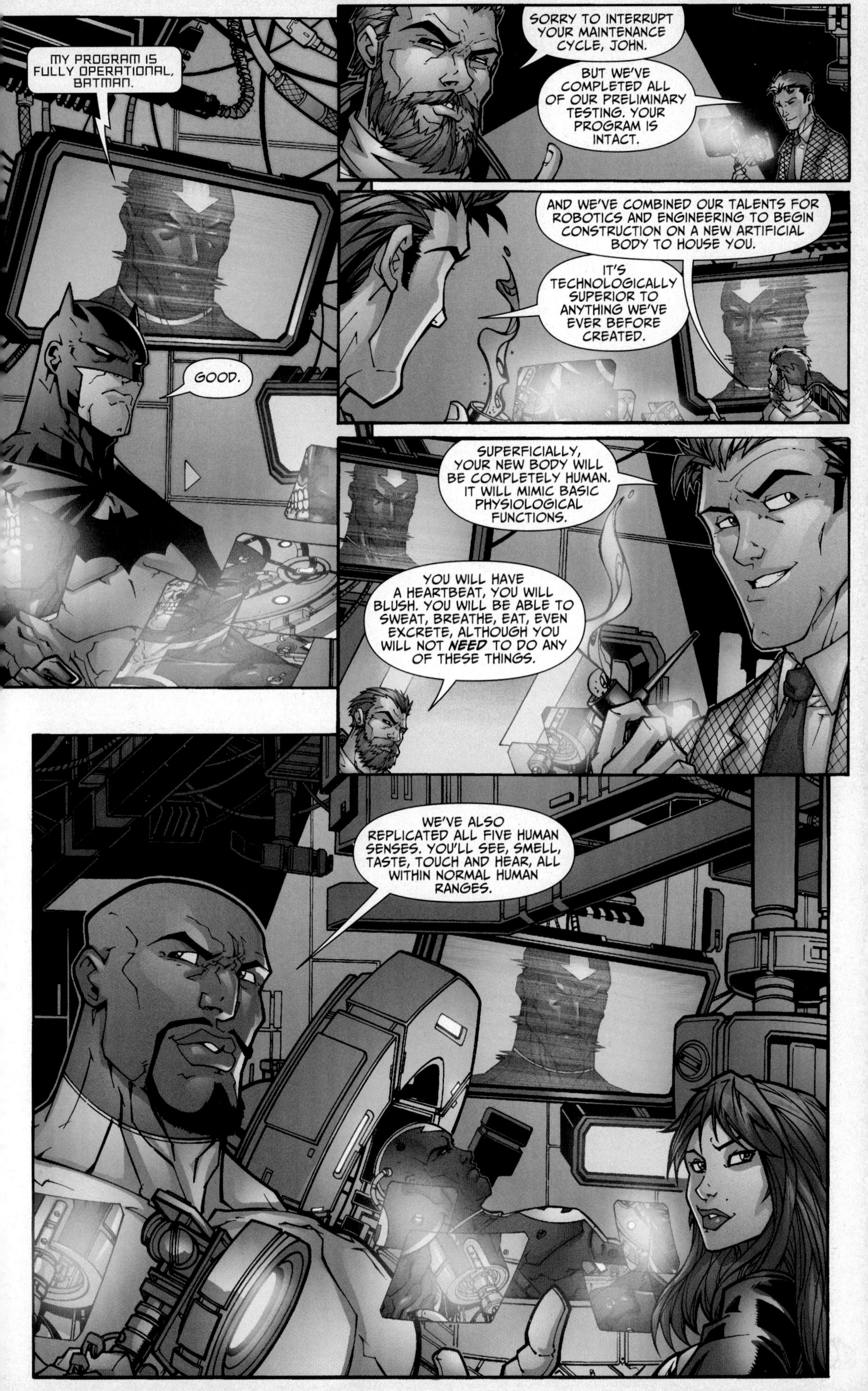
MY PROGRAM IS FULLY OPERATIONAL, BATMAN.
GOOD.
SORRY TO INTERRUPT YOUR MAINTENANCE CYCLE, JOHN.
BUT WE'VE COMPLETED ALL OF OUR PRELIMINARY TESTING. YOUR PROGRAM IS INTACT.
AND WE'VE COMBINED OUR TALENTS FOR ROBOTICS AND ENGINEERING TO BEGIN CONSTRUCTION ON A NEW ARTIFICIAL BODY TO HOUSE YOU.
IT'S TECHNOLOGICALLY SUPERIOR TO ANYTHING WE'VE EVER BEFORE CREATED.
SUPERFICIALLY, YOUR NEW BODY WILL BE COMPLETELY HUMAN. IT WILL MIMIC BASIC PHYSIOLOGICAL FUNCTIONS.
YOU WILL HAVE A HEARTBEAT, YOU WILL BLUSH. YOU WILL BE ABLE TO SWEAT, BREATHE, EAT, EVEN EXCRETE, ALTHOUGH YOU WILL NOT *NEED* TO DO ANY OF THESE THINGS.
WE'VE ALSO REPLICATED ALL FIVE HUMAN SENSES. YOU'LL SEE, SMELL, TASTE, TOUCH AND HEAR, ALL WITHIN NORMAL HUMAN RANGES.

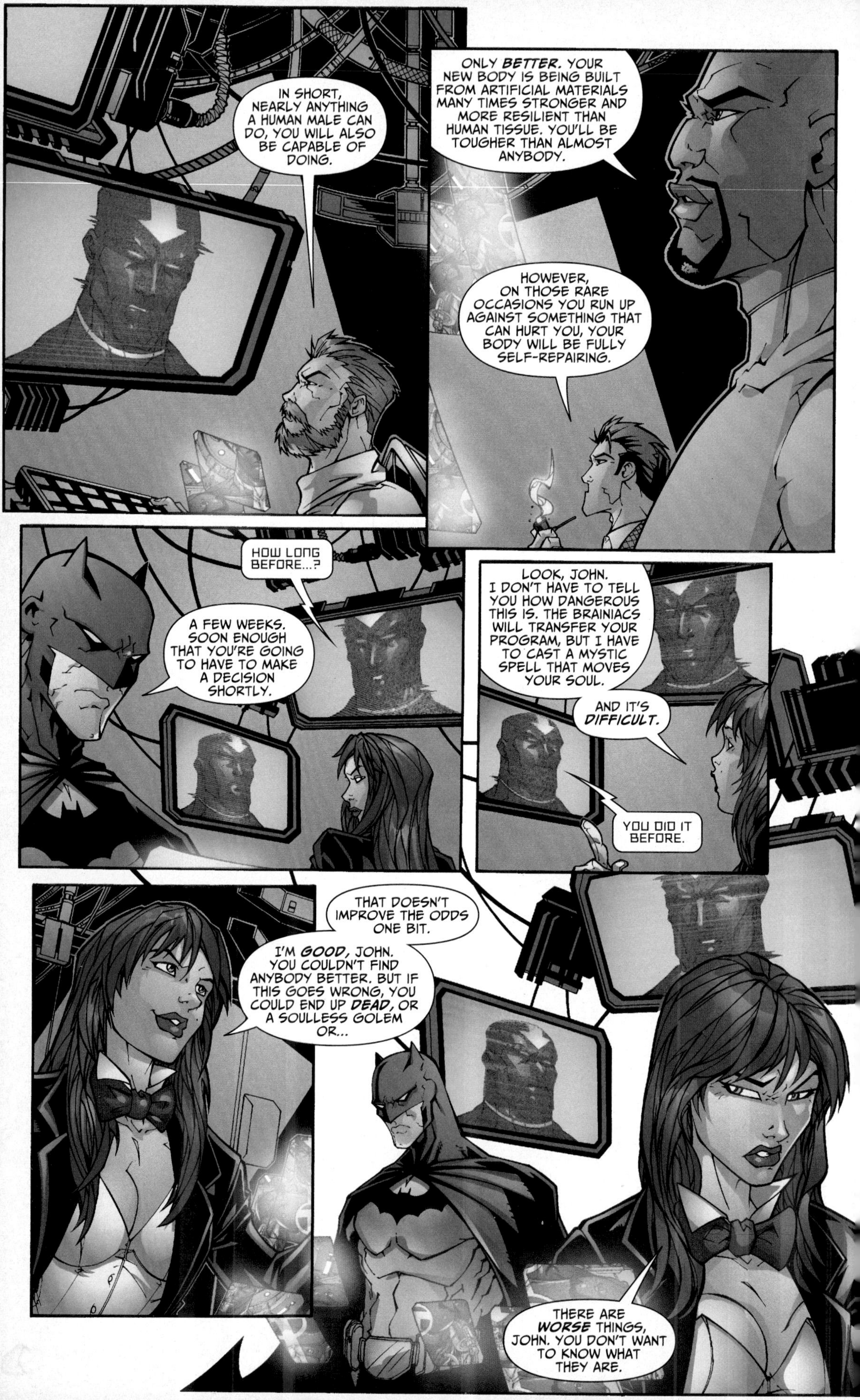
IN SHORT, NEARLY ANYTHING A HUMAN MALE CAN DO, YOU WILL ALSO BE CAPABLE OF DOING.
ONLY BETTER. YOUR NEW BODY IS BEING BUILT FROM ARTIFICIAL MATERIALS MANY TIMES STRONGER AND MORE RESILIENT THAN HUMAN TISSUE. YOU'LL BE TOUGHER THAN ALMOST ANYBODY.
HOWEVER, ON THOSE RARE OCCASIONS YOU RUN UP AGAINST SOMETHING THAT CAN HURT YOU, YOUR BODY WILL BE FULLY SELF-REPAIRING.
HOW LONG BEFORE...?
A FEW WEEKS. SOON ENOUGH THAT YOU'RE GOING TO HAVE TO MAKE A DECISION SHORTLY.
LOOK, JOHN. I DON'T HAVE TO TELL YOU HOW DANGEROUS THIS IS. THE BRAINIACS WILL TRANSFER YOUR PROGRAM, BUT I HAVE TO CAST A MYSTIC SPELL THAT MOVES YOUR SOUL.
AND IT'S DIFFICULT.
YOU DID IT BEFORE.
THAT DOESN'T IMPROVE THE ODDS ONE BIT.
I'M GOOD, JOHN. YOU COULDN'T FIND ANYBODY BETTER. BUT IF THIS GOES WRONG, YOU COULD END UP DEAD, OR A SOULLESS GOLEM OR...
THERE ARE WORSE THINGS, JOHN. YOU DON'T WANT TO KNOW WHAT THEY ARE.

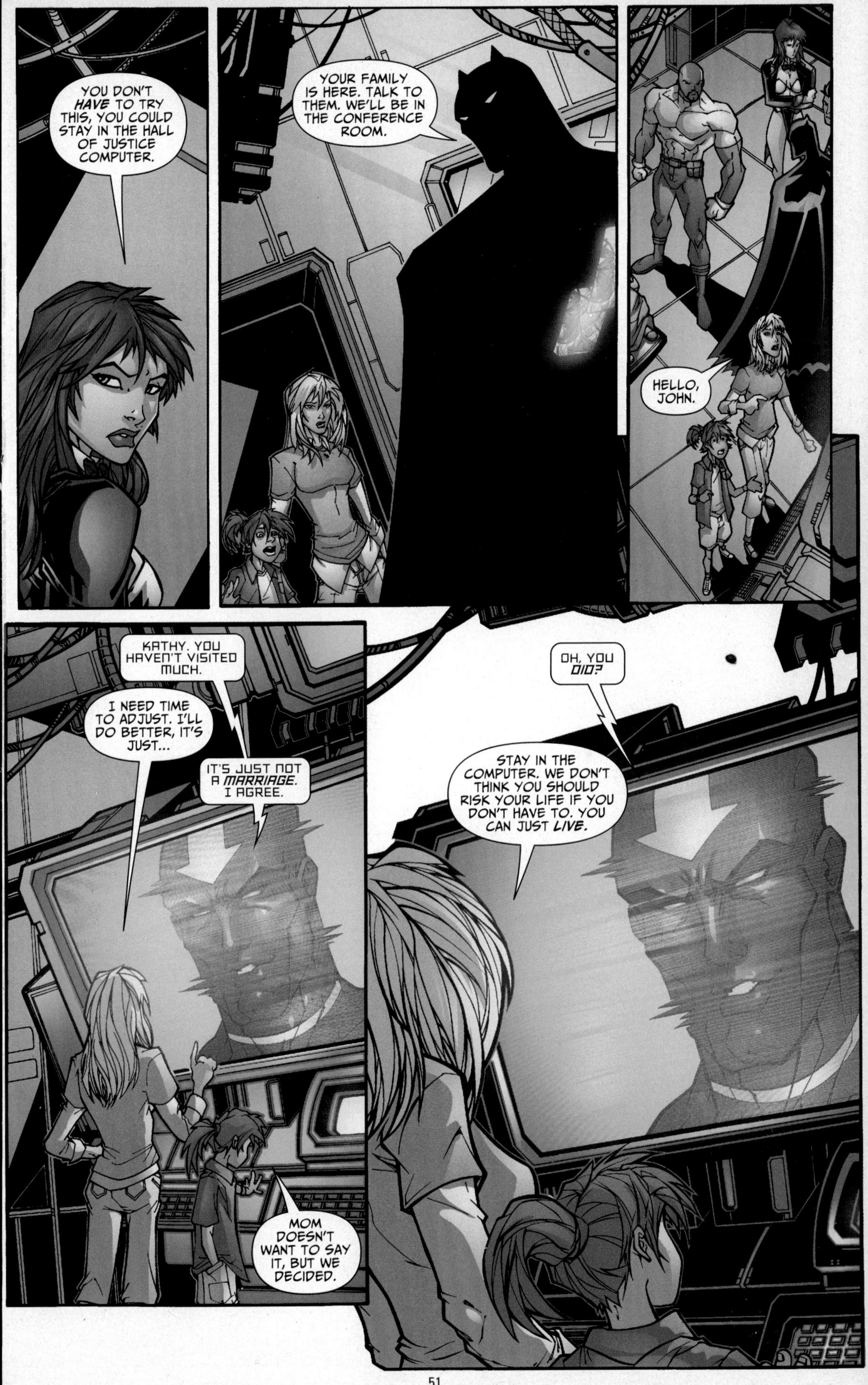
YOU DON'T *HAVE* TO TRY THIS, YOU COULD STAY IN THE HALL OF JUSTICE COMPUTER.
YOUR FAMILY IS HERE. TALK TO THEM. WE'LL BE IN THE CONFERENCE ROOM.
HELLO, JOHN.
KATHY. YOU HAVEN'T VISITED MUCH.
I NEED TIME TO ADJUST. I'LL DO BETTER, IT'S JUST...
IT'S JUST NOT A *MARRIAGE*. I AGREE.
MOM DOESN'T WANT TO SAY IT, BUT WE DECIDED.
OH, YOU *DID?*
STAY IN THE COMPUTER. WE DON'T THINK YOU SHOULD RISK YOUR LIFE IF YOU DON'T HAVE TO. YOU CAN JUST *LIVE*.

THIS ISN'T LIFE, KATHY. LIFE IS PICKING UP MY DAUGHTER AND GIVING HER A RIDE ON MY SHOULDERS.

LIFE IS USING MY POWERS TO HELP SOMEONE WHO WOULDN'T HAVE A CHANCE IF I WEREN'T THERE.

LIFE IS MAKING LOVE WITH MY WIFE AND SMELLING HER SCENT ON MY SKIN AFTERWARDS.

THERE'S NO CHOICE TO MAKE HERE. I CAN'T BE WHO I AM LIKE *THIS*. IF I *CAN'T* GO BACK INTO A BODY, I'M ALREADY DEAD.

I'M COMING BACK TO YOU. THAT'S ALL THERE IS TO IT.

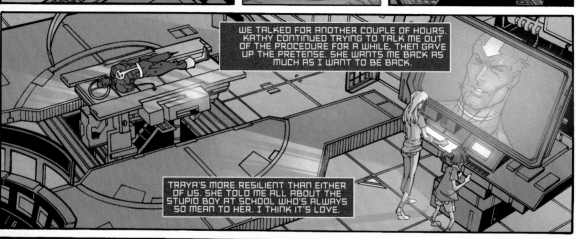

WE TALKED FOR ANOTHER COUPLE OF HOURS. KATHY CONTINUED TRYING TO TALK ME OUT OF THE PROCEDURE FOR A WHILE, THEN GAVE UP THE PRETENSE. SHE WANTS ME BACK AS MUCH AS I WANT TO BE BACK.

TRAYA'S MORE RESILIENT THAN EITHER OF US. SHE TOLD ME ALL ABOUT THE STUPID BOY AT SCHOOL WHO'S ALWAYS SO MEAN TO HER. I THINK IT'S LOVE.

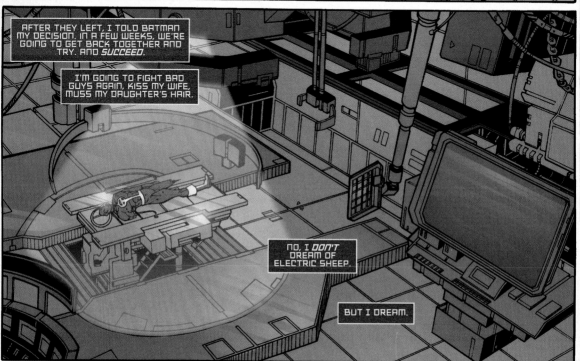

AFTER THEY LEFT, I TOLD BATMAN MY DECISION. IN A FEW WEEKS, WE'RE GOING TO GET BACK TOGETHER AND TRY. AND *SUCCEED*.

I'M GOING TO FIGHT BAD GUYS AGAIN, KISS MY WIFE, MUSS MY DAUGHTER'S HAIR.

NO, I *DON'T* DREAM OF ELECTRIC SHEEP.

BUT I DREAM.

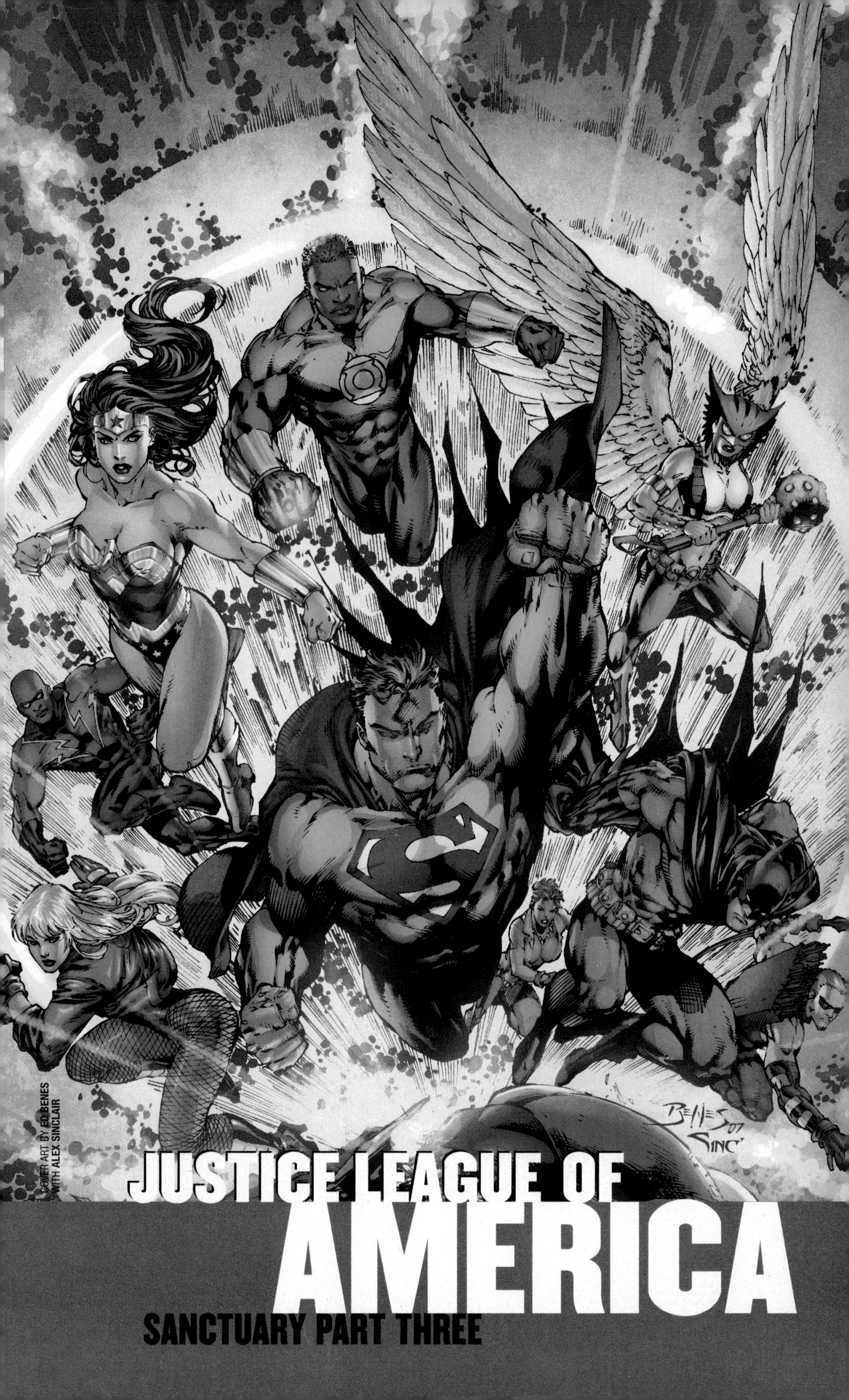
COVER ART BY ED BENES
WITH ALEX SINCLAIR

JUSTICE LEAGUE OF AMERICA

SANCTUARY PART THREE

Sanctuary Part Three

Alan Burnett
Writer

Ed Benes
Penciller

Sandra Hope
Mariah Benes
Ruy José
Inkers

Rob Leigh
Letterer

Pete Pantazis
Colorist

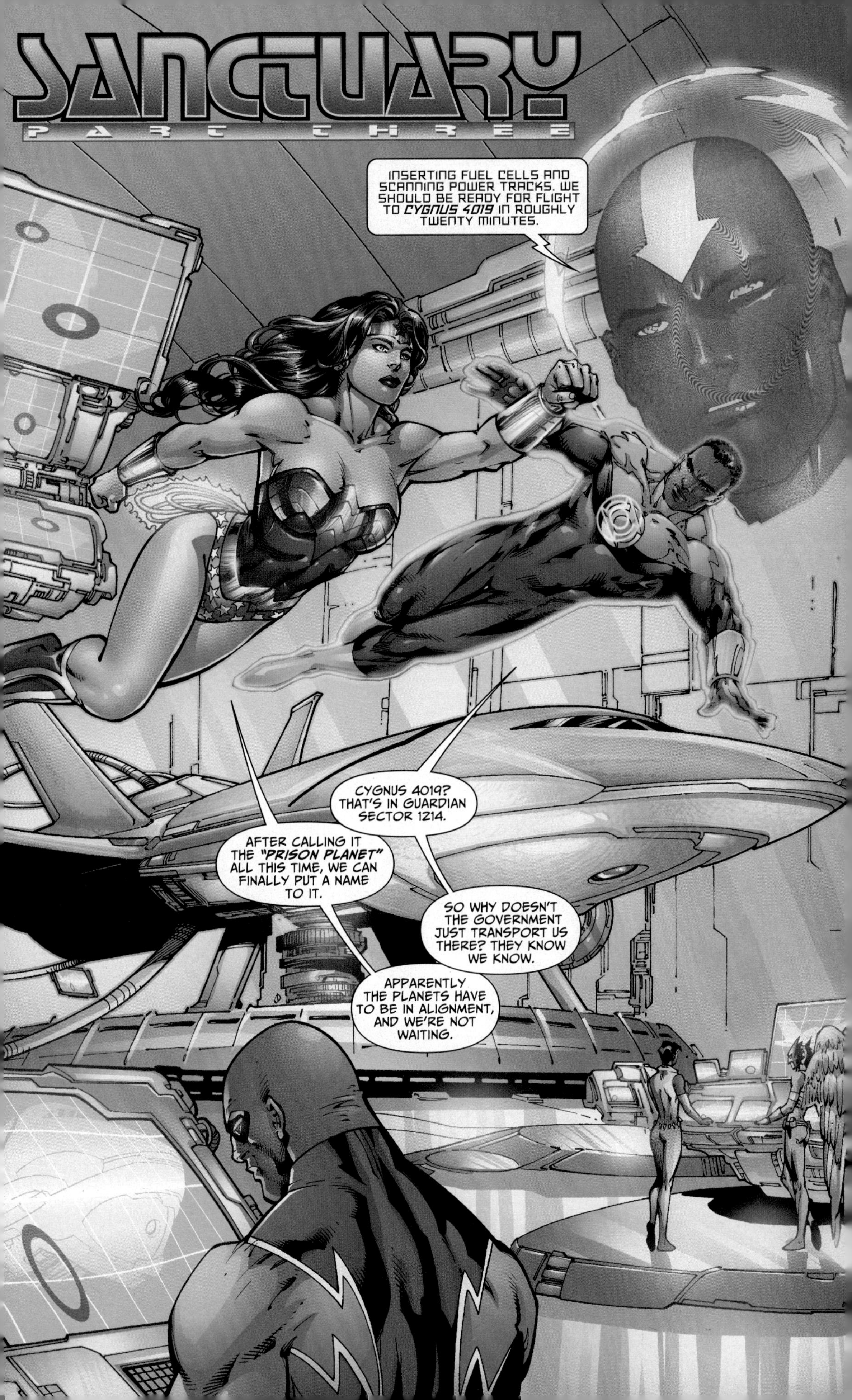
SANCTUARY
PART THREE
INSERTING FUEL CELLS AND SCANNING POWER TRACKS. WE SHOULD BE READY FOR FLIGHT TO CYGNUS 4019 IN ROUGHLY TWENTY MINUTES.
CYGNUS 4019? THAT'S IN GUARDIAN SECTOR 1214.
AFTER CALLING IT THE "PRISON PLANET" ALL THIS TIME, WE CAN FINALLY PUT A NAME TO IT.
SO WHY DOESN'T THE GOVERNMENT JUST TRANSPORT US THERE? THEY KNOW WE KNOW.
APPARENTLY THE PLANETS HAVE TO BE IN ALIGNMENT, AND WE'RE NOT WAITING.

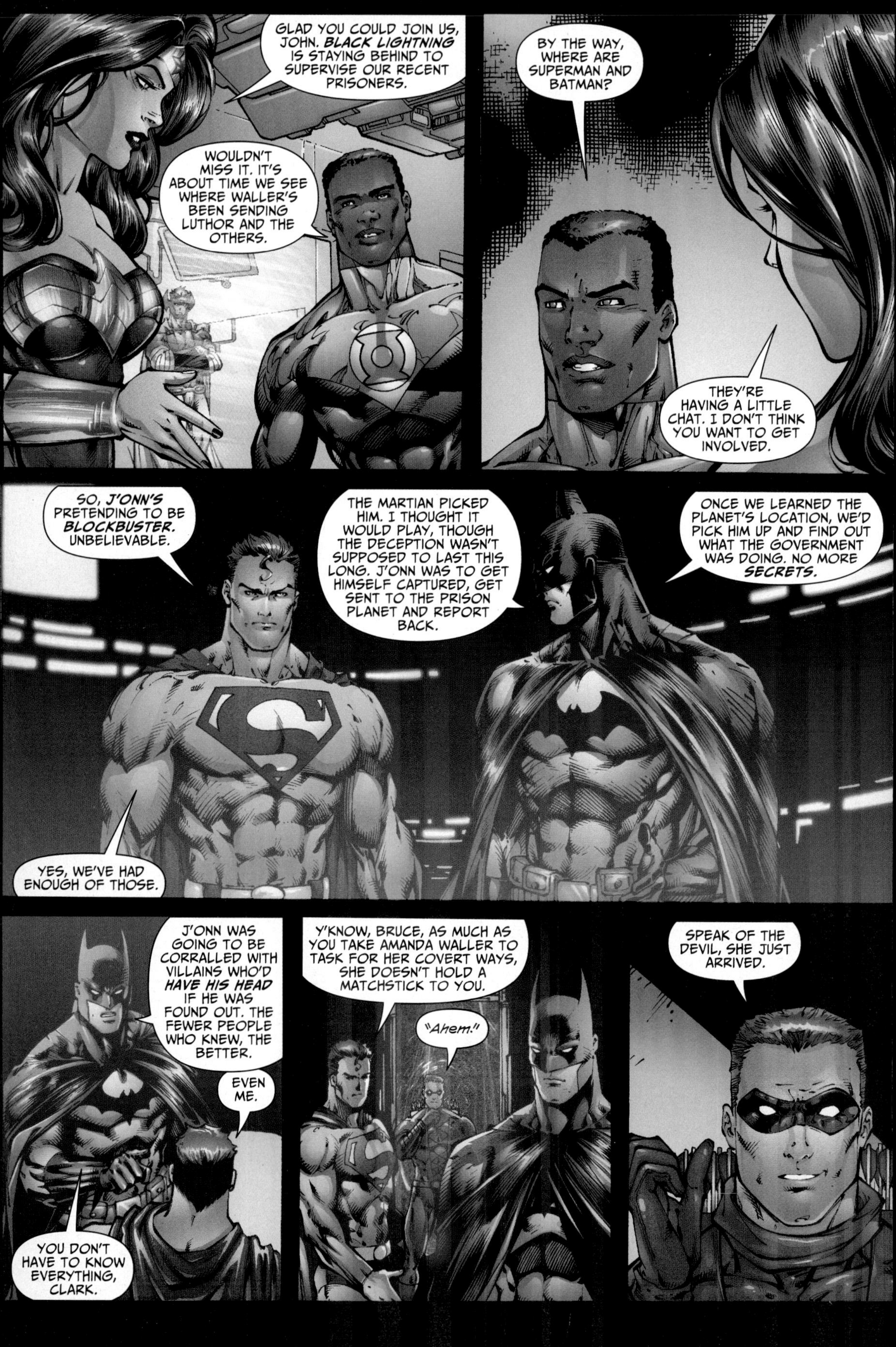
GLAD YOU COULD JOIN US, JOHN. BLACK LIGHTNING IS STAYING BEHIND TO SUPERVISE OUR RECENT PRISONERS.
WOULDN'T MISS IT. IT'S ABOUT TIME WE SEE WHERE WALLER'S BEEN SENDING LUTHOR AND THE OTHERS.
BY THE WAY, WHERE ARE SUPERMAN AND BATMAN?
THEY'RE HAVING A LITTLE CHAT. I DON'T THINK YOU WANT TO GET INVOLVED.
SO, J'ONN'S PRETENDING TO BE BLOCKBUSTER. UNBELIEVABLE.
THE MARTIAN PICKED HIM. I THOUGHT IT WOULD PLAY, THOUGH THE DECEPTION WASN'T SUPPOSED TO LAST THIS LONG. J'ONN WAS TO GET HIMSELF CAPTURED, GET SENT TO THE PRISON PLANET AND REPORT BACK.
ONCE WE LEARNED THE PLANET'S LOCATION, WE'D PICK HIM UP AND FIND OUT WHAT THE GOVERNMENT WAS DOING. NO MORE SECRETS.
YES, WE'VE HAD ENOUGH OF THOSE.
J'ONN WAS GOING TO BE CORRALLED WITH VILLAINS WHO'D HAVE HIS HEAD IF HE WAS FOUND OUT. THE FEWER PEOPLE WHO KNEW, THE BETTER.
EVEN ME.
YOU DON'T HAVE TO KNOW EVERYTHING, CLARK.
Y'KNOW, BRUCE, AS MUCH AS YOU TAKE AMANDA WALLER TO TASK FOR HER COVERT WAYS, SHE DOESN'T HOLD A MATCHSTICK TO YOU.
"Ahem."
SPEAK OF THE DEVIL, SHE JUST ARRIVED.

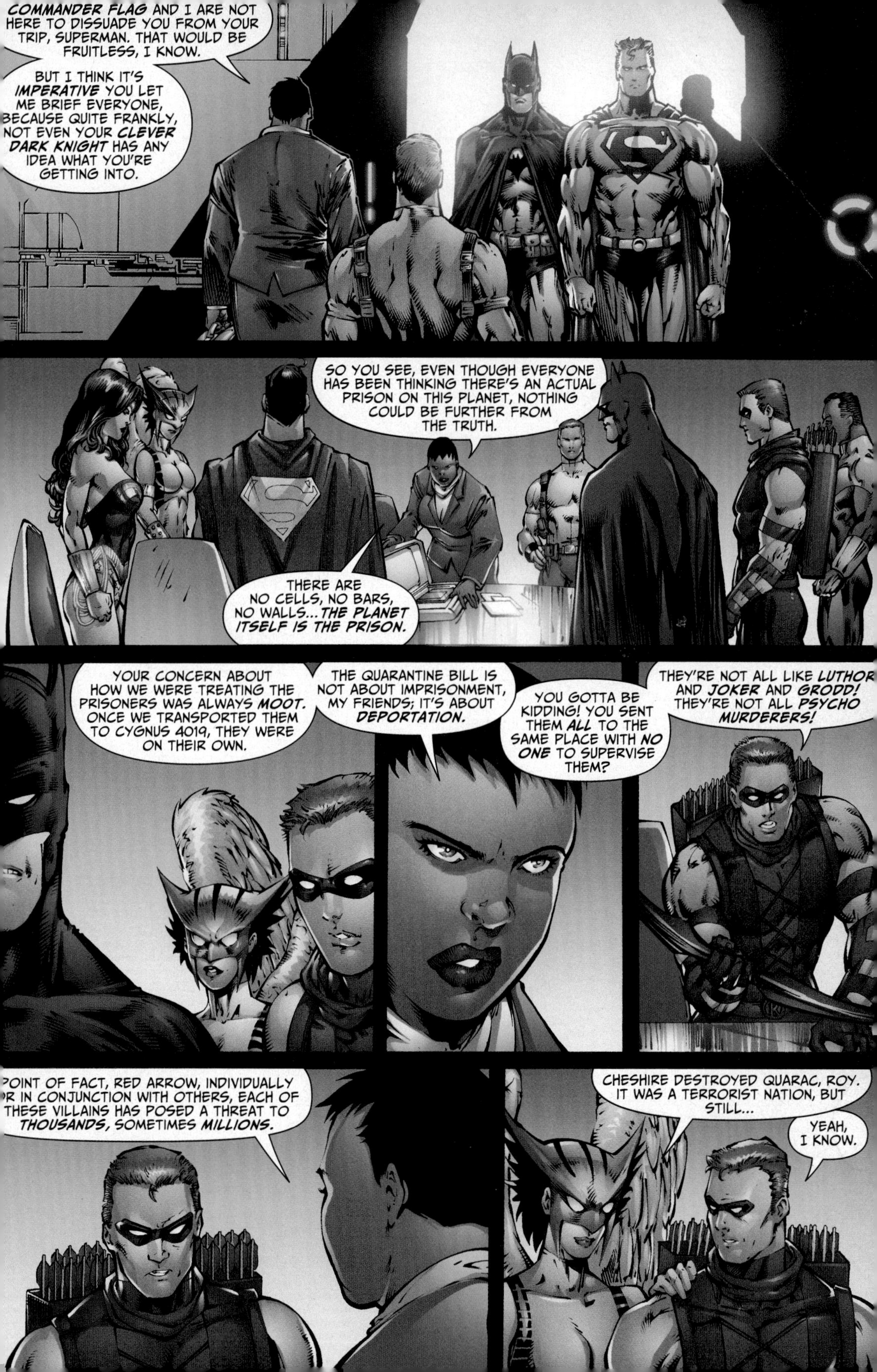
COMMANDER FLAG AND I ARE NOT HERE TO DISSUADE YOU FROM YOUR TRIP, SUPERMAN. THAT WOULD BE FRUITLESS, I KNOW.
BUT I THINK IT'S IMPERATIVE YOU LET ME BRIEF EVERYONE, BECAUSE QUITE FRANKLY, NOT EVEN YOUR CLEVER DARK KNIGHT HAS ANY IDEA WHAT YOU'RE GETTING INTO.
SO YOU SEE, EVEN THOUGH EVERYONE HAS BEEN THINKING THERE'S AN ACTUAL PRISON ON THIS PLANET, NOTHING COULD BE FURTHER FROM THE TRUTH.
THERE ARE NO CELLS, NO BARS, NO WALLS...THE PLANET ITSELF IS THE PRISON.
YOUR CONCERN ABOUT HOW WE WERE TREATING THE PRISONERS WAS ALWAYS MOOT. ONCE WE TRANSPORTED THEM TO CYGNUS 4019, THEY WERE ON THEIR OWN.
THE QUARANTINE BILL IS NOT ABOUT IMPRISONMENT, MY FRIENDS; IT'S ABOUT DEPORTATION.
YOU GOTTA BE KIDDING! YOU SENT THEM ALL TO THE SAME PLACE WITH NO ONE TO SUPERVISE THEM?
THEY'RE NOT ALL LIKE LUTHOR AND JOKER AND GRODD! THEY'RE NOT ALL PSYCHO MURDERERS!
POINT OF FACT, RED ARROW, INDIVIDUALLY OR IN CONJUNCTION WITH OTHERS, EACH OF THESE VILLAINS HAS POSED A THREAT TO THOUSANDS, SOMETIMES MILLIONS.
CHESHIRE DESTROYED QUARAC, ROY. IT WAS A TERRORIST NATION, BUT STILL...
YEAH, I KNOW.

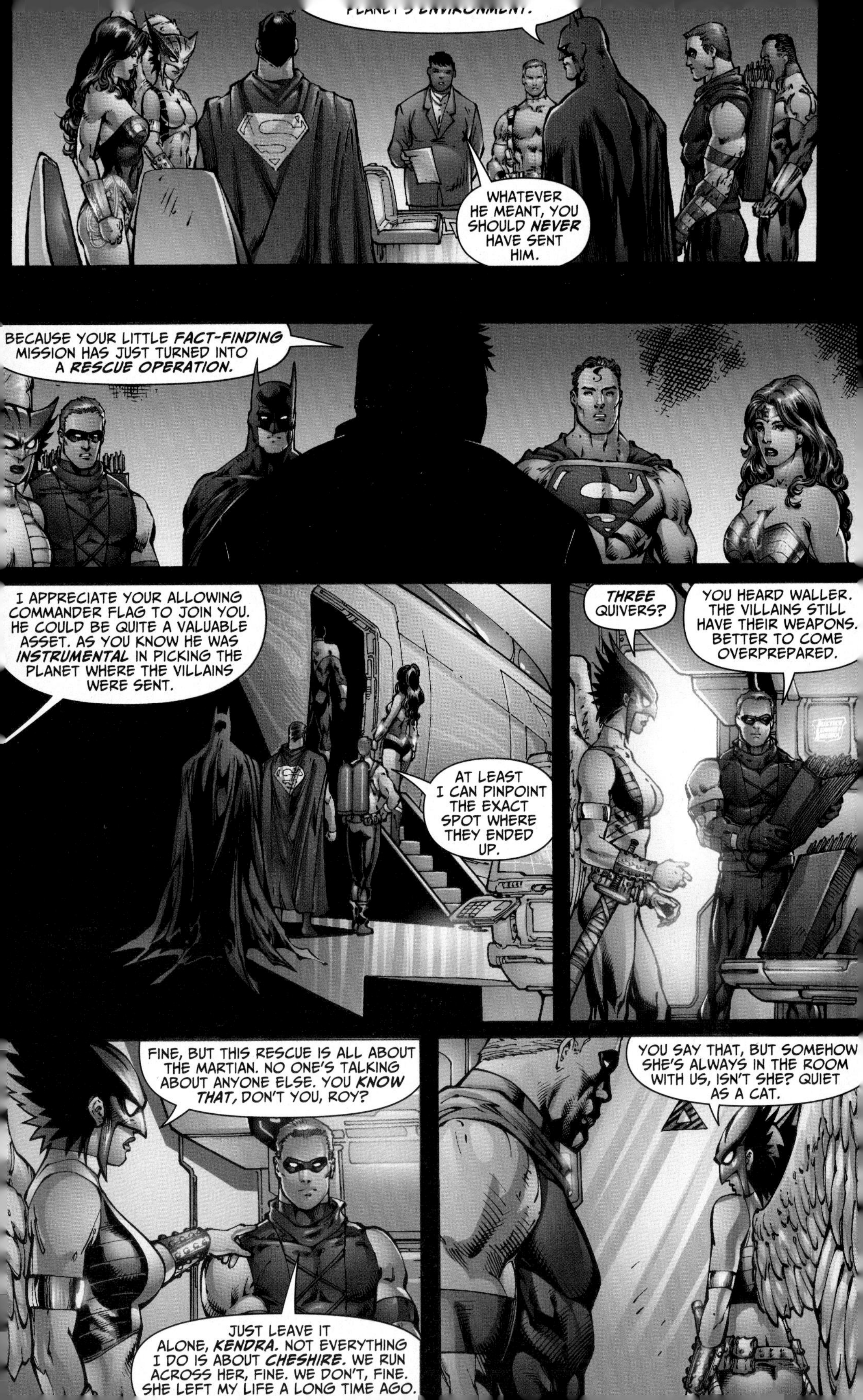
WHATEVER HE MEANT, YOU SHOULD NEVER HAVE SENT HIM.
BECAUSE YOUR LITTLE FACT-FINDING MISSION HAS JUST TURNED INTO A RESCUE OPERATION.
I APPRECIATE YOUR ALLOWING COMMANDER FLAG TO JOIN YOU. HE COULD BE QUITE A VALUABLE ASSET. AS YOU KNOW HE WAS INSTRUMENTAL IN PICKING THE PLANET WHERE THE VILLAINS WERE SENT.
AT LEAST I CAN PINPOINT THE EXACT SPOT WHERE THEY ENDED UP.
THREE QUIVERS?
YOU HEARD WALLER. THE VILLAINS STILL HAVE THEIR WEAPONS. BETTER TO COME OVERPREPARED.
FINE, BUT THIS RESCUE IS ALL ABOUT THE MARTIAN. NO ONE'S TALKING ABOUT ANYONE ELSE. YOU KNOW THAT, DON'T YOU, ROY?
JUST LEAVE IT ALONE, KENDRA. NOT EVERYTHING I DO IS ABOUT CHESHIRE. WE RUN ACROSS HER, FINE. WE DON'T, FINE. SHE LEFT MY LIFE A LONG TIME AGO.
YOU SAY THAT, BUT SOMEHOW SHE'S ALWAYS IN THE ROOM WITH US, ISN'T SHE? QUIET AS A CAT.

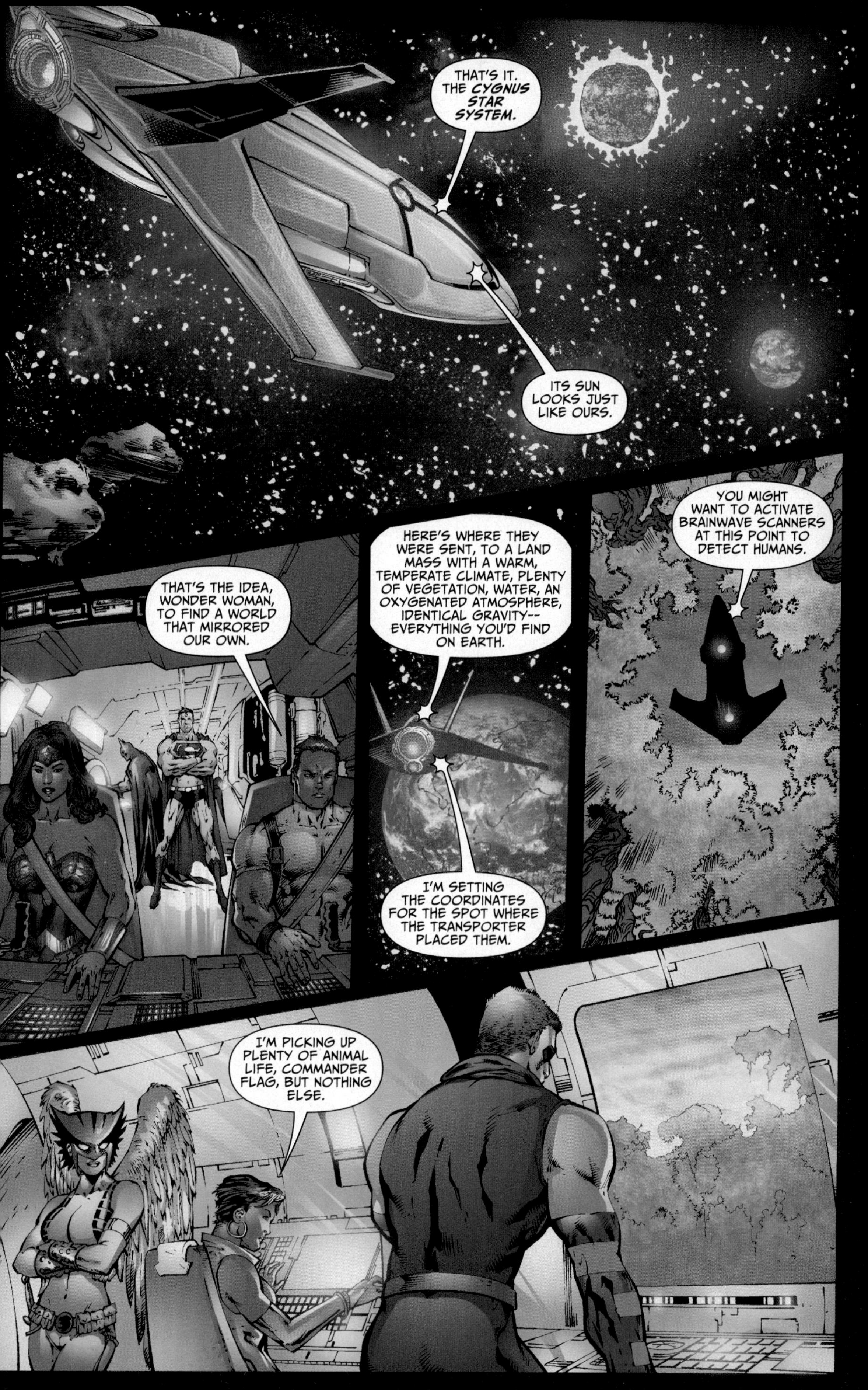
THAT'S IT. THE CYGNUS STAR SYSTEM.
ITS SUN LOOKS JUST LIKE OURS.
THAT'S THE IDEA, WONDER WOMAN, TO FIND A WORLD THAT MIRRORED OUR OWN.
HERE'S WHERE THEY WERE SENT, TO A LAND MASS WITH A WARM, TEMPERATE CLIMATE, PLENTY OF VEGETATION, WATER, AN OXYGENATED ATMOSPHERE, IDENTICAL GRAVITY-- EVERYTHING YOU'D FIND ON EARTH.
I'M SETTING THE COORDINATES FOR THE SPOT WHERE THE TRANSPORTER PLACED THEM.
YOU MIGHT WANT TO ACTIVATE BRAINWAVE SCANNERS AT THIS POINT TO DETECT HUMANS.
I'M PICKING UP PLENTY OF ANIMAL LIFE, COMMANDER FLAG, BUT NOTHING ELSE.

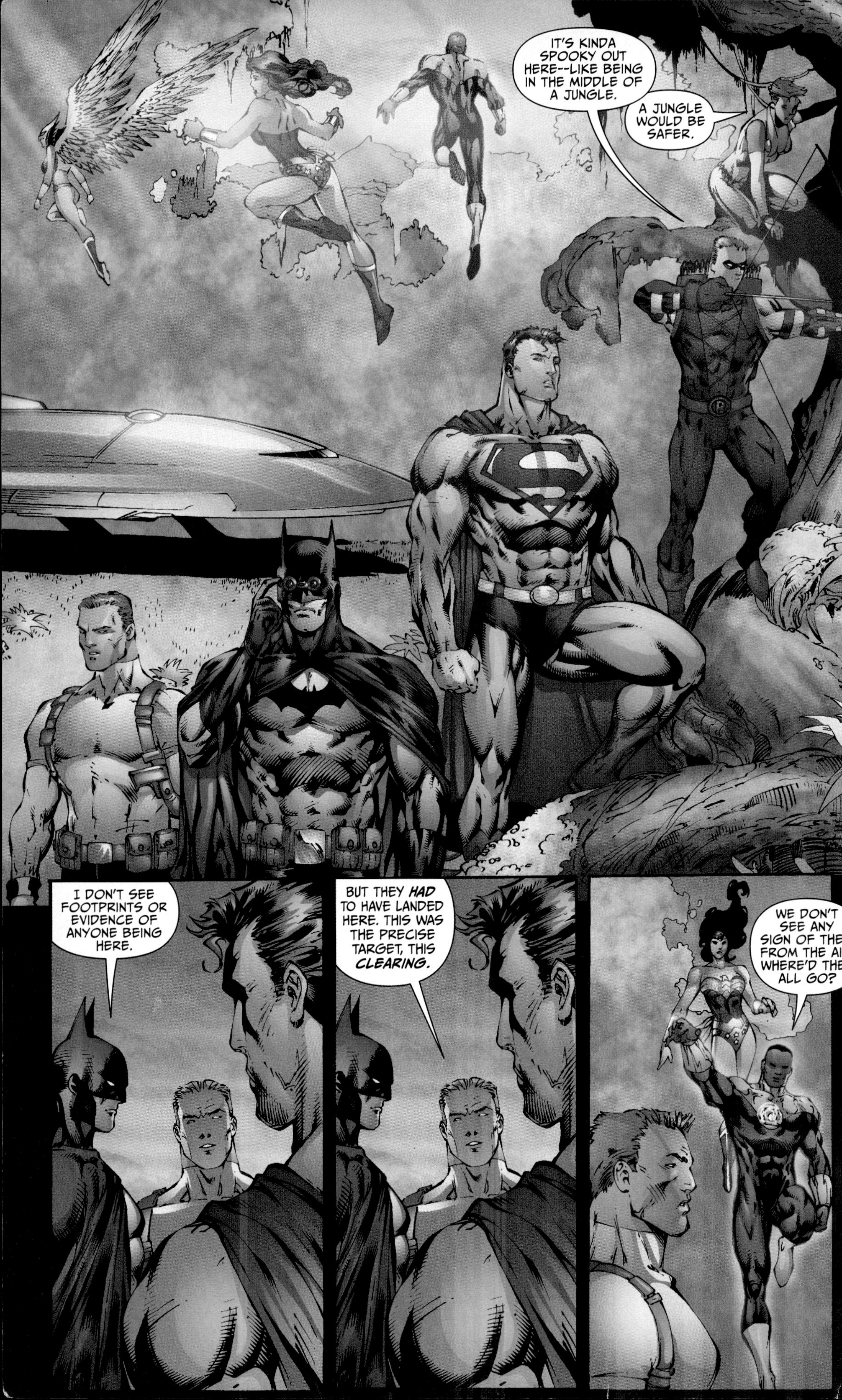

IT'S KINDA SPOOKY OUT HERE--LIKE BEING IN THE MIDDLE OF A JUNGLE.
A JUNGLE WOULD BE SAFER.
I DON'T SEE FOOTPRINTS OR EVIDENCE OF ANYONE BEING HERE.
BUT THEY HAD TO HAVE LANDED HERE. THIS WAS THE PRECISE TARGET, THIS CLEARING.
WE DON'T SEE ANY SIGN OF THE FROM THE AI WHERE'D THE ALL GO?

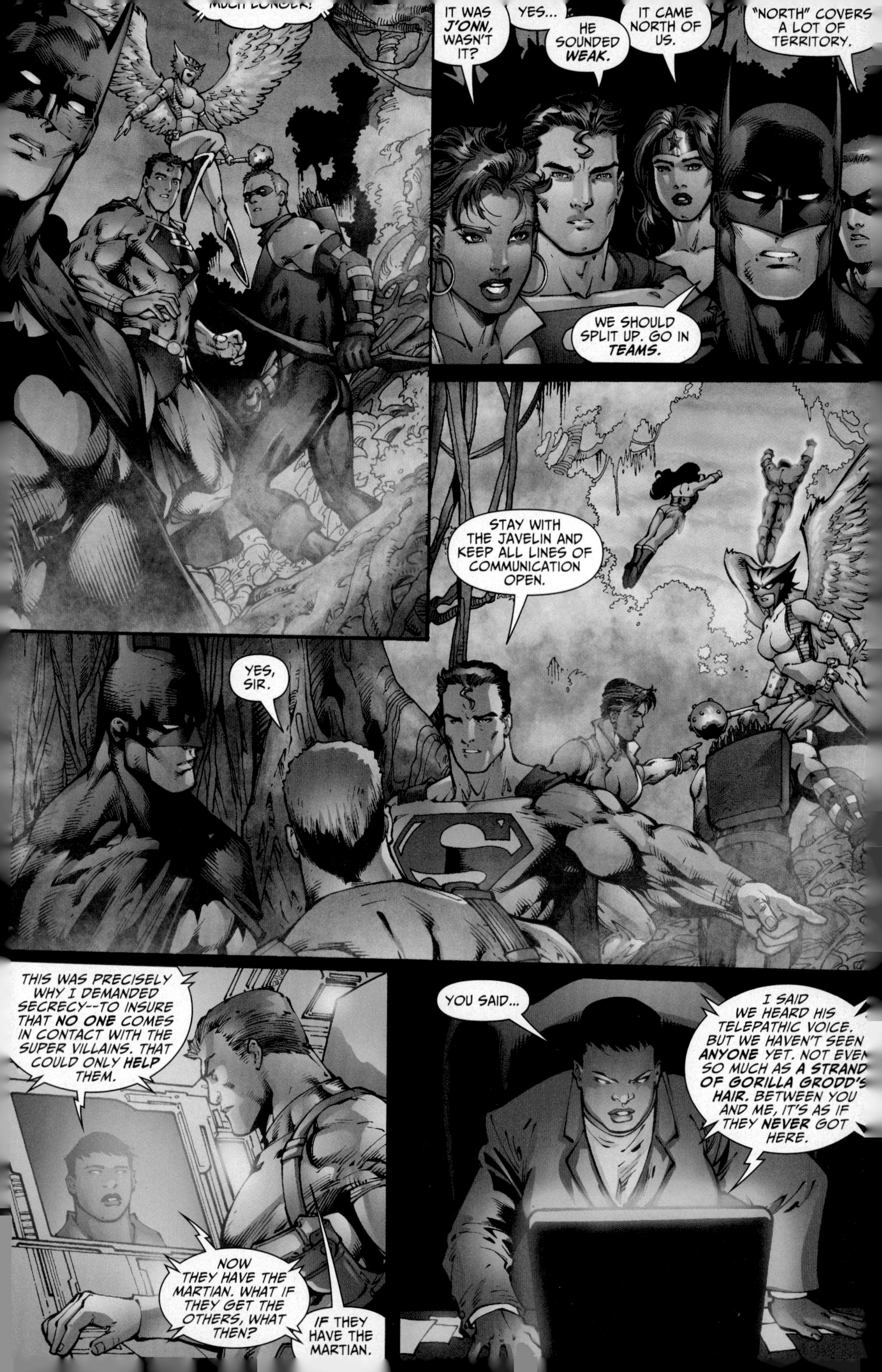
IT WAS **J'ONN,** WASN'T IT?
YES... HE SOUNDED **WEAK.**
IT CAME NORTH OF US.
"NORTH" COVERS A LOT OF TERRITORY.
WE SHOULD SPLIT UP. GO IN **TEAMS.**
STAY WITH THE JAVELIN AND KEEP ALL LINES OF COMMUNICATION OPEN.
YES, SIR.
THIS WAS PRECISELY WHY I DEMANDED SECRECY--TO INSURE THAT **NO ONE** COMES IN CONTACT WITH THE SUPER VILLAINS. THAT COULD ONLY **HELP** THEM.
NOW THEY HAVE THE MARTIAN. WHAT IF THEY GET THE OTHERS, WHAT THEN?
IF THEY HAVE THE MARTIAN.
YOU SAID...
I SAID WE HEARD HIS TELEPATHIC VOICE. BUT WE HAVEN'T SEEN **ANYONE** YET. NOT EVEN SO MUCH AS **A STRAND OF GORILLA GRODD'S HAIR.** BETWEEN YOU AND ME, IT'S AS IF THEY **NEVER** GOT HERE.

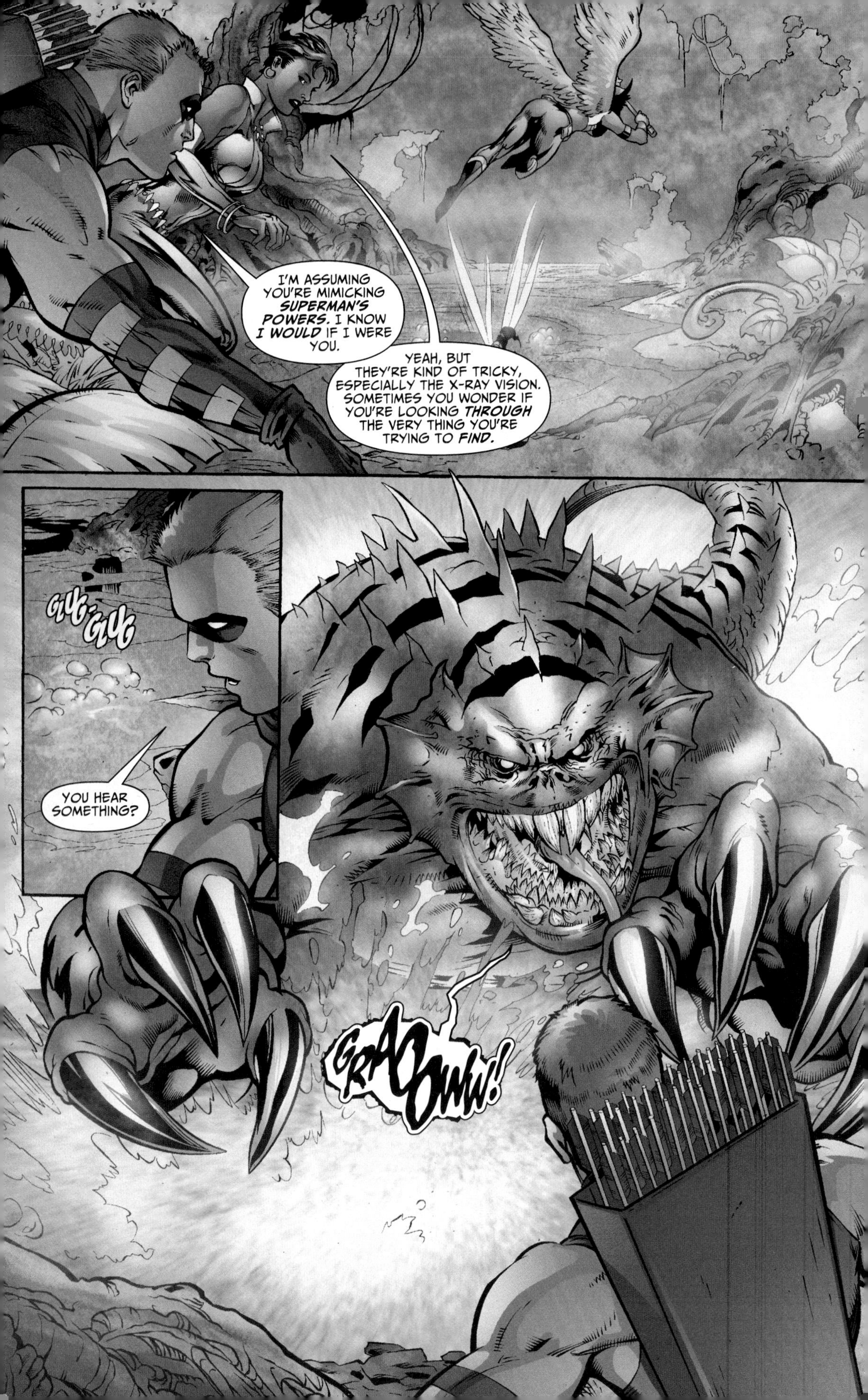
I'M ASSUMING YOU'RE MIMICKING **SUPERMAN'S POWERS.** I KNOW **I WOULD** IF I WERE YOU.
YEAH, BUT THEY'RE KIND OF TRICKY, ESPECIALLY THE X-RAY VISION. SOMETIMES YOU WONDER IF YOU'RE LOOKING **THROUGH** THE VERY THING YOU'RE TRYING TO **FIND.**
GLUG-GLUG
YOU HEAR SOMETHING?
GRAOWW!

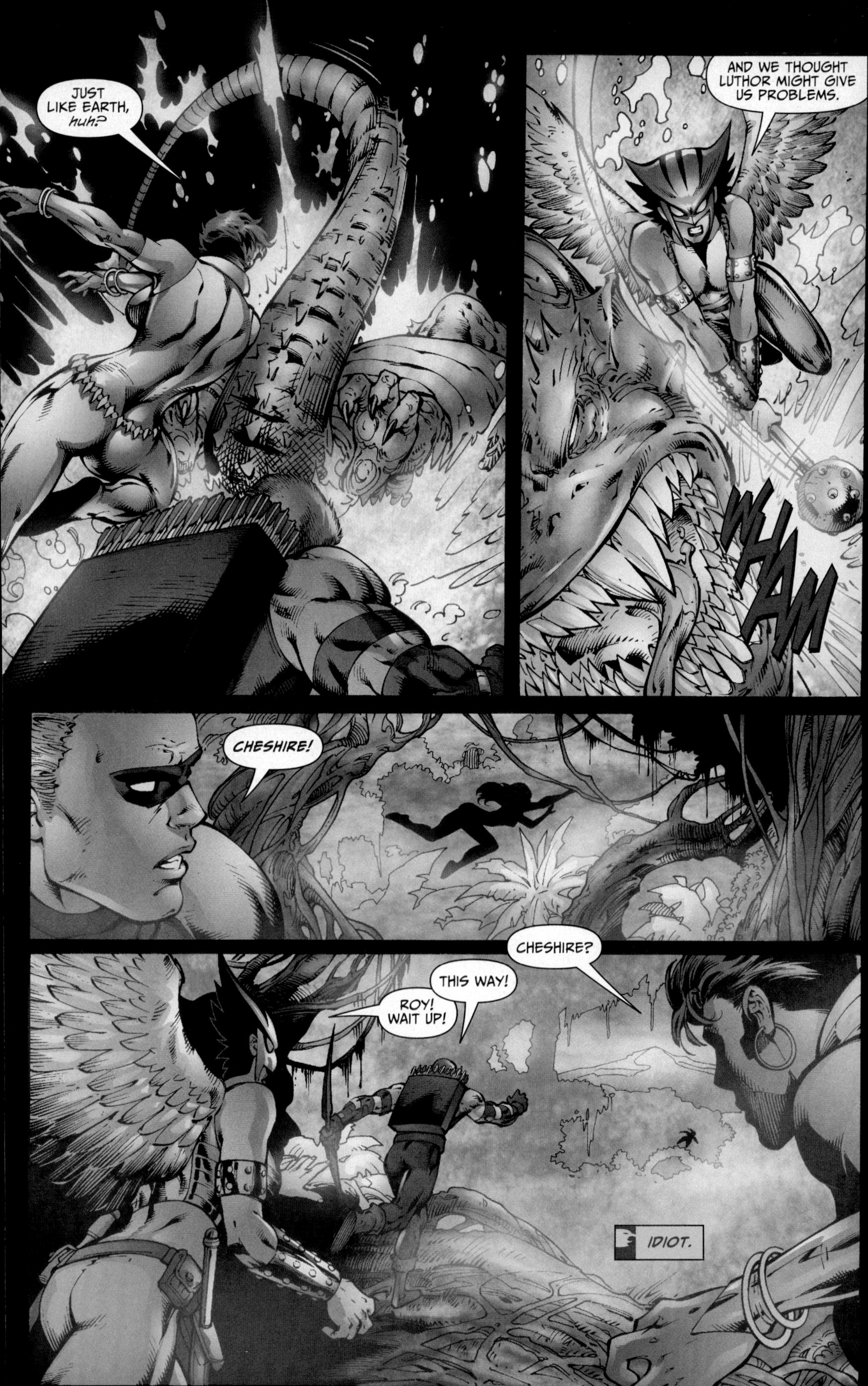
JUST LIKE EARTH, *huh?*
AND WE THOUGHT LUTHOR MIGHT GIVE US PROBLEMS.
WHAM
CHESHIRE!
CHESHIRE?
THIS WAY!
ROY! WAIT UP!
IDIOT.

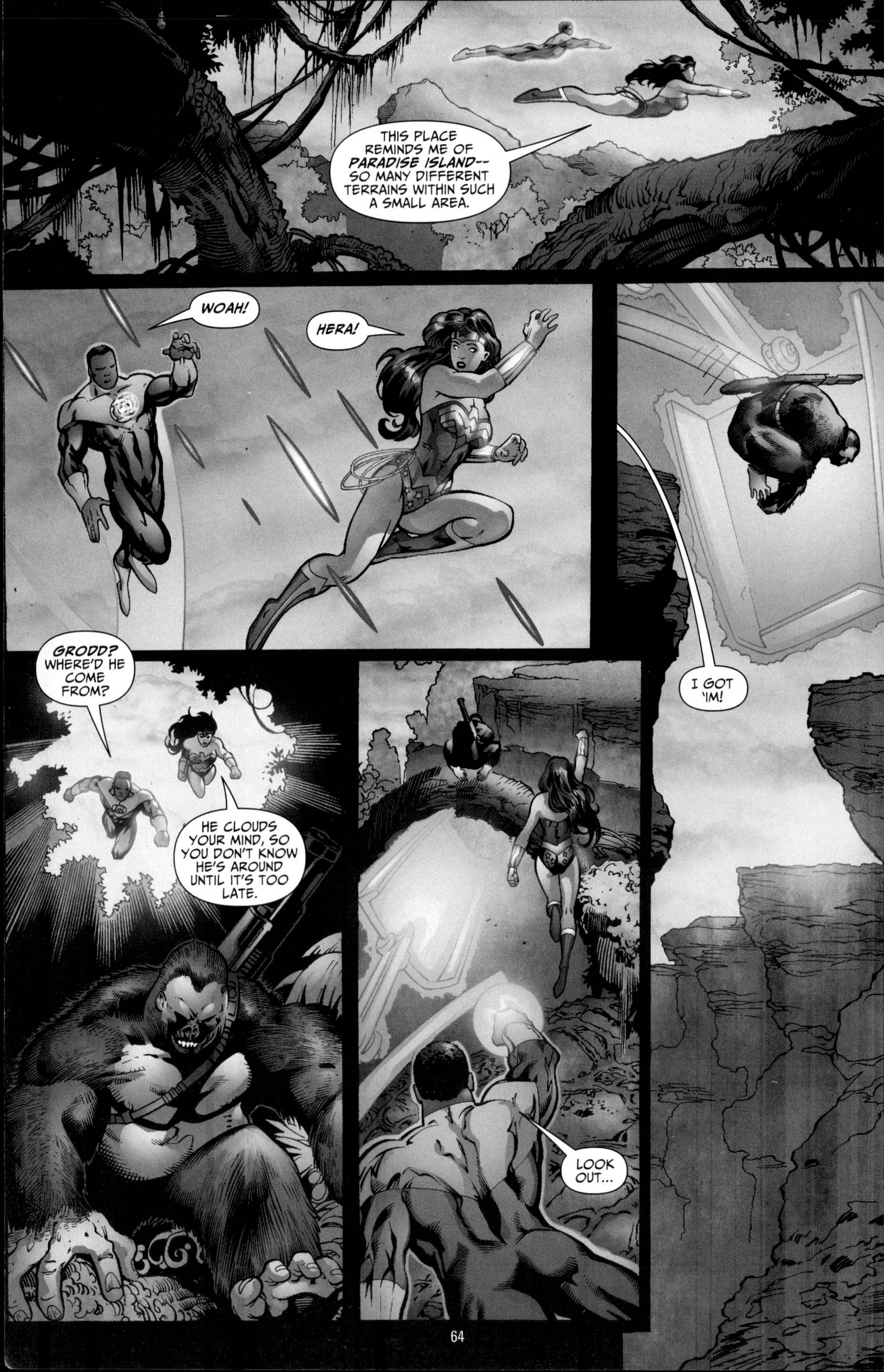
THIS PLACE REMINDS ME OF PARADISE ISLAND-- SO MANY DIFFERENT TERRAINS WITHIN SUCH A SMALL AREA.
WOAH!
HERA!
I GOT 'IM!
GRODD? WHERE'D HE COME FROM?
HE CLOUDS YOUR MIND, SO YOU DON'T KNOW HE'S AROUND UNTIL IT'S TOO LATE.
LOOK OUT...

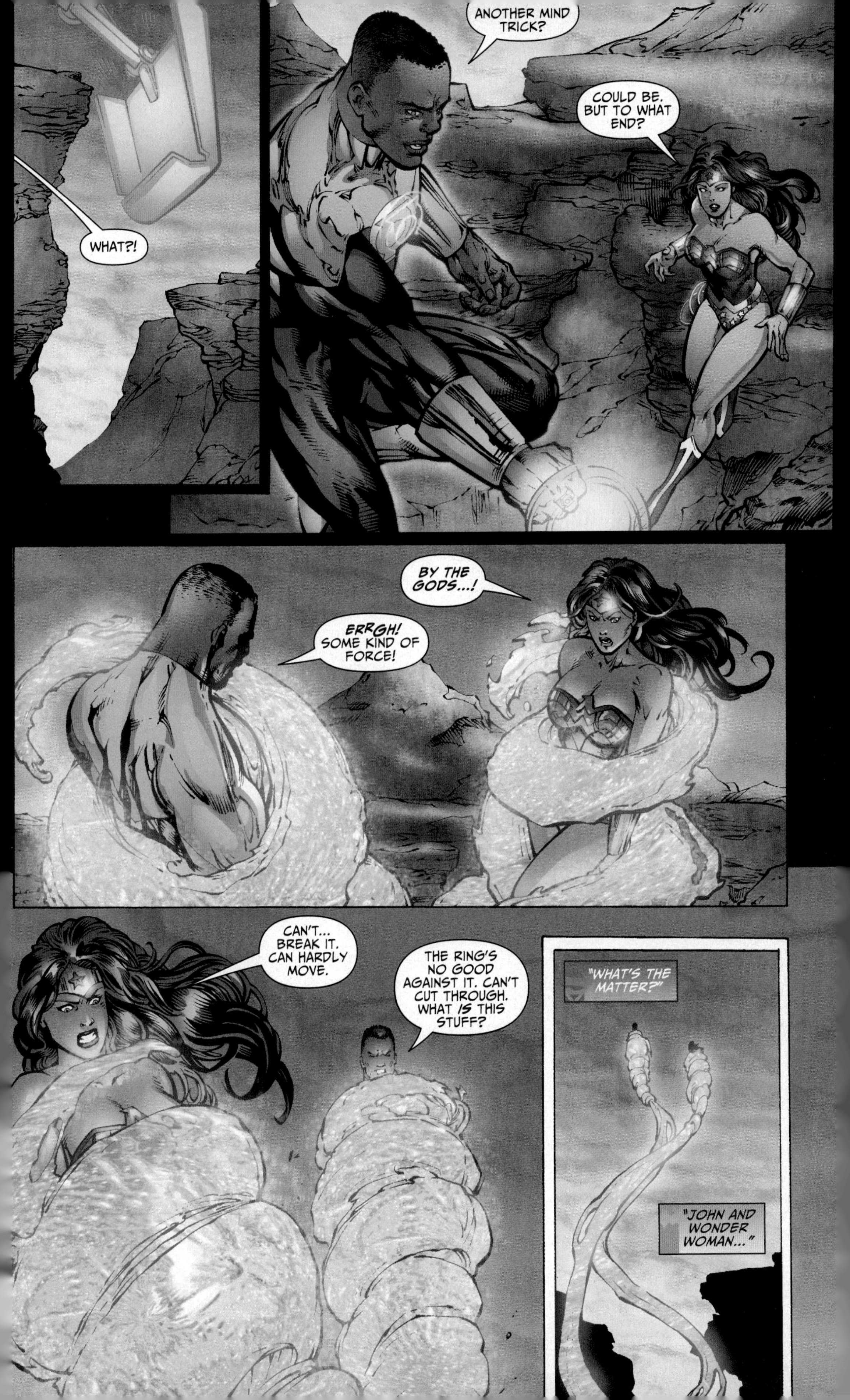
WHAT?!
ANOTHER MIND TRICK?
COULD BE. BUT TO WHAT END?
BY THE GODS...!
ERRGH! SOME KIND OF FORCE!
CAN'T... BREAK IT. CAN HARDLY MOVE.
THE RING'S NO GOOD AGAINST IT. CAN'T CUT THROUGH. WHAT IS THIS STUFF?
"WHAT'S THE MATTER?"
"JOHN AND WONDER WOMAN..."

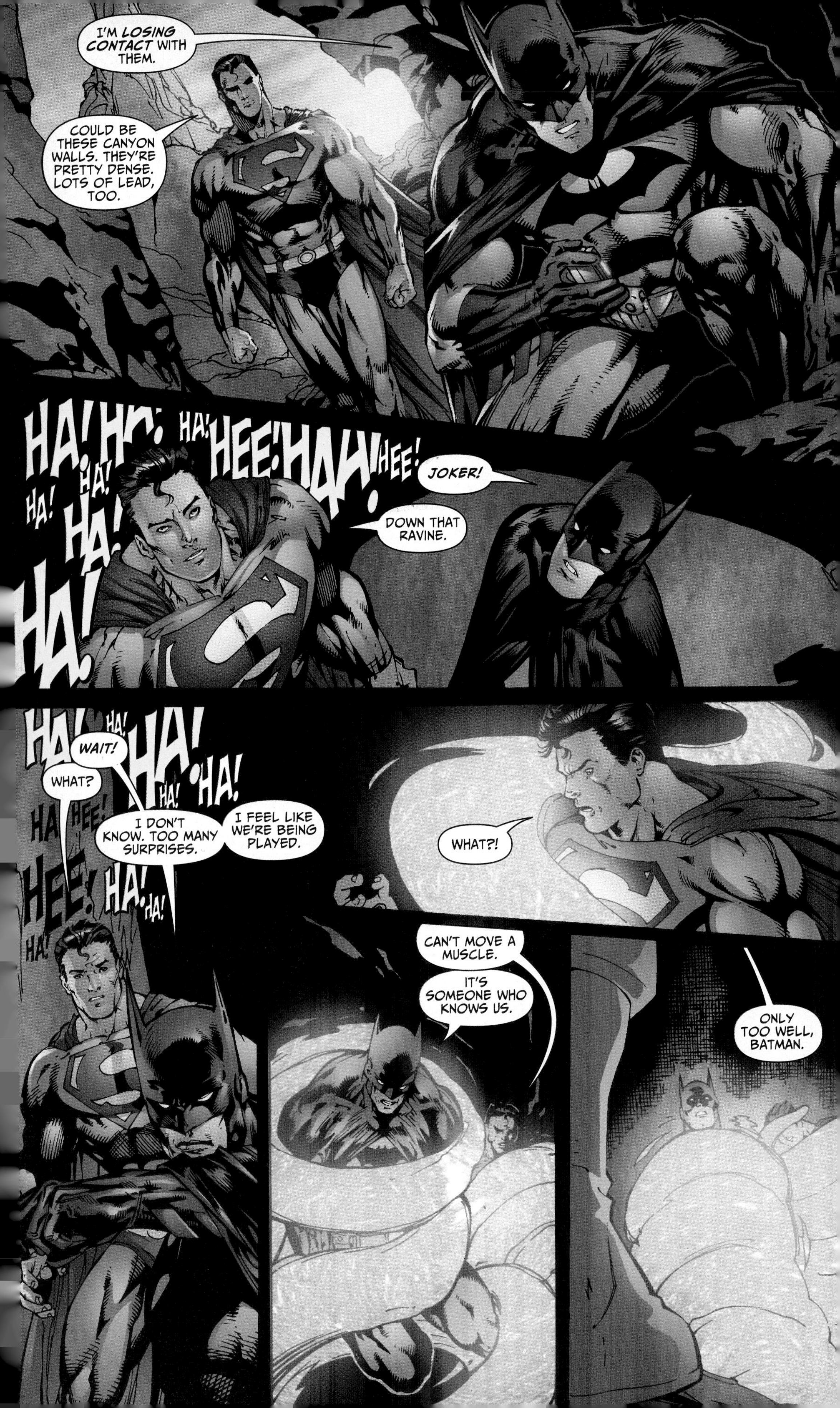
I'M LOSING CONTACT WITH THEM.
COULD BE THESE CANYON WALLS. THEY'RE PRETTY DENSE. LOTS OF LEAD, TOO.
HA! HO! HA! HEE! HAH! HEE! HA! HA! HA! HA!
JOKER!
DOWN THAT RAVINE.
HA! HA! HA! HA! HA!
WAIT!
WHAT?
HA! HEE! HEE! HA! HA! HA!
I DON'T KNOW. TOO MANY SURPRISES.
I FEEL LIKE WE'RE BEING PLAYED.
WHAT?!
CAN'T MOVE A MUSCLE.
IT'S SOMEONE WHO KNOWS US.
ONLY TOO WELL, BATMAN.

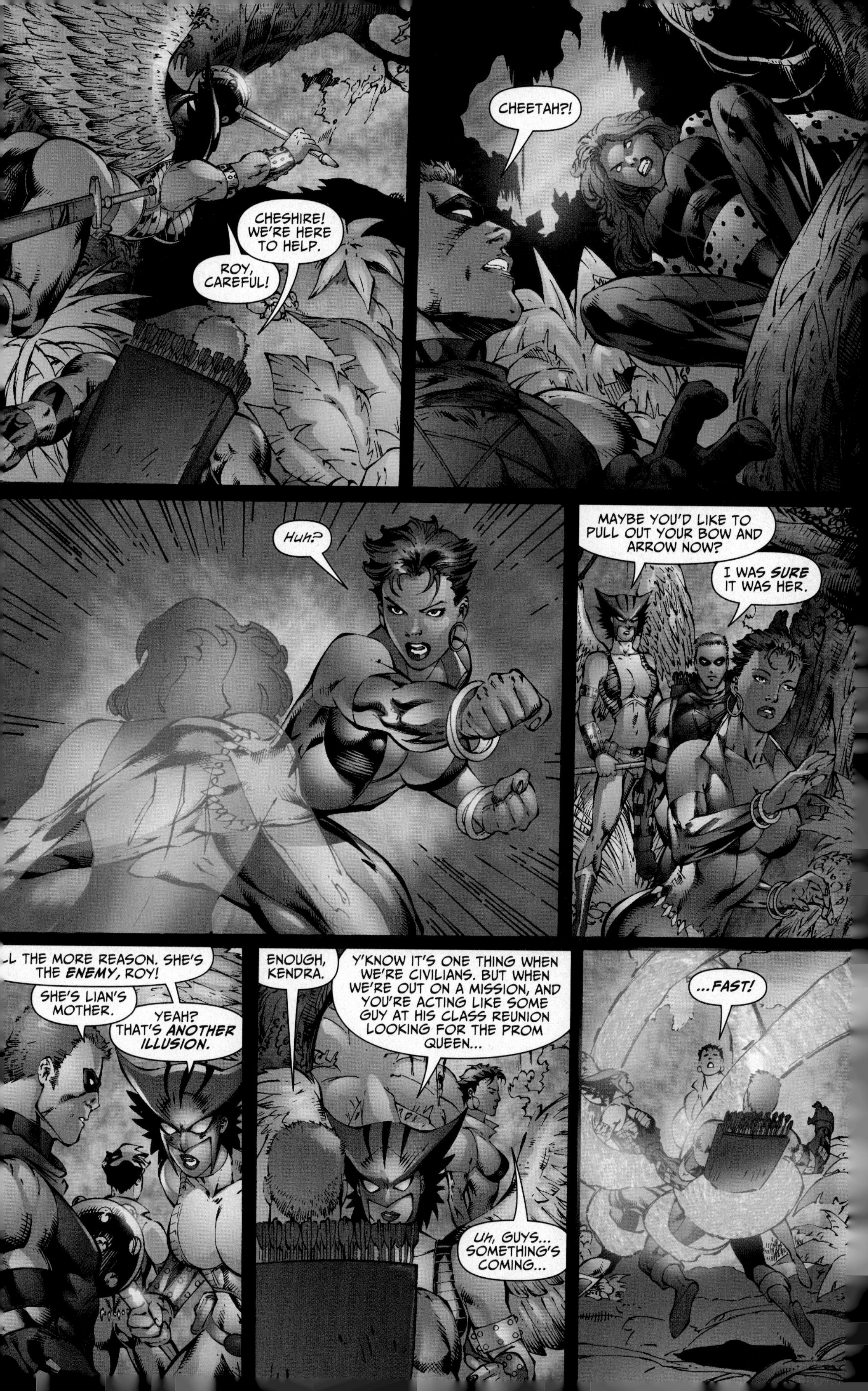
CHESHIRE! WE'RE HERE TO HELP.
ROY, CAREFUL!
CHEETAH?!
Huh?
MAYBE YOU'D LIKE TO PULL OUT YOUR BOW AND ARROW NOW?
I WAS SURE IT WAS HER.
L THE MORE REASON. SHE'S THE ENEMY, ROY!
SHE'S LIAN'S MOTHER.
YEAH? THAT'S ANOTHER ILLUSION.
ENOUGH, KENDRA.
Y'KNOW IT'S ONE THING WHEN WE'RE CIVILIANS. BUT WHEN WE'RE OUT ON A MISSION, AND YOU'RE ACTING LIKE SOME GUY AT HIS CLASS REUNION LOOKING FOR THE PROM QUEEN...
Uh, GUYS... SOMETHING'S COMING...
...FAST!

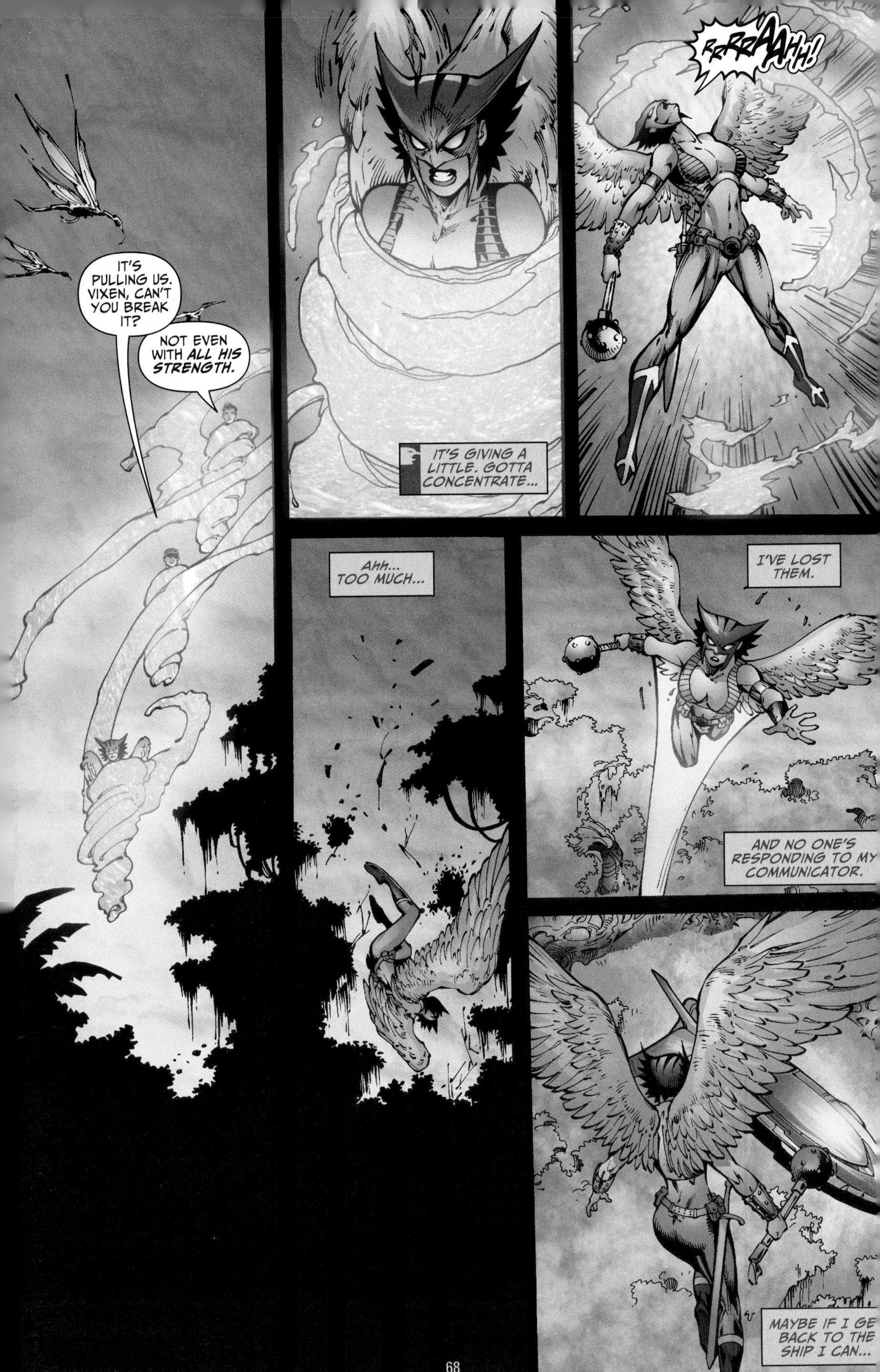
IT'S PULLING US. VIXEN, CAN'T YOU BREAK IT?
NOT EVEN WITH ALL HIS STRENGTH.
IT'S GIVING A LITTLE. GOTTA CONCENTRATE...
RRRRAAHH!
Ahh... TOO MUCH...
I'VE LOST THEM.
AND NO ONE'S RESPONDING TO MY COMMUNICATOR.
MAYBE IF I GET BACK TO THE SHIP I CAN...

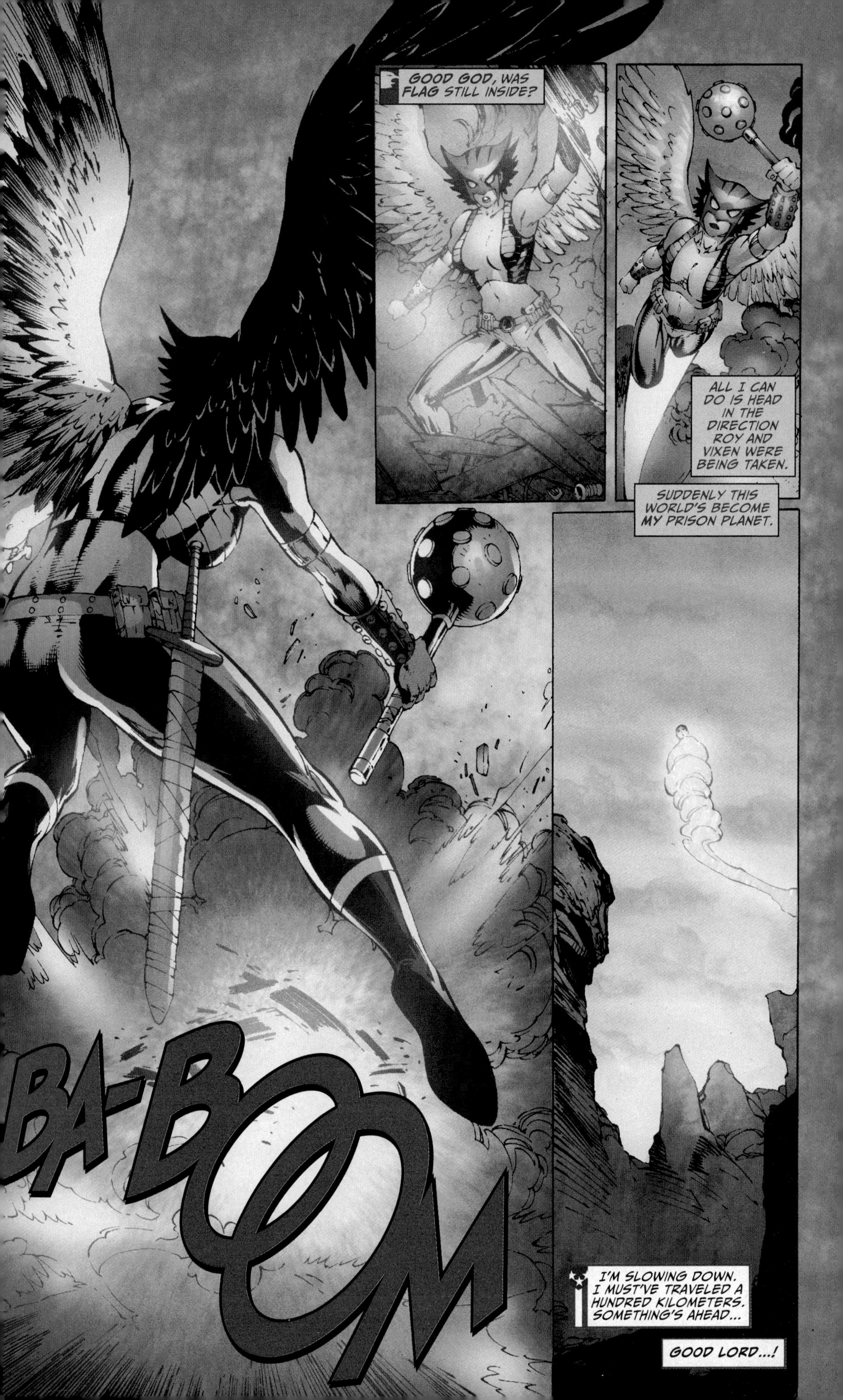

GOOD GOD, WAS FLAG STILL INSIDE?
ALL I CAN DO IS HEAD IN THE DIRECTION ROY AND VIXEN WERE BEING TAKEN.
SUDDENLY THIS WORLD'S BECOME MY PRISON PLANET.
BA-BOOM
I'M SLOWING DOWN. I MUST'VE TRAVELED A HUNDRED KILOMETERS. SOMETHING'S AHEAD...
GOOD LORD...!

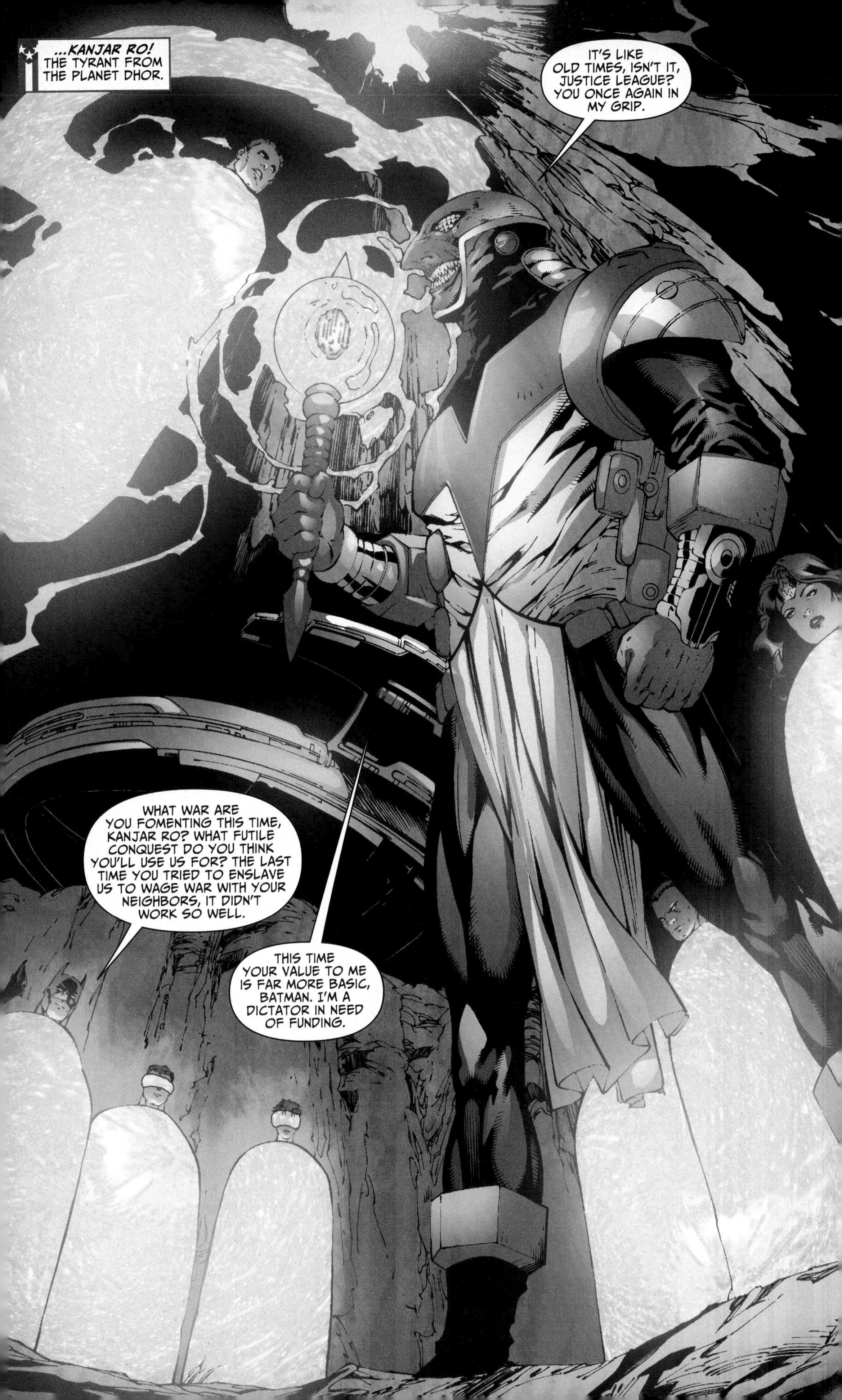
...KANJAR RO! THE TYRANT FROM THE PLANET DHOR.
IT'S LIKE OLD TIMES, ISN'T IT, JUSTICE LEAGUE? YOU ONCE AGAIN IN MY GRIP.
WHAT WAR ARE YOU FOMENTING THIS TIME, KANJAR RO? WHAT FUTILE CONQUEST DO YOU THINK YOU'LL USE US FOR? THE LAST TIME YOU TRIED TO ENSLAVE US TO WAGE WAR WITH YOUR NEIGHBORS, IT DIDN'T WORK SO WELL.
THIS TIME YOUR VALUE TO ME IS FAR MORE BASIC, BATMAN. I'M A DICTATOR IN NEED OF FUNDING.

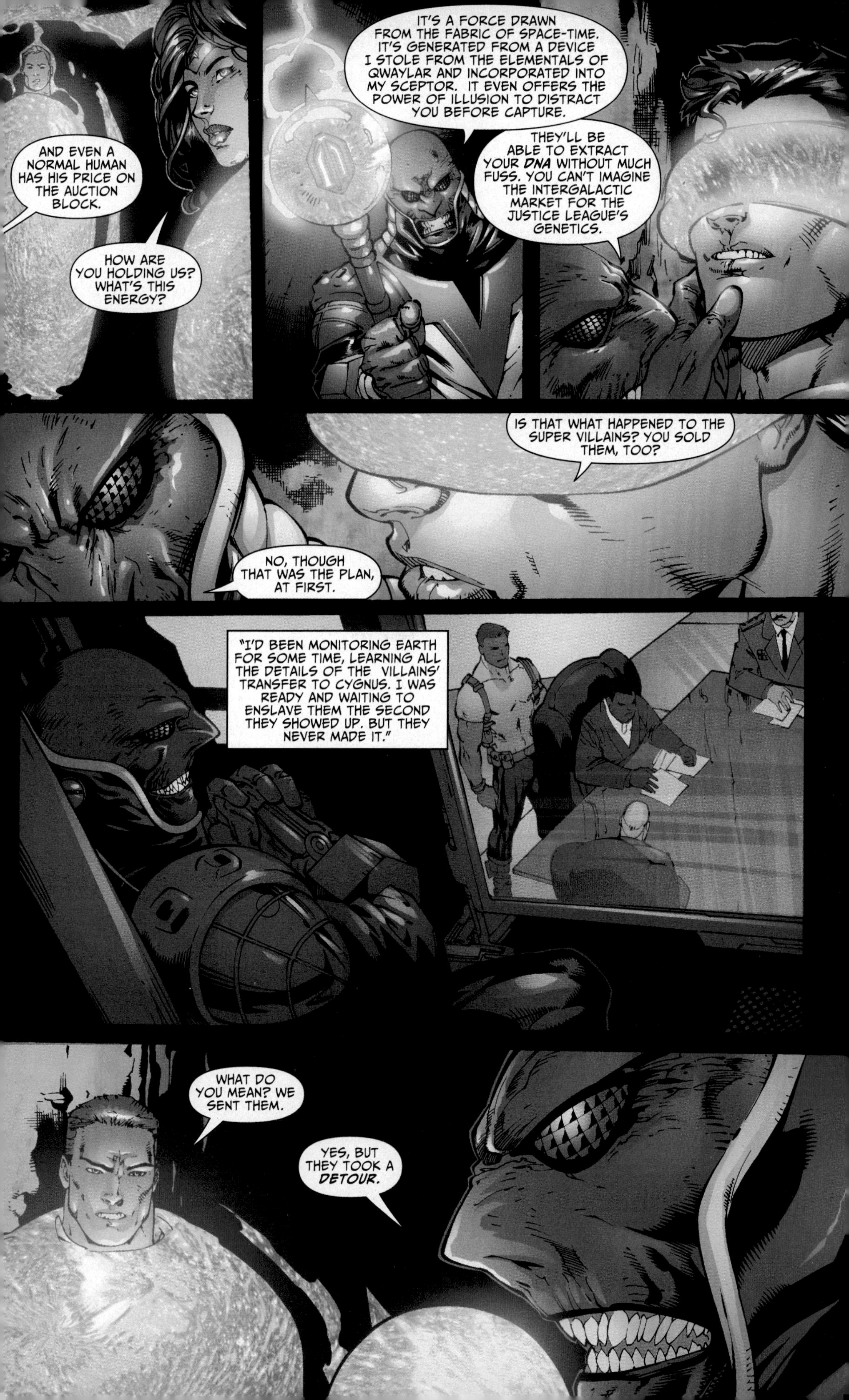
AND EVEN A NORMAL HUMAN HAS HIS PRICE ON THE AUCTION BLOCK.
HOW ARE YOU HOLDING US? WHAT'S THIS ENERGY?
IT'S A FORCE DRAWN FROM THE FABRIC OF SPACE-TIME. IT'S GENERATED FROM A DEVICE I STOLE FROM THE ELEMENTALS OF QWAYLAR AND INCORPORATED INTO MY SCEPTOR. IT EVEN OFFERS THE POWER OF ILLUSION TO DISTRACT YOU BEFORE CAPTURE.
THEY'LL BE ABLE TO EXTRACT YOUR DNA WITHOUT MUCH FUSS. YOU CAN'T IMAGINE THE INTERGALACTIC MARKET FOR THE JUSTICE LEAGUE'S GENETICS.
IS THAT WHAT HAPPENED TO THE SUPER VILLAINS? YOU SOLD THEM, TOO?
NO, THOUGH THAT WAS THE PLAN, AT FIRST.
"I'D BEEN MONITORING EARTH FOR SOME TIME, LEARNING ALL THE DETAILS OF THE VILLAINS' TRANSFER TO CYGNUS. I WAS READY AND WAITING TO ENSLAVE THEM THE SECOND THEY SHOWED UP. BUT THEY NEVER MADE IT."
WHAT DO YOU MEAN? WE SENT THEM.
YES, BUT THEY TOOK A DETOUR.

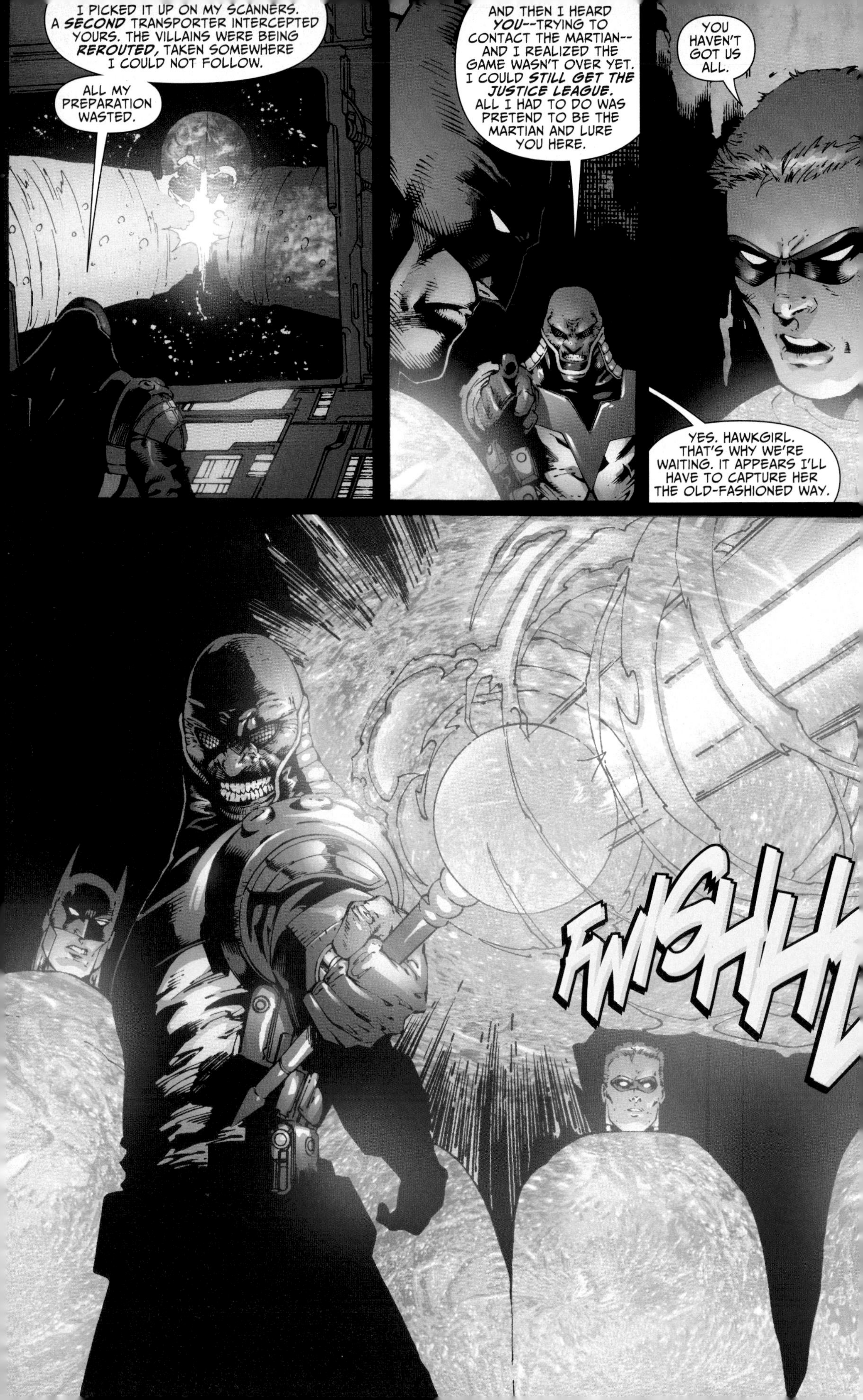
I PICKED IT UP ON MY SCANNERS. A *SECOND* TRANSPORTER INTERCEPTED YOURS. THE VILLAINS WERE BEING *REROUTED,* TAKEN SOMEWHERE I COULD NOT FOLLOW.
ALL MY PREPARATION WASTED.
AND THEN I HEARD *YOU*--TRYING TO CONTACT THE MARTIAN--AND I REALIZED THE GAME WASN'T OVER YET. I COULD *STILL GET THE JUSTICE LEAGUE.* ALL I HAD TO DO WAS PRETEND TO BE THE MARTIAN AND LURE YOU HERE.
YOU HAVEN'T GOT US ALL.
YES. HAWKGIRL. THAT'S WHY WE'RE WAITING. IT APPEARS I'LL HAVE TO CAPTURE HER THE OLD-FASHIONED WAY.
FWISHHH

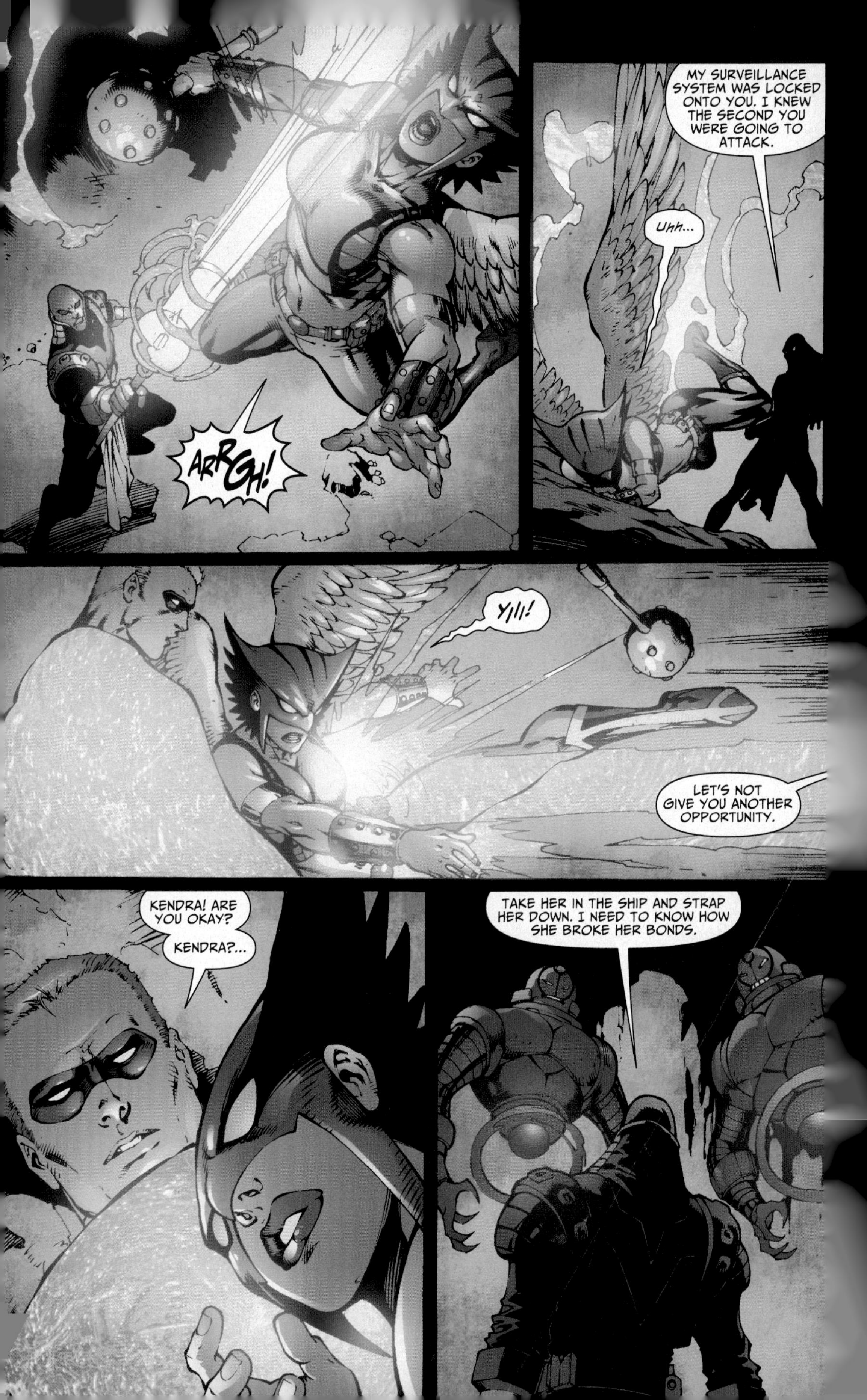
ARRGH!
MY SURVEILLANCE SYSTEM WAS LOCKED ONTO YOU. I KNEW THE SECOND YOU WERE GOING TO ATTACK.
Uhh...
YIII!
LET'S NOT GIVE YOU ANOTHER OPPORTUNITY.
KENDRA! ARE YOU OKAY?
KENDRA?...
TAKE HER IN THE SHIP AND STRAP HER DOWN. I NEED TO KNOW HOW SHE BROKE HER BONDS.

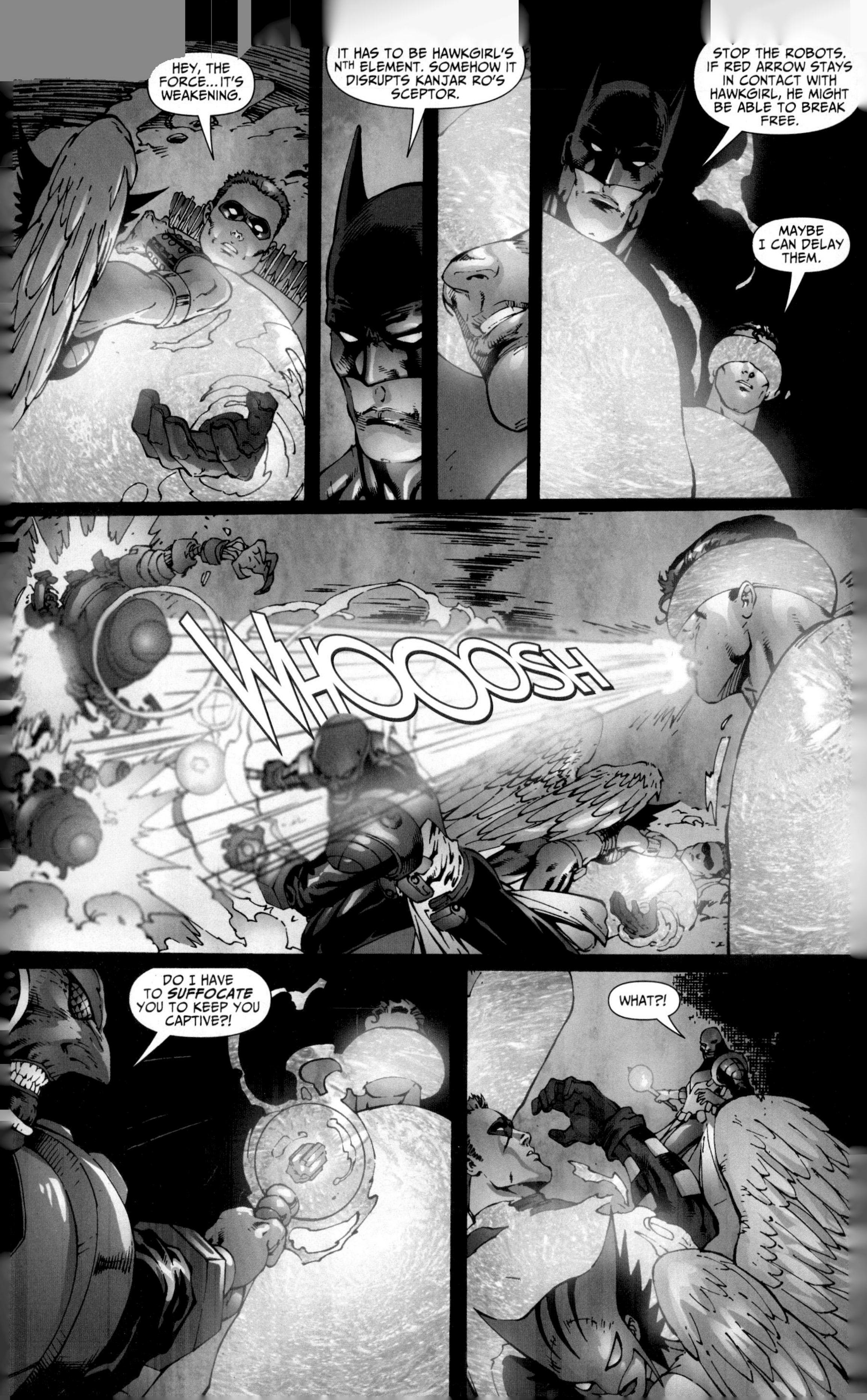
HEY, THE FORCE...IT'S WEAKENING.
IT HAS TO BE HAWKGIRL'S Nth ELEMENT. SOMEHOW IT DISRUPTS KANJAR RO'S SCEPTOR.
STOP THE ROBOTS. IF RED ARROW STAYS IN CONTACT WITH HAWKGIRL, HE MIGHT BE ABLE TO BREAK FREE.
MAYBE I CAN DELAY THEM.
WHOOOSH
DO I HAVE TO SUFFOCATE YOU TO KEEP YOU CAPTIVE?!
WHAT?!

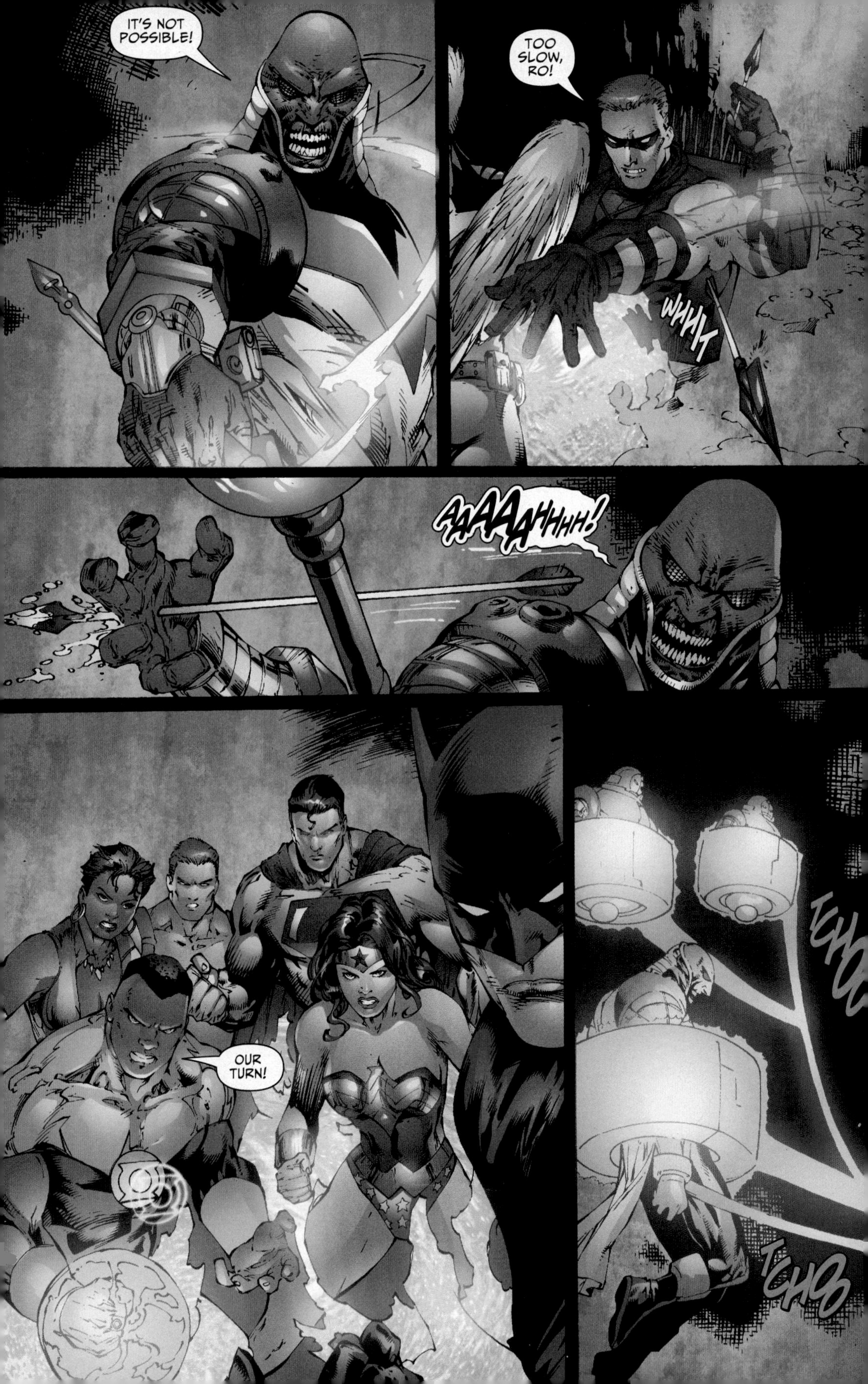
IT'S NOT POSSIBLE!
TOO SLOW, RO!
WHHK
AAAAAHHHH!
OUR TURN!
TCHOO
TCHOO

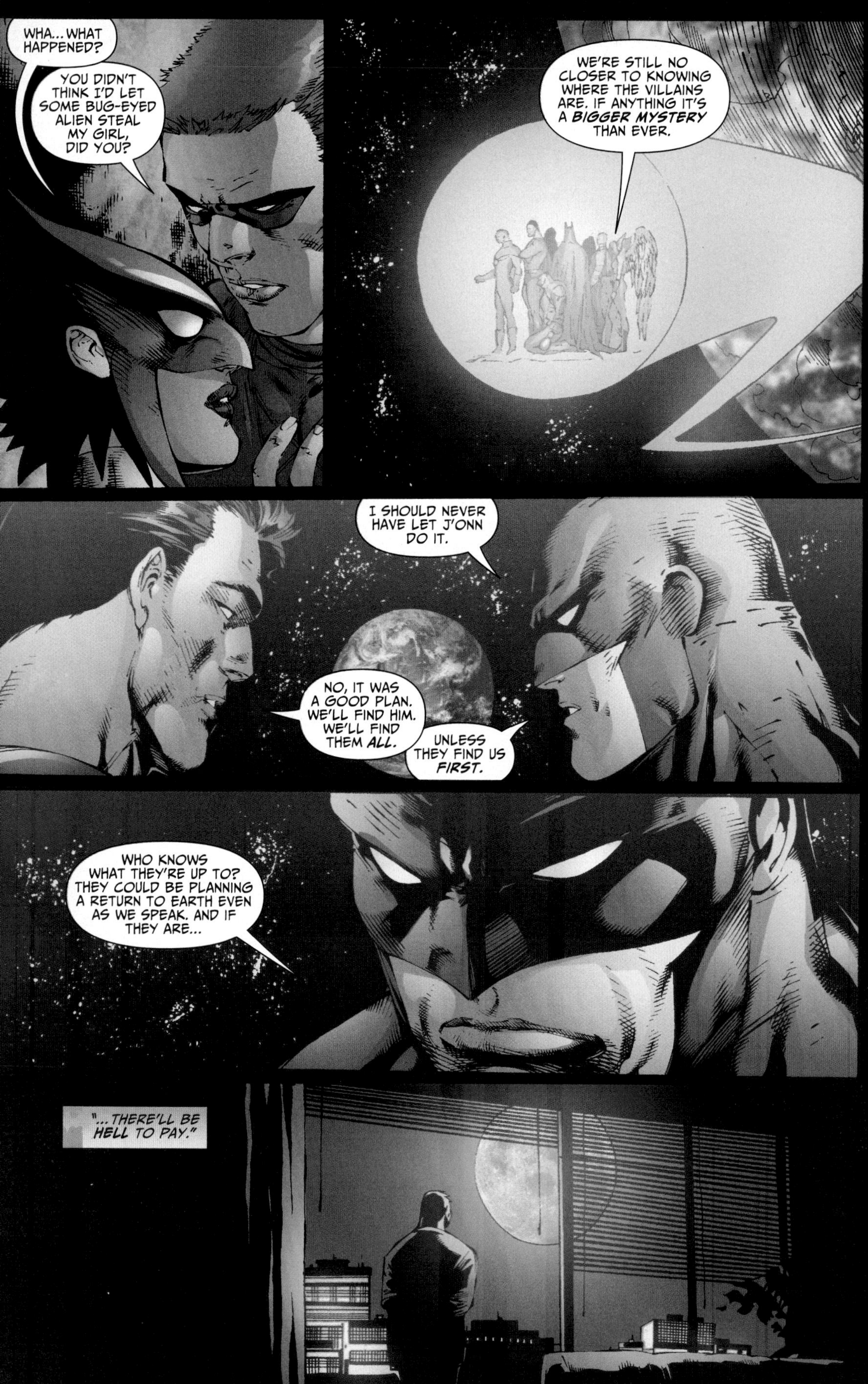
WHA...WHAT HAPPENED?
YOU DIDN'T THINK I'D LET SOME BUG-EYED ALIEN STEAL MY GIRL, DID YOU?
WE'RE STILL NO CLOSER TO KNOWING WHERE THE VILLAINS ARE. IF ANYTHING IT'S A BIGGER MYSTERY THAN EVER.
I SHOULD NEVER HAVE LET J'ONN DO IT.
NO, IT WAS A GOOD PLAN. WE'LL FIND HIM. WE'LL FIND THEM ALL.
UNLESS THEY FIND US FIRST.
WHO KNOWS WHAT THEY'RE UP TO? THEY COULD BE PLANNING A RETURN TO EARTH EVEN AS WE SPEAK. AND IF THEY ARE...
"...THERE'LL BE HELL TO PAY."

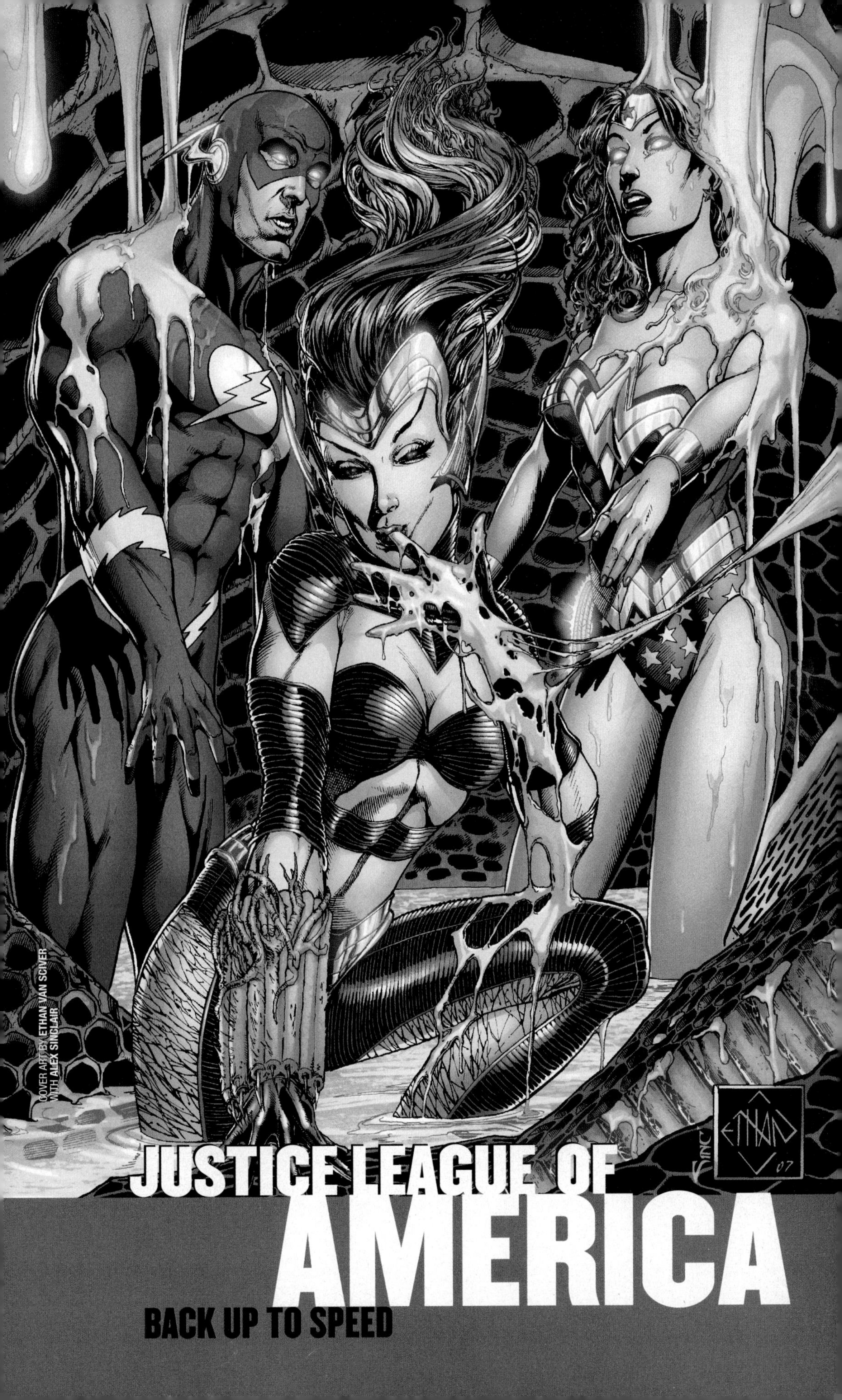
COVER ART BY ETHAN VAN SCIVER
WITH ALEX SINCLAIR

JUSTICE LEAGUE OF AMERICA

BACK UP TO SPEED

Back Up to Speed

Dwayne McDuffie
Writer

Ethan Van Sciver
Artist

Rob Leigh
Letterer

Brian Miller (Hi-Fi)
Colorist

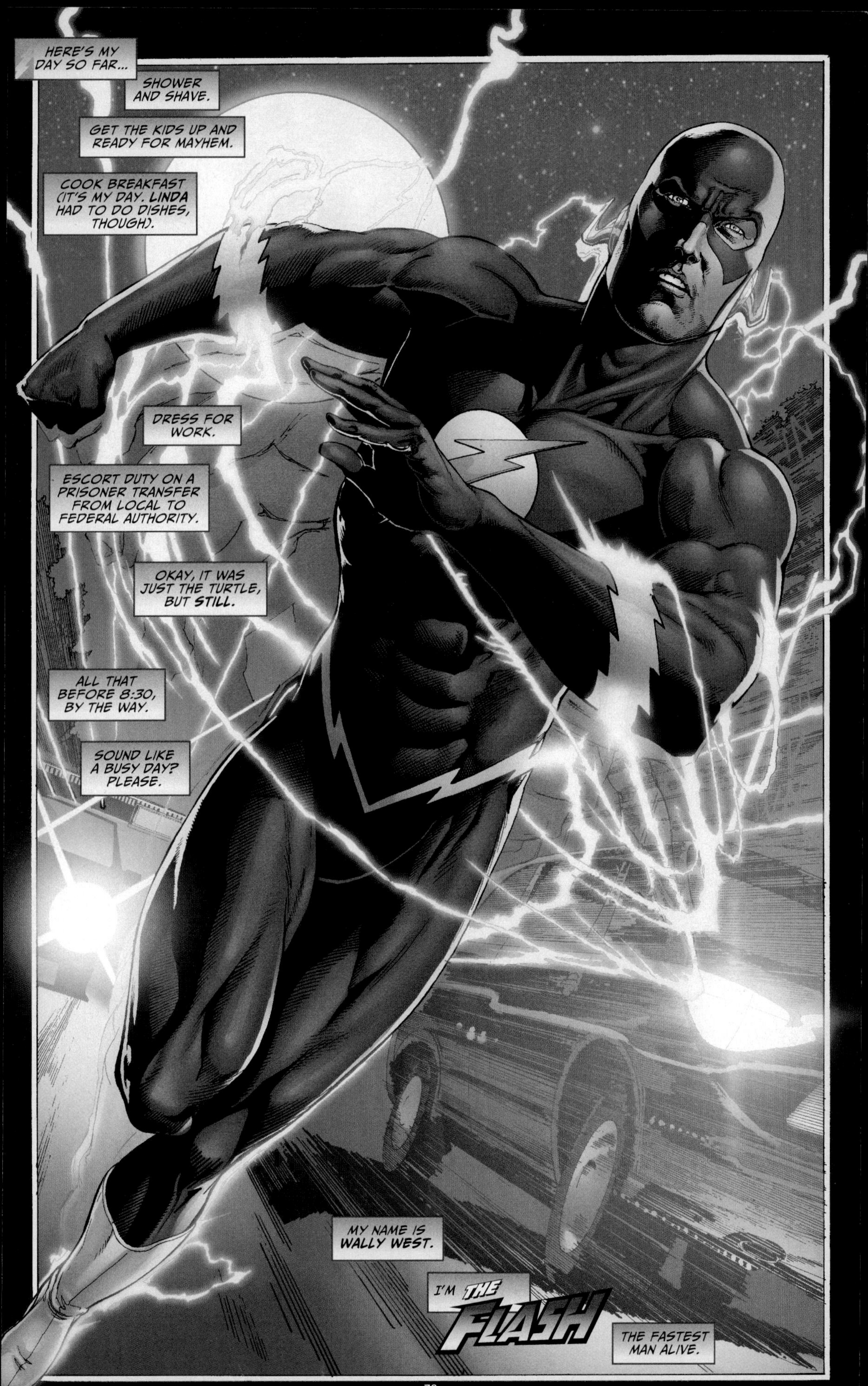
HERE'S MY DAY SO FAR...
SHOWER AND SHAVE.
GET THE KIDS UP AND READY FOR MAYHEM.
COOK BREAKFAST (IT'S MY DAY. LINDA HAD TO DO DISHES, THOUGH).
DRESS FOR WORK.
ESCORT DUTY ON A PRISONER TRANSFER FROM LOCAL TO FEDERAL AUTHORITY.
OKAY, IT WAS JUST THE TURTLE, BUT STILL.
ALL THAT BEFORE 8:30, BY THE WAY.
SOUND LIKE A BUSY DAY? PLEASE.
MY NAME IS WALLY WEST.
I'M THE FLASH
THE FASTEST MAN ALIVE.

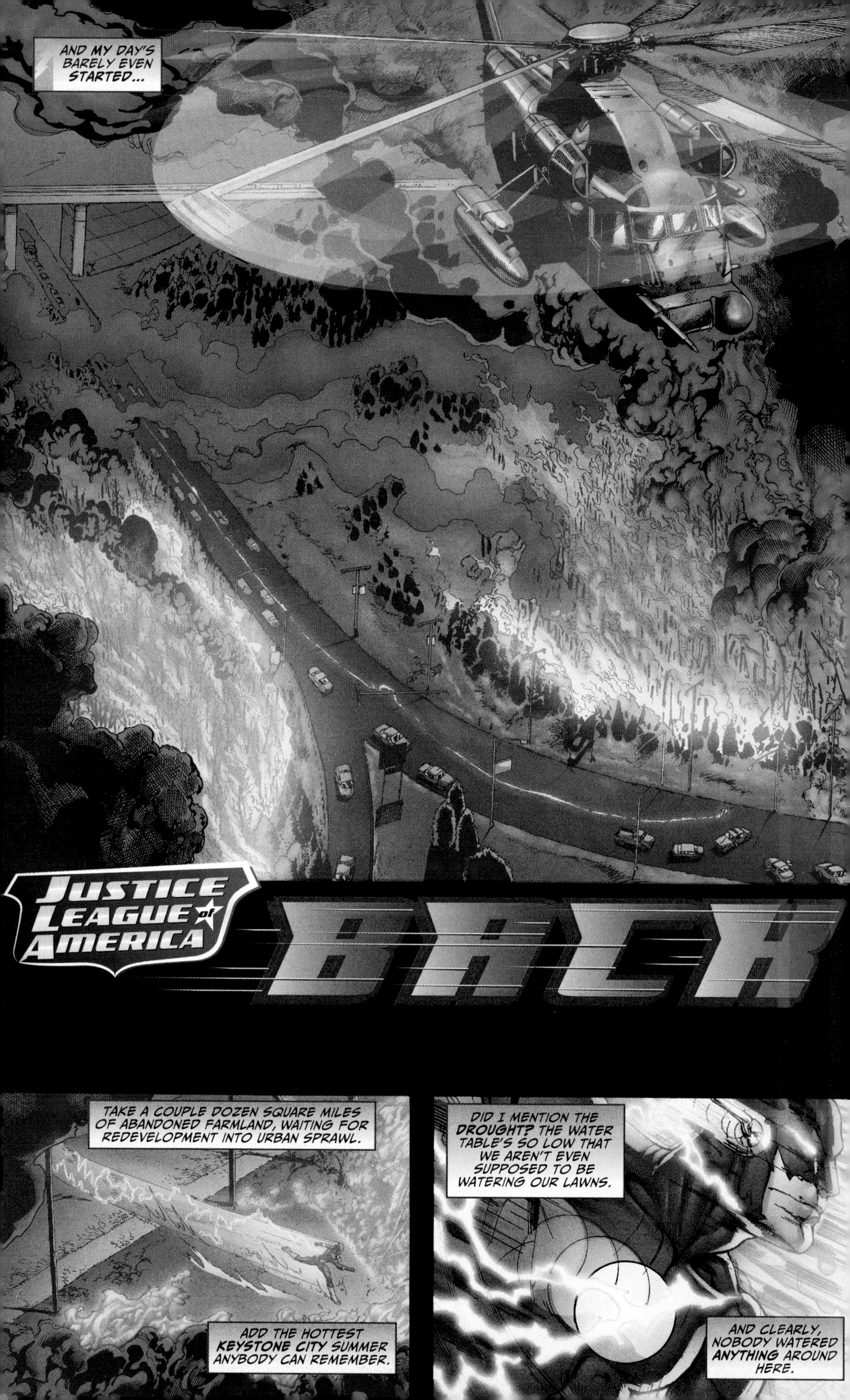

AND MY DAY'S BARELY EVEN STARTED...
JUSTICE LEAGUE of AMERICA
BACK
TAKE A COUPLE DOZEN SQUARE MILES OF ABANDONED FARMLAND, WAITING FOR REDEVELOPMENT INTO URBAN SPRAWL.
ADD THE HOTTEST KEYSTONE CITY SUMMER ANYBODY CAN REMEMBER.
DID I MENTION THE DROUGHT? THE WATER TABLE'S SO LOW THAT WE AREN'T EVEN SUPPOSED TO BE WATERING OUR LAWNS.
AND CLEARLY, NOBODY WATERED ANYTHING AROUND HERE.

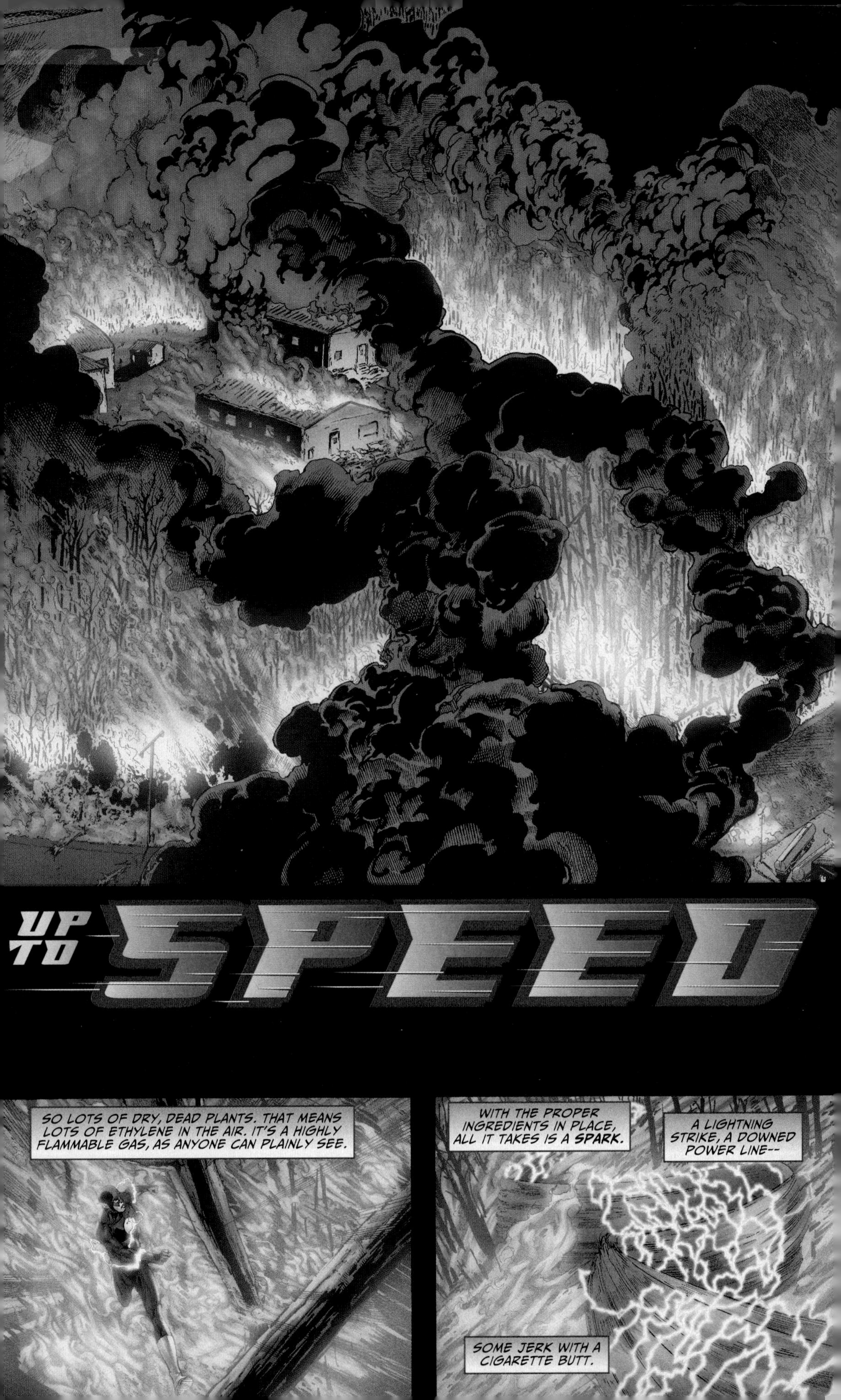
UP TO SPEED
SO LOTS OF DRY, DEAD PLANTS. THAT MEANS LOTS OF ETHYLENE IN THE AIR. IT'S A HIGHLY FLAMMABLE GAS, AS ANYONE CAN PLAINLY SEE.
WITH THE PROPER INGREDIENTS IN PLACE, ALL IT TAKES IS A SPARK.
A LIGHTNING STRIKE, A DOWNED POWER LINE--
SOME JERK WITH A CIGARETTE BUTT.

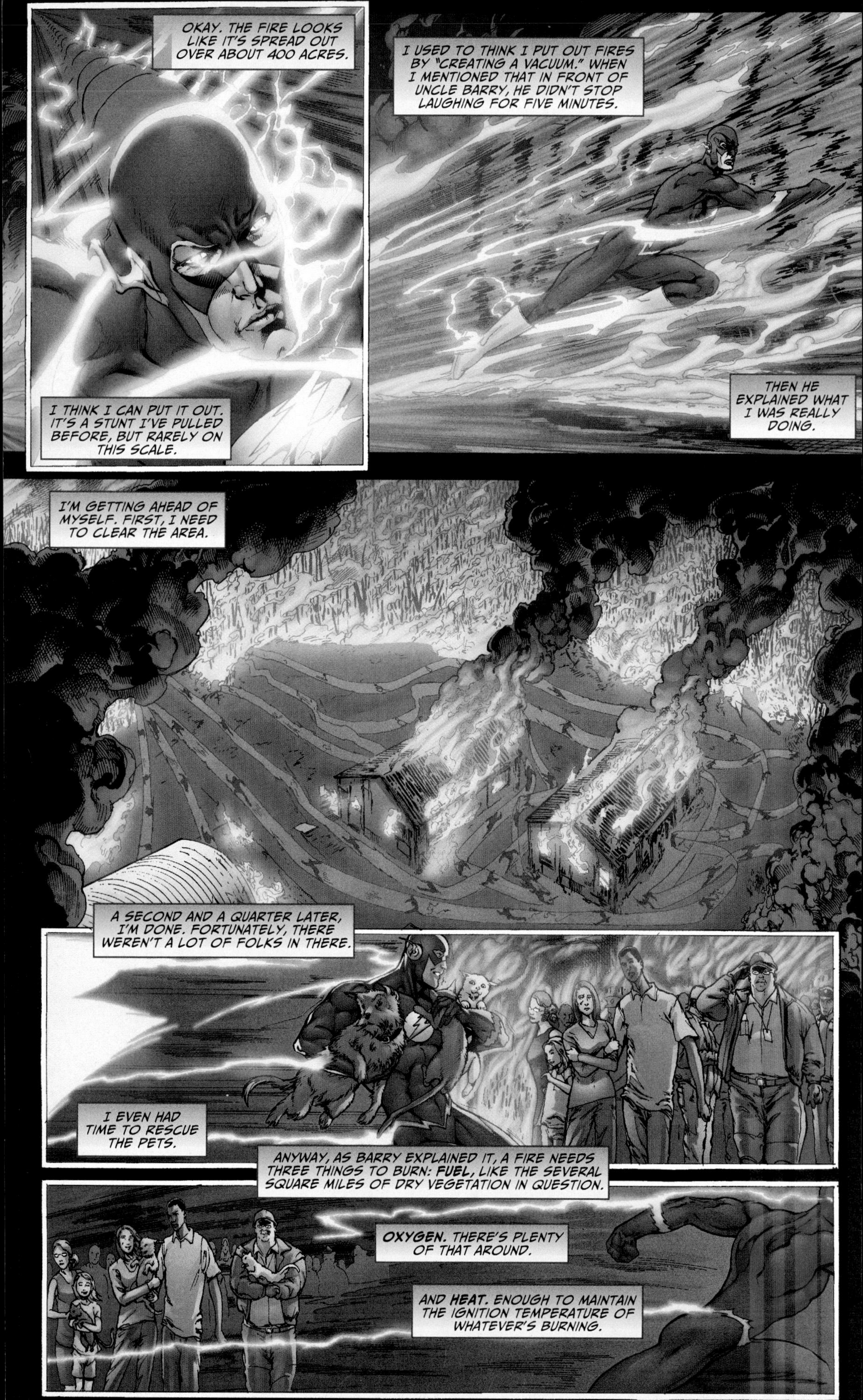

OKAY. THE FIRE LOOKS LIKE IT'S SPREAD OUT OVER ABOUT 400 ACRES.
I THINK I CAN PUT IT OUT. IT'S A STUNT I'VE PULLED BEFORE, BUT RARELY ON THIS SCALE.
I USED TO THINK I PUT OUT FIRES BY "CREATING A VACUUM." WHEN I MENTIONED THAT IN FRONT OF UNCLE BARRY, HE DIDN'T STOP LAUGHING FOR FIVE MINUTES.
THEN HE EXPLAINED WHAT I WAS REALLY DOING.
I'M GETTING AHEAD OF MYSELF. FIRST, I NEED TO CLEAR THE AREA.
A SECOND AND A QUARTER LATER, I'M DONE. FORTUNATELY, THERE WEREN'T A LOT OF FOLKS IN THERE.
I EVEN HAD TIME TO RESCUE THE PETS.
ANYWAY, AS BARRY EXPLAINED IT, A FIRE NEEDS THREE THINGS TO BURN: FUEL, LIKE THE SEVERAL SQUARE MILES OF DRY VEGETATION IN QUESTION.
OXYGEN. THERE'S PLENTY OF THAT AROUND.
AND HEAT. ENOUGH TO MAINTAIN THE IGNITION TEMPERATURE OF WHATEVER'S BURNING.

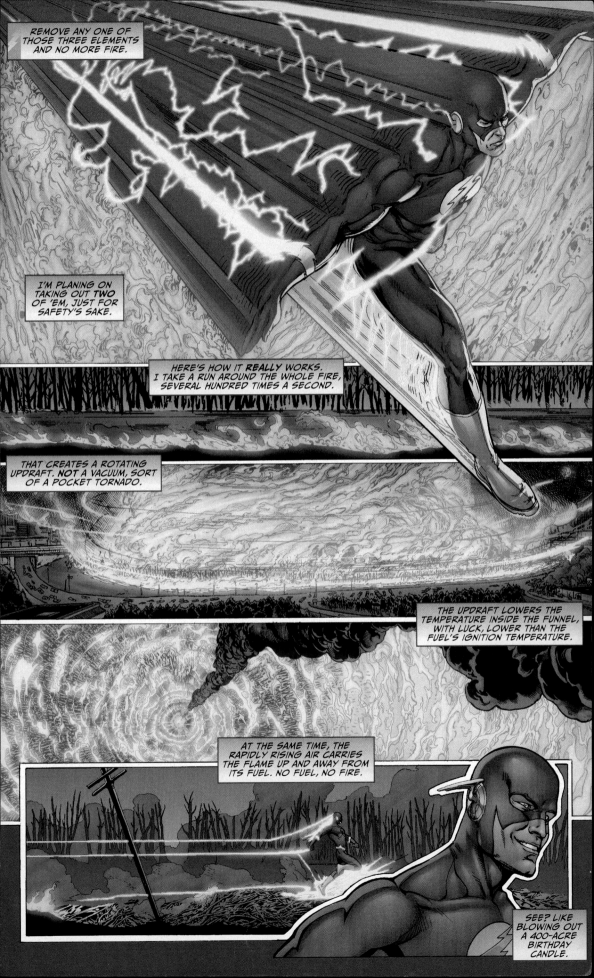

REMOVE ANY ONE OF THOSE THREE ELEMENTS AND NO MORE FIRE.

I'M PLANING ON TAKING OUT *TWO* OF 'EM, JUST FOR SAFETY'S SAKE.

HERE'S HOW IT *REALLY* WORKS. I TAKE A RUN AROUND THE WHOLE FIRE, SEVERAL HUNDRED TIMES A SECOND.

THAT CREATES A ROTATING UPDRAFT. *NOT A VACUUM,* SORT OF A POCKET TORNADO.

THE UPDRAFT LOWERS THE TEMPERATURE INSIDE THE FUNNEL, WITH LUCK, LOWER THAN THE FUEL'S IGNITION TEMPERATURE.

AT THE SAME TIME, THE RAPIDLY RISING AIR CARRIES THE FLAME UP AND AWAY FROM ITS FUEL. NO FUEL, NO FIRE.

SEE? LIKE BLOWING OUT A 400-ACRE BIRTHDAY CANDLE.

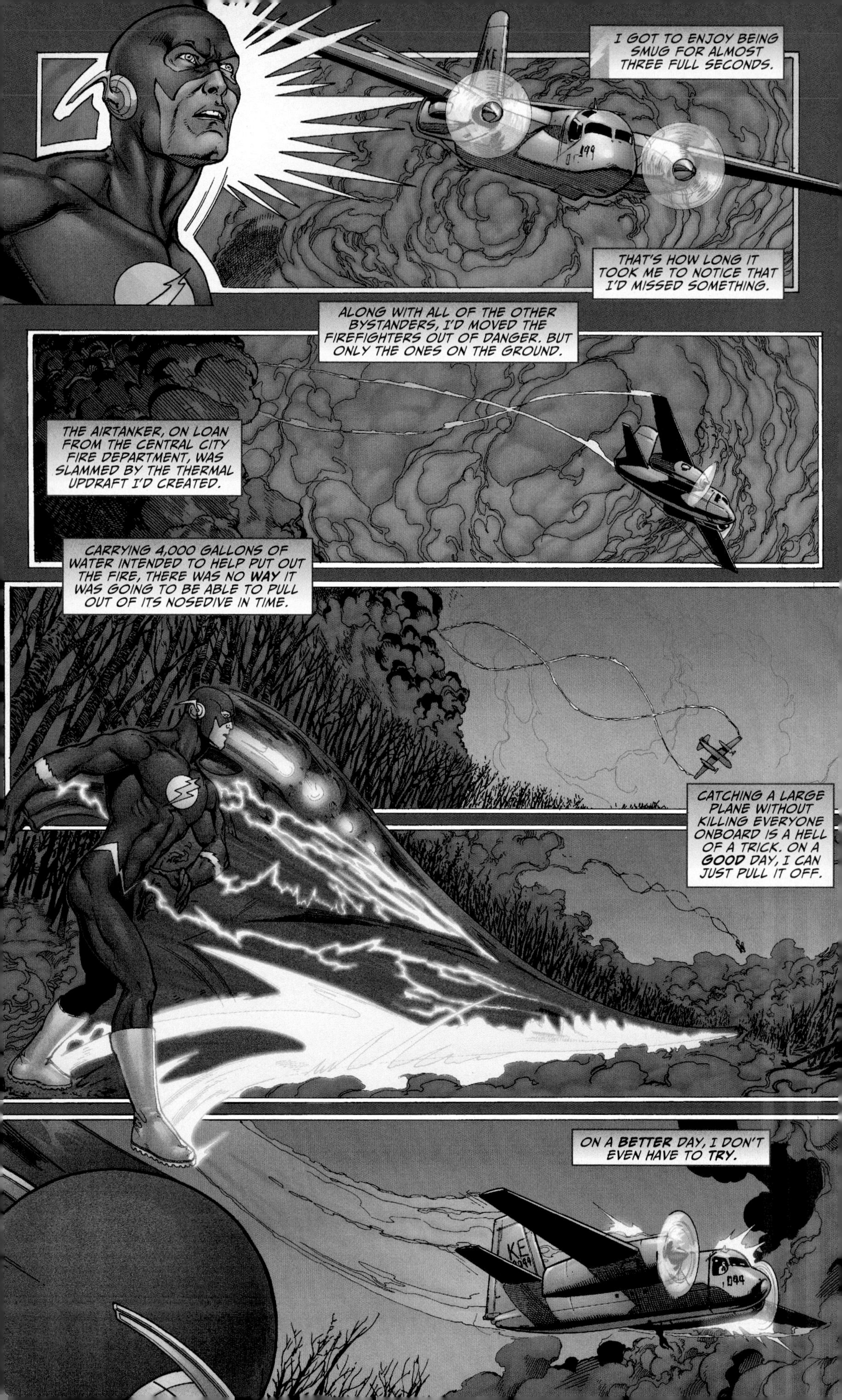

I GOT TO ENJOY BEING SMUG FOR ALMOST THREE FULL SECONDS.
THAT'S HOW LONG IT TOOK ME TO NOTICE THAT I'D MISSED SOMETHING.
ALONG WITH ALL OF THE OTHER BYSTANDERS, I'D MOVED THE FIREFIGHTERS OUT OF DANGER. BUT ONLY THE ONES ON THE GROUND.
THE AIRTANKER, ON LOAN FROM THE CENTRAL CITY FIRE DEPARTMENT, WAS SLAMMED BY THE THERMAL UPDRAFT I'D CREATED.
CARRYING 4,000 GALLONS OF WATER INTENDED TO HELP PUT OUT THE FIRE, THERE WAS NO WAY IT WAS GOING TO BE ABLE TO PULL OUT OF ITS NOSEDIVE IN TIME.
CATCHING A LARGE PLANE WITHOUT KILLING EVERYONE ONBOARD IS A HELL OF A TRICK. ON A GOOD DAY, I CAN JUST PULL IT OFF.
ON A BETTER DAY, I DON'T EVEN HAVE TO TRY.

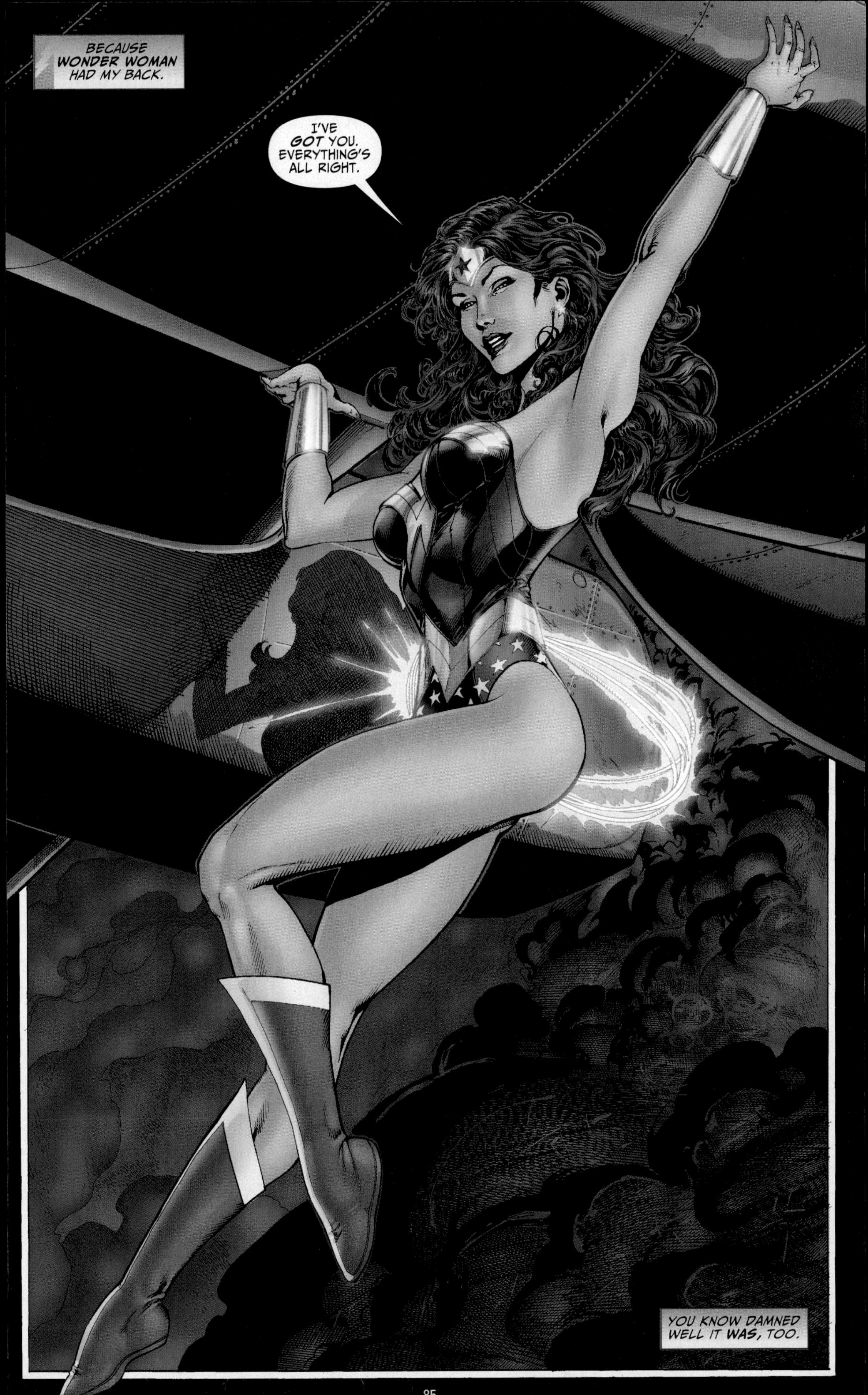
BECAUSE WONDER WOMAN HAD MY BACK.
I'VE GOT YOU. EVERYTHING'S ALL RIGHT.
YOU KNOW DAMNED WELL IT WAS, TOO.

I DON'T KNOW HOW MUCH THE PLANE WEIGHS BUT WHATEVER IT WAS, SHE CARRIED IT AND ITS CARGO, ANOTHER 30,000 POUNDS PLUS OF WATER IN FOR A SAFE LANDING.

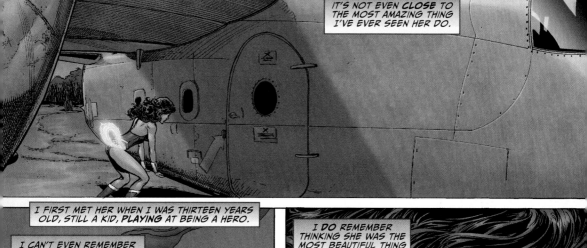

IT'S NOT EVEN **CLOSE** TO THE MOST AMAZING THING I'VE EVER SEEN HER DO.

I FIRST MET HER WHEN I WAS THIRTEEN YEARS OLD, STILL A KID, **PLAYING** AT BEING A HERO.

I CAN'T EVEN REMEMBER WHAT I WAS DOING THAT DAY. SOMETHING WITH THE TITANS, PROBABLY.

I **DO** REMEMBER THINKING SHE WAS THE MOST BEAUTIFUL THING I'D EVER SEEN.

I WANTED TO IMPRESS HER. I WANTED HER **RESPECT.**

SOME THINGS NEVER CHANGE.

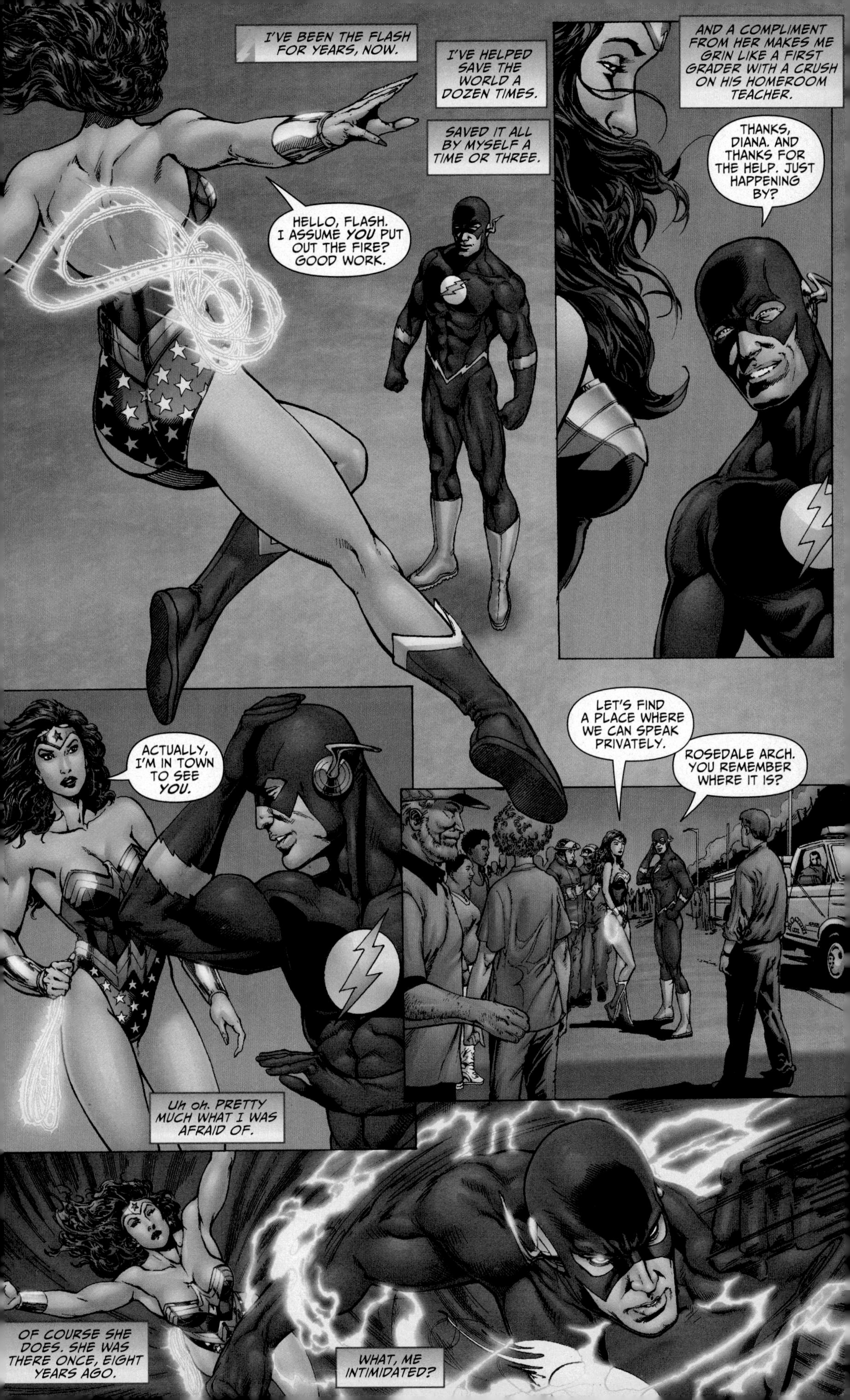
I'VE BEEN THE FLASH FOR YEARS, NOW.
I'VE HELPED SAVE THE WORLD A DOZEN TIMES.
SAVED IT ALL BY MYSELF A TIME OR THREE.
HELLO, FLASH. I ASSUME YOU PUT OUT THE FIRE? GOOD WORK.
AND A COMPLIMENT FROM HER MAKES ME GRIN LIKE A FIRST GRADER WITH A CRUSH ON HIS HOMEROOM TEACHER.
THANKS, DIANA. AND THANKS FOR THE HELP. JUST HAPPENING BY?
ACTUALLY, I'M IN TOWN TO SEE YOU.
Uh oh. PRETTY MUCH WHAT I WAS AFRAID OF.
LET'S FIND A PLACE WHERE WE CAN SPEAK PRIVATELY.
ROSEDALE ARCH. YOU REMEMBER WHERE IT IS?
OF COURSE SHE DOES. SHE WAS THERE ONCE, EIGHT YEARS AGO.
WHAT, ME INTIMIDATED?

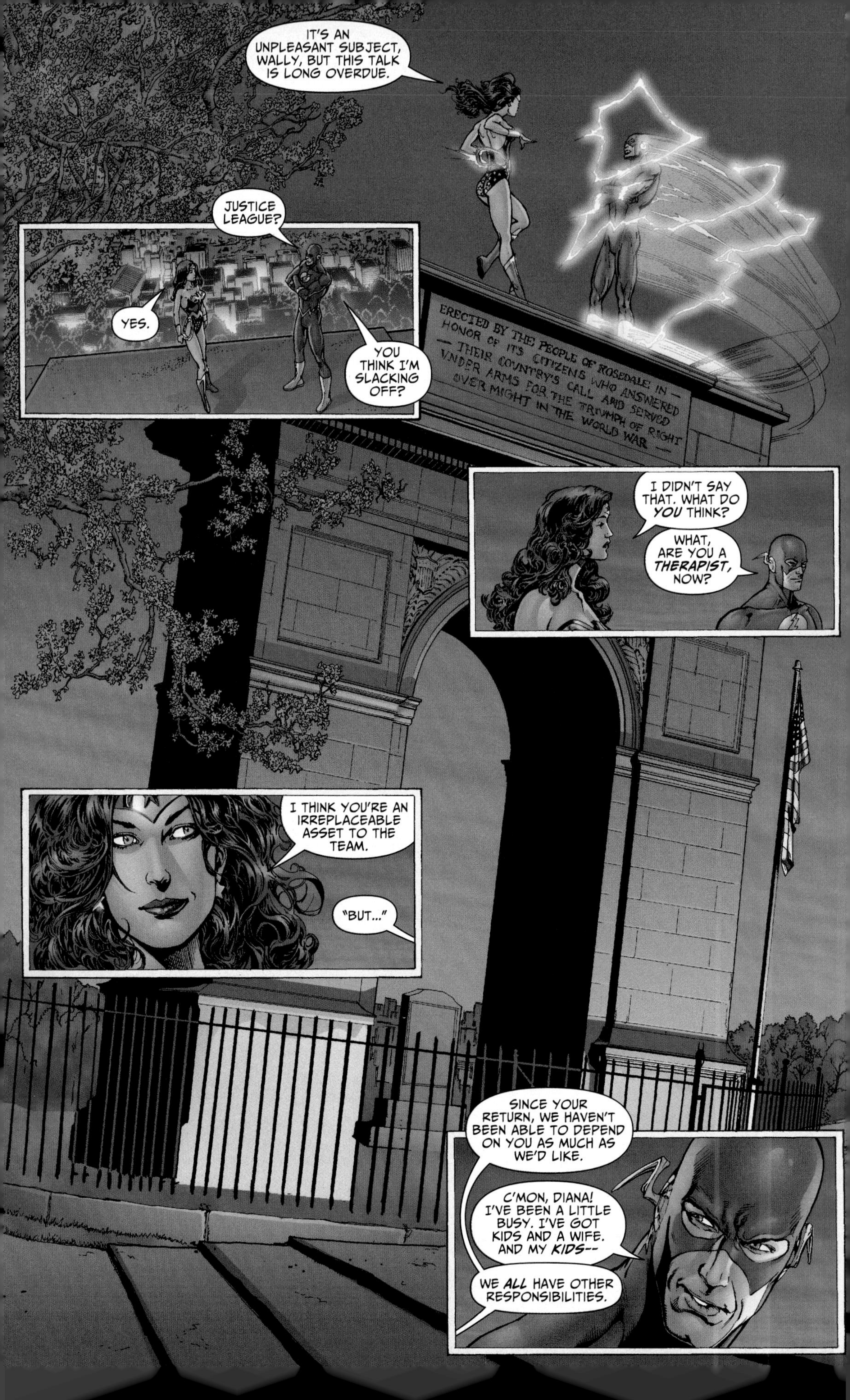
IT'S AN UNPLEASANT SUBJECT, WALLY, BUT THIS TALK IS LONG OVERDUE.
ERECTED BY THE PEOPLE OF ROSEDALE IN HONOR OF ITS CITIZENS WHO ANSWERED — THEIR COUNTRY'S CALL AND SERVED VNDER ARMS FOR THE TRIVMPH OF RIGHT OVER MIGHT IN THE WORLD WAR —
JUSTICE LEAGUE?
YES.
YOU THINK I'M SLACKING OFF?
I DIDN'T SAY THAT. WHAT DO *YOU* THINK?
WHAT, ARE YOU A ***THERAPIST,*** NOW?
I THINK YOU'RE AN IRREPLACEABLE ASSET TO THE TEAM.
"BUT..."
SINCE YOUR RETURN, WE HAVEN'T BEEN ABLE TO DEPEND ON YOU AS MUCH AS WE'D LIKE.
C'MON, DIANA! I'VE BEEN A LITTLE BUSY. I'VE GOT KIDS AND A WIFE. AND MY ***KIDS--***
WE ***ALL*** HAVE OTHER RESPONSIBILITIES.

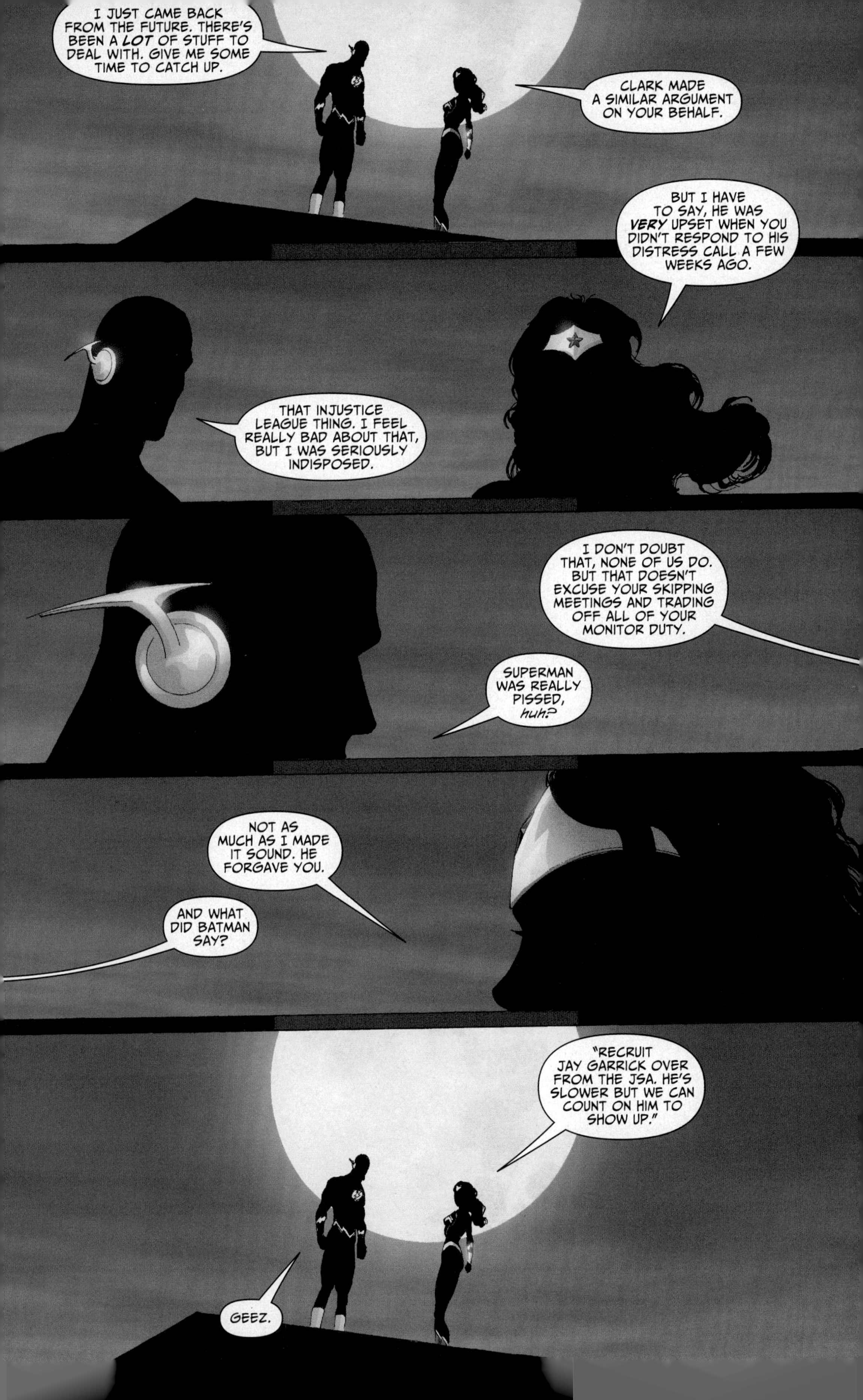

I JUST CAME BACK FROM THE FUTURE. THERE'S BEEN A *LOT* OF STUFF TO DEAL WITH. GIVE ME SOME TIME TO CATCH UP.
CLARK MADE A SIMILAR ARGUMENT ON YOUR BEHALF.
BUT I HAVE TO SAY, HE WAS ***VERY*** UPSET WHEN YOU DIDN'T RESPOND TO HIS DISTRESS CALL A FEW WEEKS AGO.
THAT INJUSTICE LEAGUE THING. I FEEL REALLY BAD ABOUT THAT, BUT I WAS SERIOUSLY INDISPOSED.
I DON'T DOUBT THAT, NONE OF US DO. BUT THAT DOESN'T EXCUSE YOUR SKIPPING MEETINGS AND TRADING OFF ALL OF YOUR MONITOR DUTY.
SUPERMAN WAS REALLY PISSED, *huh?*
NOT AS MUCH AS I MADE IT SOUND. HE FORGAVE YOU.
AND WHAT DID BATMAN SAY?
"RECRUIT JAY GARRICK OVER FROM THE JSA. HE'S SLOWER BUT WE CAN COUNT ON HIM TO SHOW UP."
GEEZ.

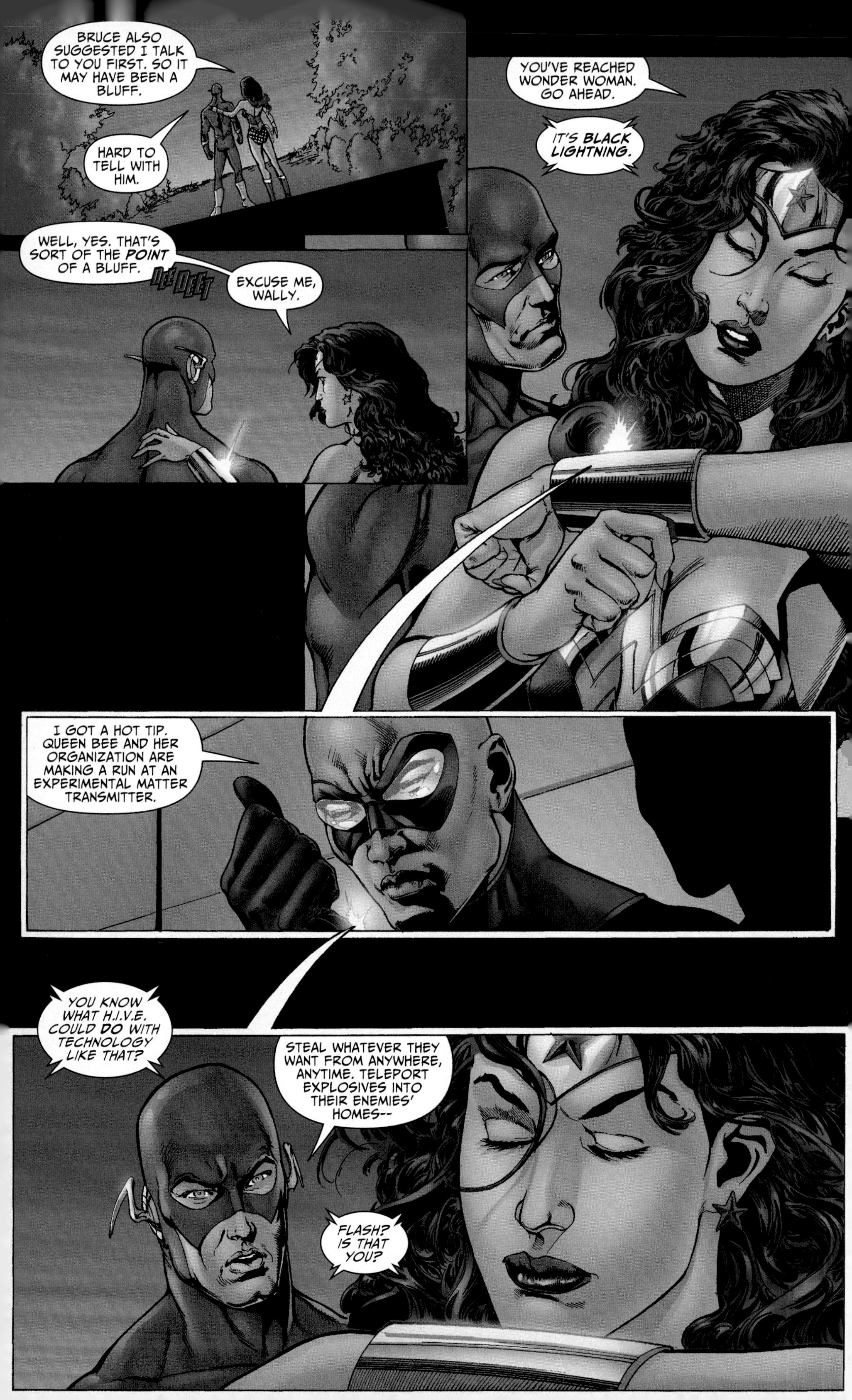
BRUCE ALSO SUGGESTED I TALK TO YOU FIRST. SO IT MAY HAVE BEEN A BLUFF.
HARD TO TELL WITH HIM.
WELL, YES. THAT'S SORT OF THE POINT OF A BLUFF.
DEE DEET
EXCUSE ME, WALLY.
YOU'VE REACHED WONDER WOMAN. GO AHEAD.
IT'S BLACK LIGHTNING.
I GOT A HOT TIP. QUEEN BEE AND HER ORGANIZATION ARE MAKING A RUN AT AN EXPERIMENTAL MATTER TRANSMITTER.
YOU KNOW WHAT H.I.V.E. COULD DO WITH TECHNOLOGY LIKE THAT?
STEAL WHATEVER THEY WANT FROM ANYWHERE, ANYTIME. TELEPORT EXPLOSIVES INTO THEIR ENEMIES' HOMES--
FLASH? IS THAT YOU?

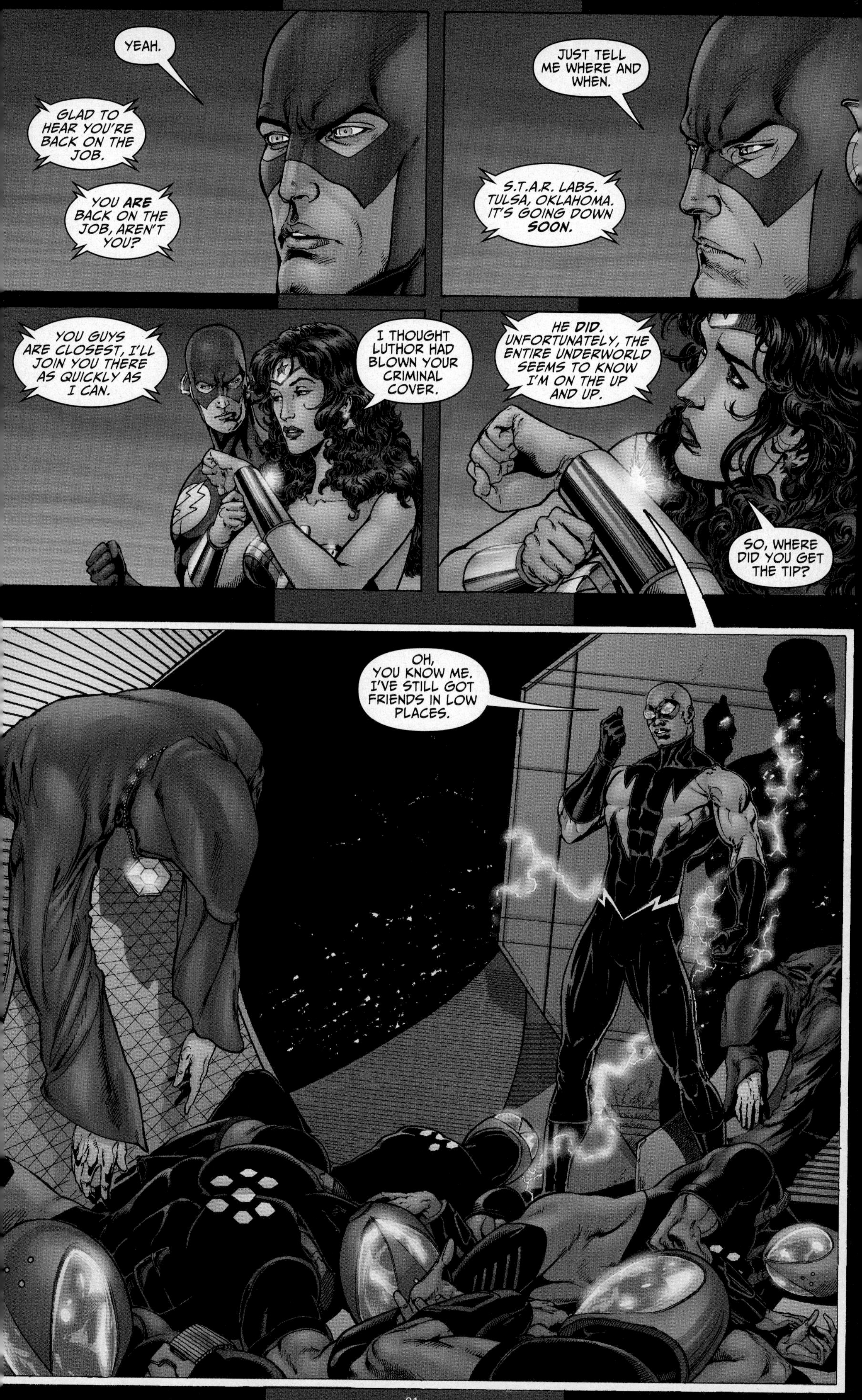
YEAH.
GLAD TO HEAR YOU'RE BACK ON THE JOB.
YOU ARE BACK ON THE JOB, AREN'T YOU?
JUST TELL ME WHERE AND WHEN.
S.T.A.R. LABS. TULSA, OKLAHOMA. IT'S GOING DOWN SOON.
YOU GUYS ARE CLOSEST, I'LL JOIN YOU THERE AS QUICKLY AS I CAN.
I THOUGHT LUTHOR HAD BLOWN YOUR CRIMINAL COVER.
HE DID. UNFORTUNATELY, THE ENTIRE UNDERWORLD SEEMS TO KNOW I'M ON THE UP AND UP.
SO, WHERE DID YOU GET THE TIP?
OH, YOU KNOW ME. I'VE STILL GOT FRIENDS IN LOW PLACES.

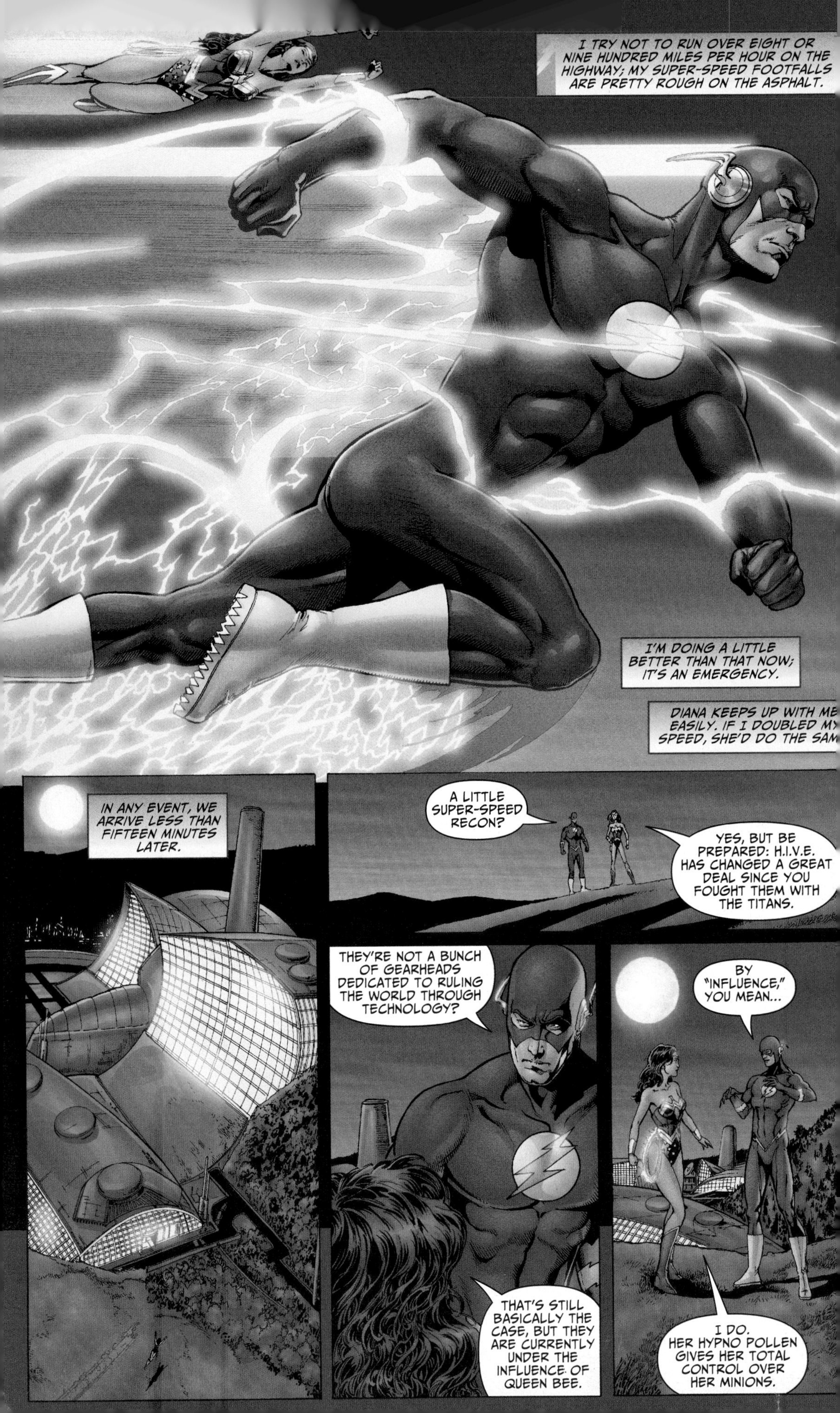
I TRY NOT TO RUN OVER EIGHT OR NINE HUNDRED MILES PER HOUR ON THE HIGHWAY; MY SUPER-SPEED FOOTFALLS ARE PRETTY ROUGH ON THE ASPHALT.
I'M DOING A LITTLE BETTER THAN THAT NOW; IT'S AN EMERGENCY.
DIANA KEEPS UP WITH ME EASILY. IF I DOUBLED MY SPEED, SHE'D DO THE SAM
IN ANY EVENT, WE ARRIVE LESS THAN FIFTEEN MINUTES LATER.
A LITTLE SUPER-SPEED RECON?
YES, BUT BE PREPARED: H.I.V.E. HAS CHANGED A GREAT DEAL SINCE YOU FOUGHT THEM WITH THE TITANS.
THEY'RE NOT A BUNCH OF GEARHEADS DEDICATED TO RULING THE WORLD THROUGH TECHNOLOGY?
THAT'S STILL BASICALLY THE CASE, BUT THEY ARE CURRENTLY UNDER THE INFLUENCE OF QUEEN BEE.
BY "INFLUENCE," YOU MEAN...
I DO. HER HYPNO POLLEN GIVES HER TOTAL CONTROL OVER HER MINIONS.

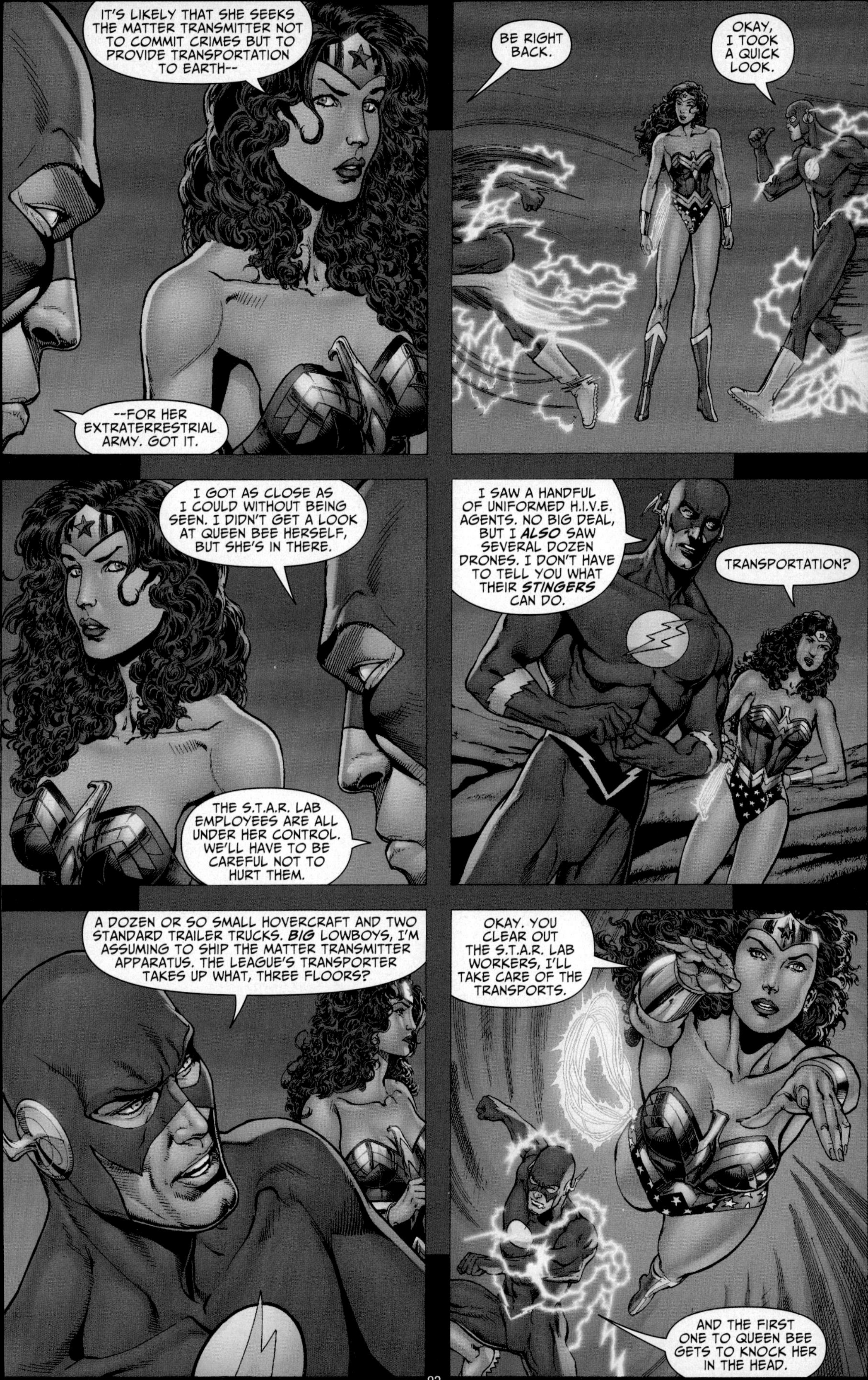
IT'S LIKELY THAT SHE SEEKS THE MATTER TRANSMITTER NOT TO COMMIT CRIMES BUT TO PROVIDE TRANSPORTATION TO EARTH--
--FOR HER EXTRATERRESTRIAL ARMY. GOT IT.
BE RIGHT BACK.
OKAY, I TOOK A QUICK LOOK.
I GOT AS CLOSE AS I COULD WITHOUT BEING SEEN. I DIDN'T GET A LOOK AT QUEEN BEE HERSELF, BUT SHE'S IN THERE.
THE S.T.A.R. LAB EMPLOYEES ARE ALL UNDER HER CONTROL. WE'LL HAVE TO BE CAREFUL NOT TO HURT THEM.
I SAW A HANDFUL OF UNIFORMED H.I.V.E. AGENTS. NO BIG DEAL, BUT I *ALSO* SAW SEVERAL DOZEN DRONES. I DON'T HAVE TO TELL YOU WHAT THEIR *STINGERS* CAN DO.
TRANSPORTATION?
A DOZEN OR SO SMALL HOVERCRAFT AND TWO STANDARD TRAILER TRUCKS. *BIG* LOWBOYS, I'M ASSUMING TO SHIP THE MATTER TRANSMITTER APPARATUS. THE LEAGUE'S TRANSPORTER TAKES UP WHAT, THREE FLOORS?
OKAY. YOU CLEAR OUT THE S.T.A.R. LAB WORKERS, I'LL TAKE CARE OF THE TRANSPORTS.
AND THE FIRST ONE TO QUEEN BEE GETS TO KNOCK HER IN THE HEAD.

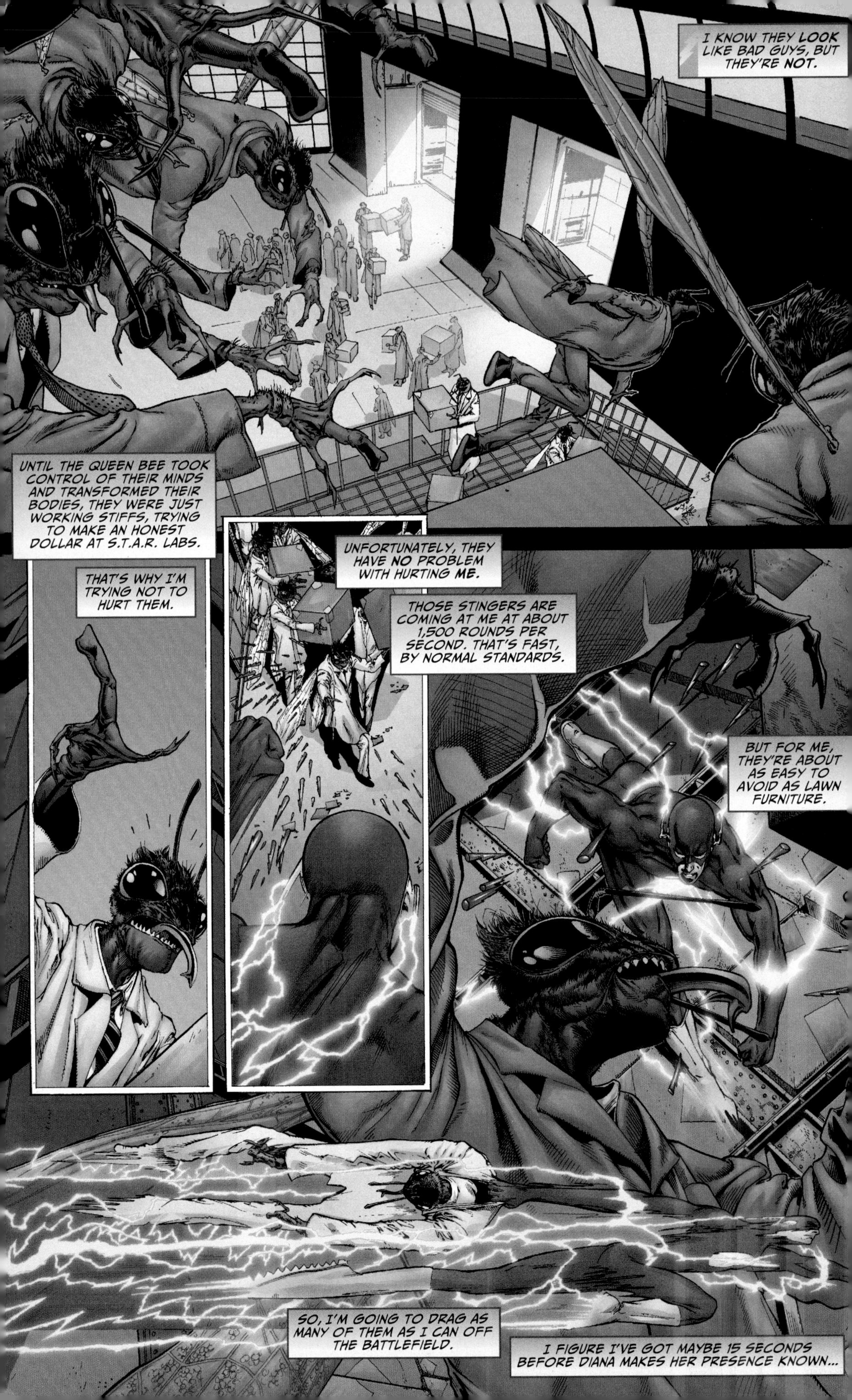
I KNOW THEY LOOK LIKE BAD GUYS, BUT THEY'RE NOT.
UNTIL THE QUEEN BEE TOOK CONTROL OF THEIR MINDS AND TRANSFORMED THEIR BODIES, THEY WERE JUST WORKING STIFFS, TRYING TO MAKE AN HONEST DOLLAR AT S.T.A.R. LABS.
THAT'S WHY I'M TRYING NOT TO HURT THEM.
UNFORTUNATELY, THEY HAVE NO PROBLEM WITH HURTING ME.
THOSE STINGERS ARE COMING AT ME AT ABOUT 1,500 ROUNDS PER SECOND. THAT'S FAST, BY NORMAL STANDARDS.
BUT FOR ME, THEY'RE ABOUT AS EASY TO AVOID AS LAWN FURNITURE.
SO, I'M GOING TO DRAG AS MANY OF THEM AS I CAN OFF THE BATTLEFIELD.
I FIGURE I'VE GOT MAYBE 15 SECONDS BEFORE DIANA MAKES HER PRESENCE KNOWN...

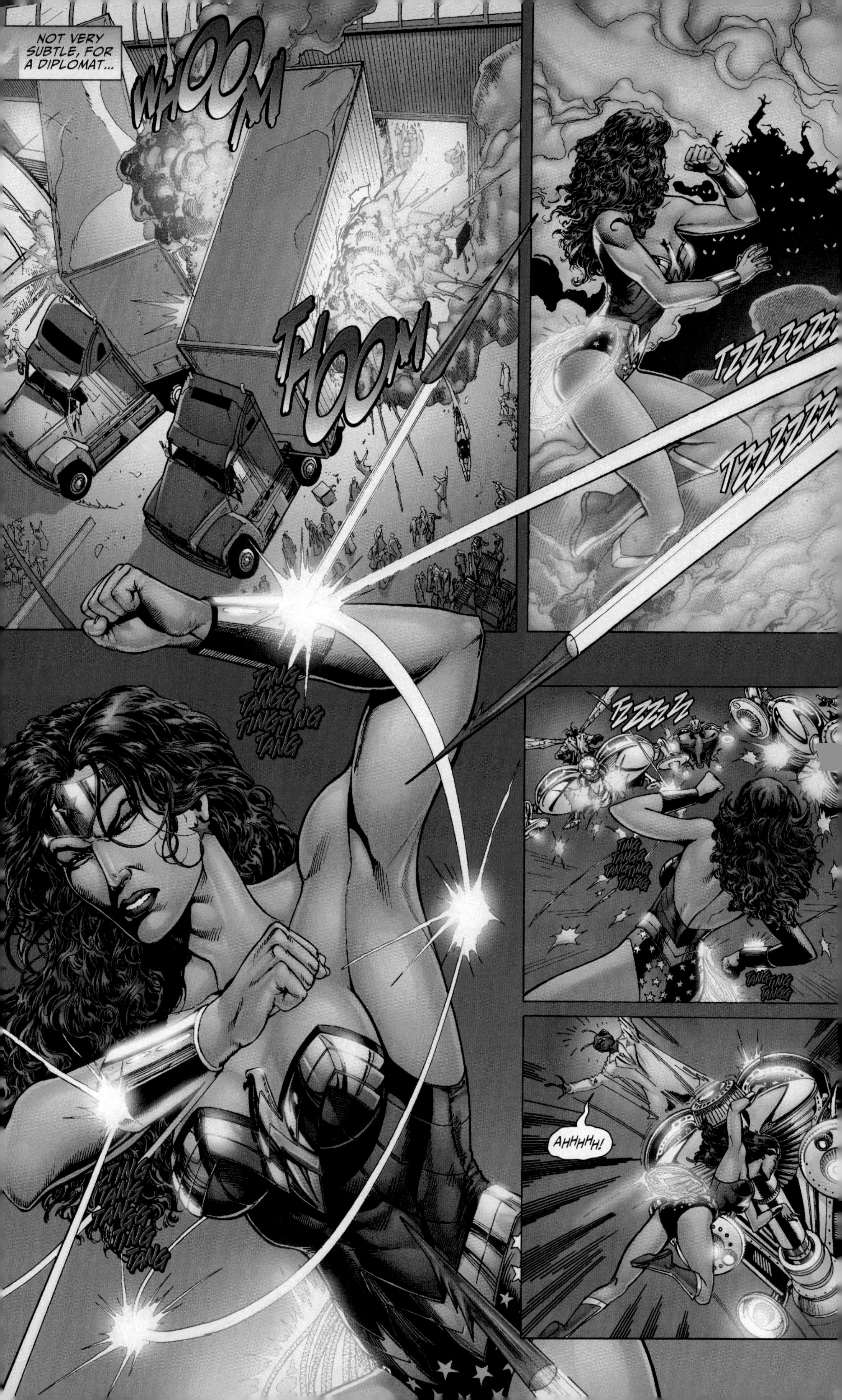
NOT VERY SUBTLE, FOR A DIPLOMAT...
WHOOM
THOOM
TZZZZZZZ
TZZZZZZZ
TANG TANGG TINGTING TANG
TZZZZZ
TANG TING TANG
AHHHHH!

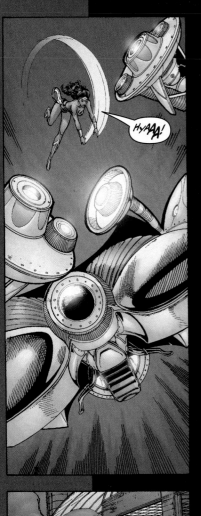

HyAAA!

WHOOM
THOOM
CHOOM

HEED MY *LASSO OF TRUTH* AND REMEMBER WHO YOU REALLY ARE.

WHAT...?

YOU'RE FREE OF THE QUEEN BEE'S CONTROL.

EXCUSE ME. THERE ARE OTHERS WHO NEED MY HELP.

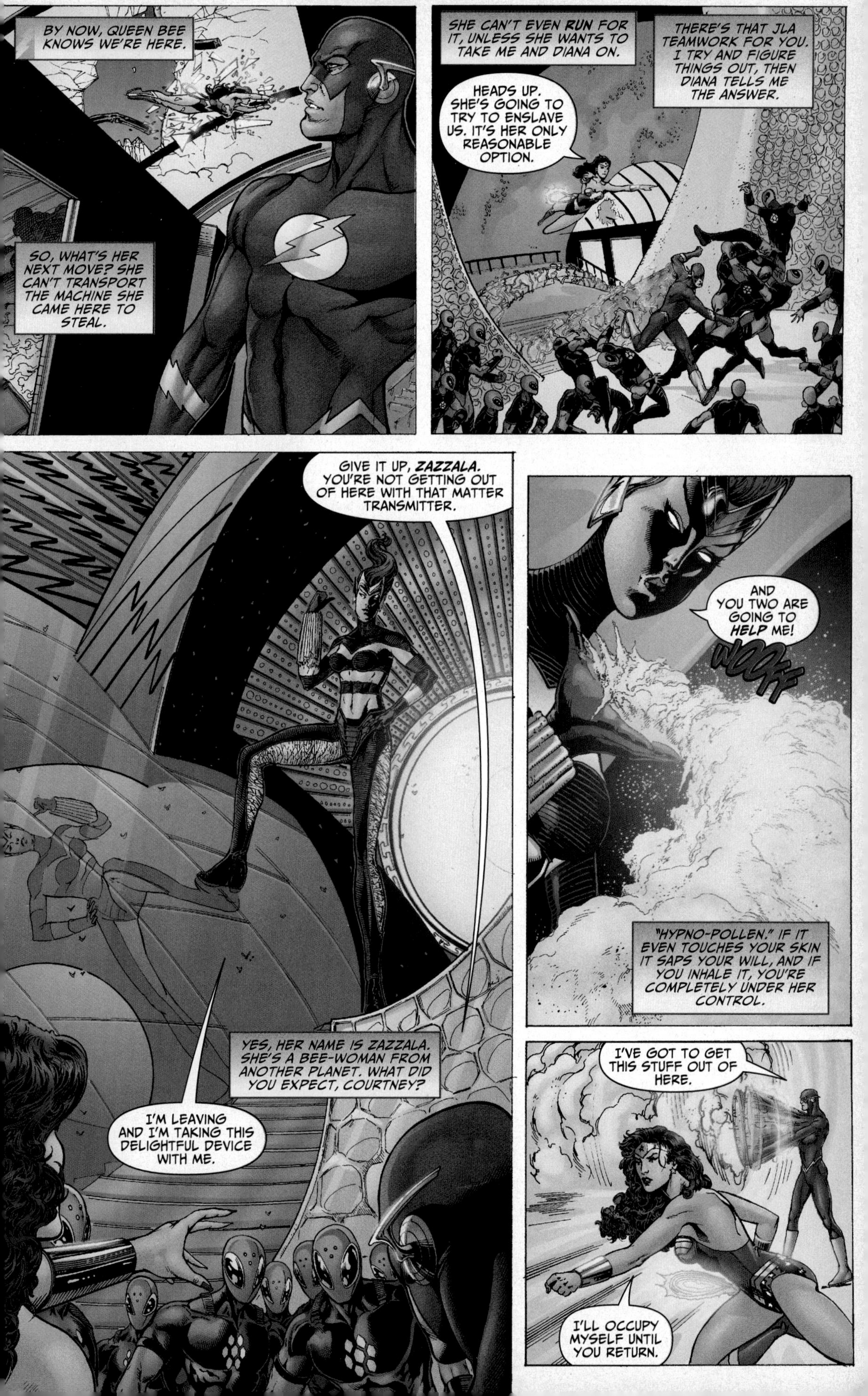

BY NOW, QUEEN BEE KNOWS WE'RE HERE.
SO, WHAT'S HER NEXT MOVE? SHE CAN'T TRANSPORT THE MACHINE SHE CAME HERE TO STEAL.
SHE CAN'T EVEN RUN FOR IT, UNLESS SHE WANTS TO TAKE ME AND DIANA ON.
HEADS UP. SHE'S GOING TO TRY TO ENSLAVE US. IT'S HER ONLY REASONABLE OPTION.
THERE'S THAT JLA TEAMWORK FOR YOU. I TRY AND FIGURE THINGS OUT, THEN DIANA TELLS ME THE ANSWER.
GIVE IT UP, ZAZZALA. YOU'RE NOT GETTING OUT OF HERE WITH THAT MATTER TRANSMITTER.
YES, HER NAME IS ZAZZALA. SHE'S A BEE-WOMAN FROM ANOTHER PLANET. WHAT DID YOU EXPECT, COURTNEY?
I'M LEAVING AND I'M TAKING THIS DELIGHTFUL DEVICE WITH ME.
AND YOU TWO ARE GOING TO HELP ME!
WOOOFF
"HYPNO-POLLEN." IF IT EVEN TOUCHES YOUR SKIN IT SAPS YOUR WILL, AND IF YOU INHALE IT, YOU'RE COMPLETELY UNDER HER CONTROL.
I'VE GOT TO GET THIS STUFF OUT OF HERE.
I'LL OCCUPY MYSELF UNTIL YOU RETURN.

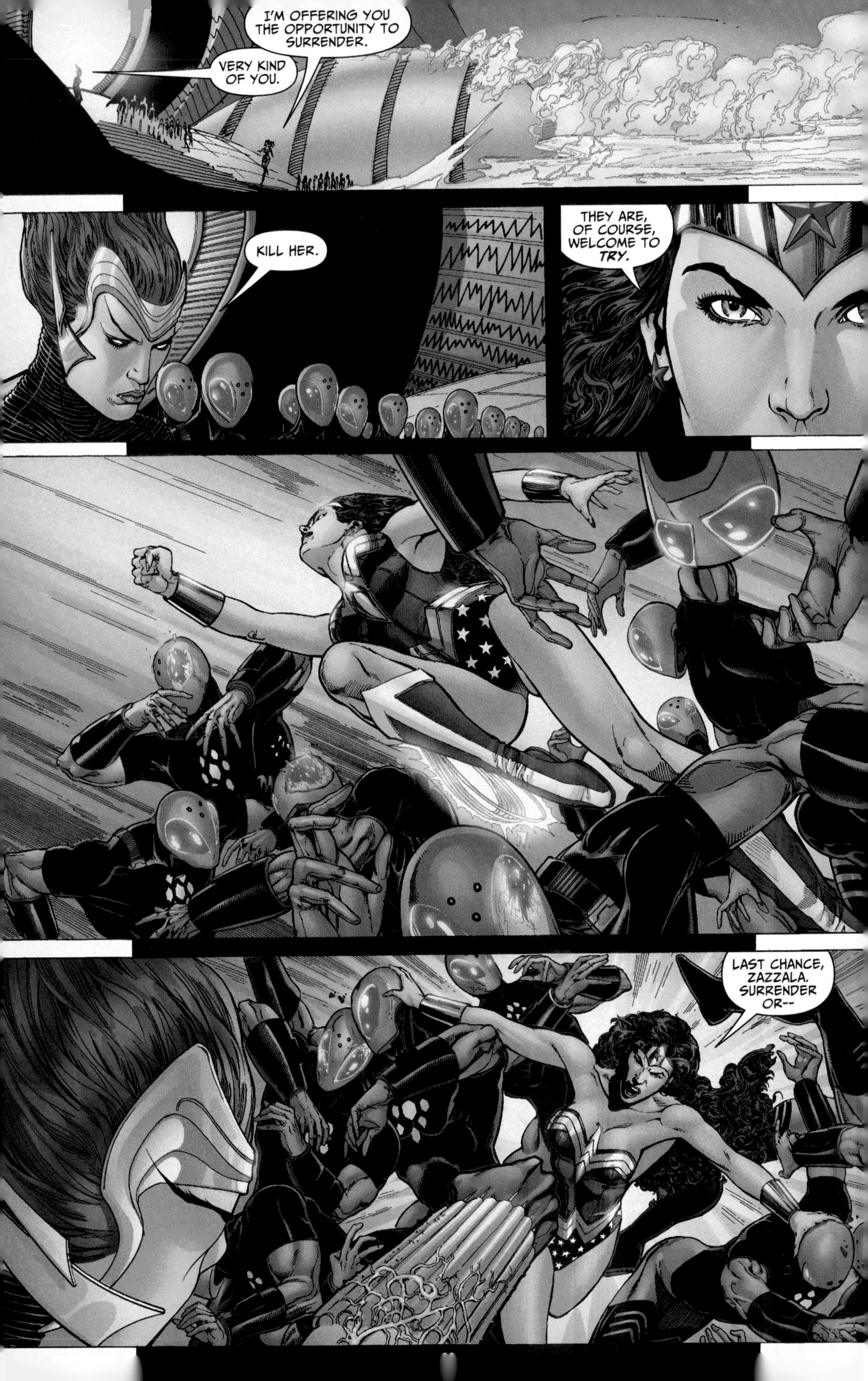
I'M OFFERING YOU THE OPPORTUNITY TO SURRENDER.
VERY KIND OF YOU.
KILL HER.
THEY ARE, OF COURSE, WELCOME TO TRY.
LAST CHANCE, ZAZZALA. SURRENDER OR--

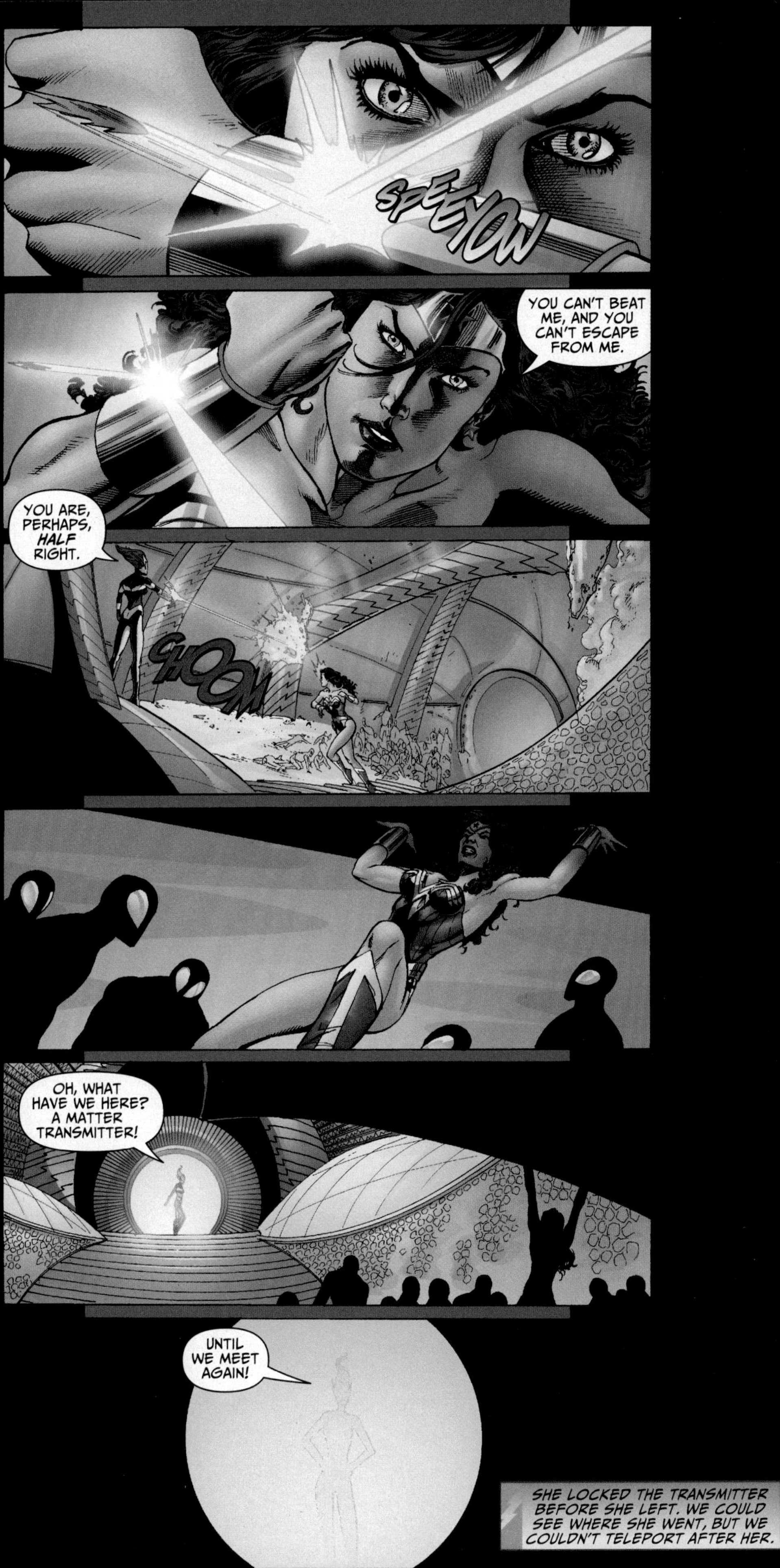
SPEEYOW
YOU CAN'T BEAT ME, AND YOU CAN'T ESCAPE FROM ME.
YOU ARE, PERHAPS, HALF RIGHT.
CHOOOM
OH, WHAT HAVE WE HERE? A MATTER TRANSMITTER!
UNTIL WE MEET AGAIN!
SHE LOCKED THE TRANSMITTER BEFORE SHE LEFT. WE COULD SEE WHERE SHE WENT, BUT WE COULDN'T TELEPORT AFTER HER.

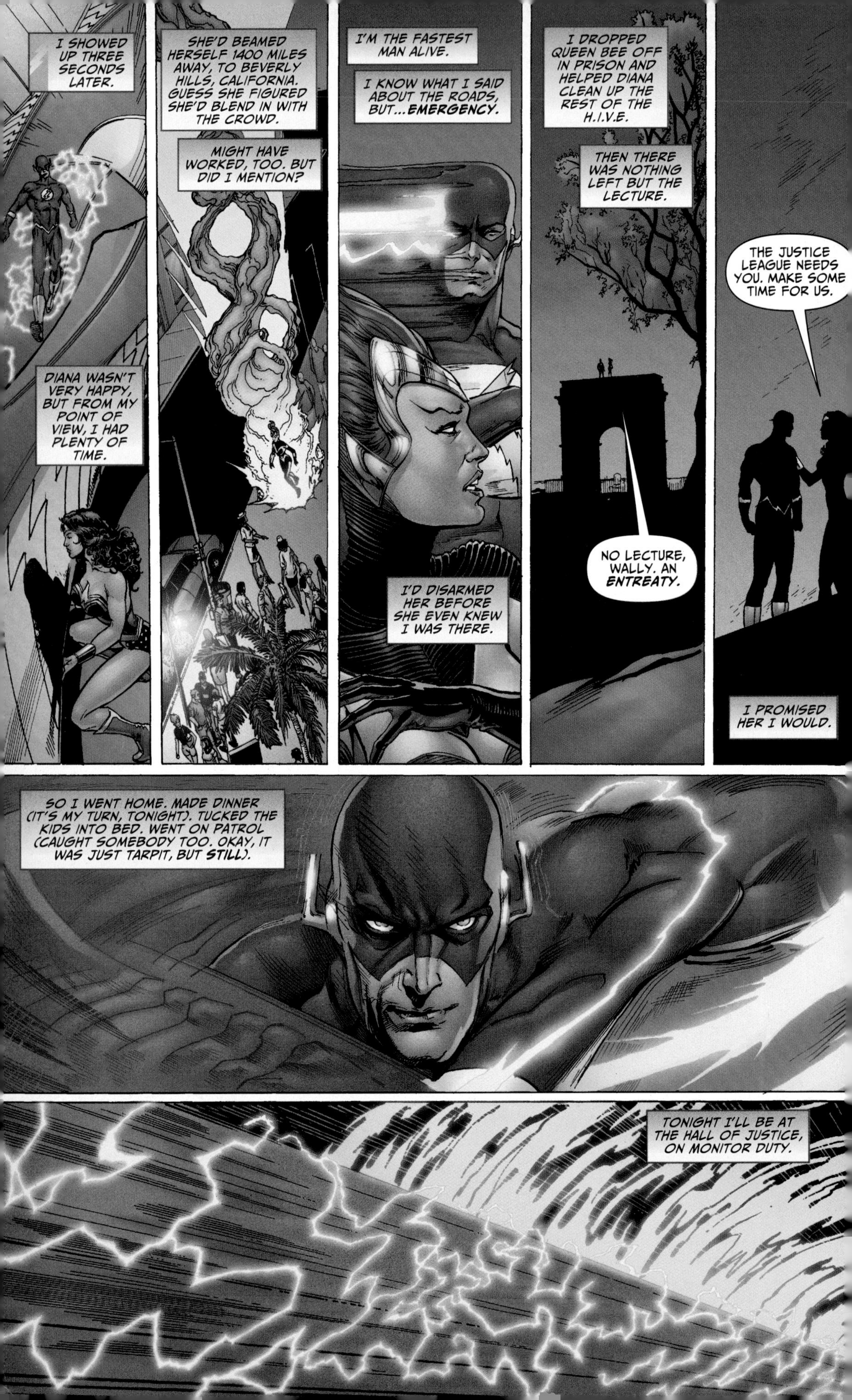
I SHOWED UP THREE SECONDS LATER.
DIANA WASN'T VERY HAPPY, BUT FROM MY POINT OF VIEW, I HAD PLENTY OF TIME.
SHE'D BEAMED HERSELF 1400 MILES AWAY, TO BEVERLY HILLS, CALIFORNIA. GUESS SHE FIGURED SHE'D BLEND IN WITH THE CROWD.
MIGHT HAVE WORKED, TOO. BUT DID I MENTION?
I'M THE FASTEST MAN ALIVE.
I KNOW WHAT I SAID ABOUT THE ROADS, BUT...EMERGENCY.
I'D DISARMED HER BEFORE SHE EVEN KNEW I WAS THERE.
I DROPPED QUEEN BEE OFF IN PRISON AND HELPED DIANA CLEAN UP THE REST OF THE H.I.V.E.
THEN THERE WAS NOTHING LEFT BUT THE LECTURE.
NO LECTURE, WALLY. AN ENTREATY.
THE JUSTICE LEAGUE NEEDS YOU. MAKE SOME TIME FOR US.
I PROMISED HER I WOULD.
SO I WENT HOME. MADE DINNER (IT'S MY TURN, TONIGHT). TUCKED THE KIDS INTO BED. WENT ON PATROL (CAUGHT SOMEBODY TOO. OKAY, IT WAS JUST TARPIT, BUT STILL).
TONIGHT I'LL BE AT THE HALL OF JUSTICE, ON MONITOR DUTY.

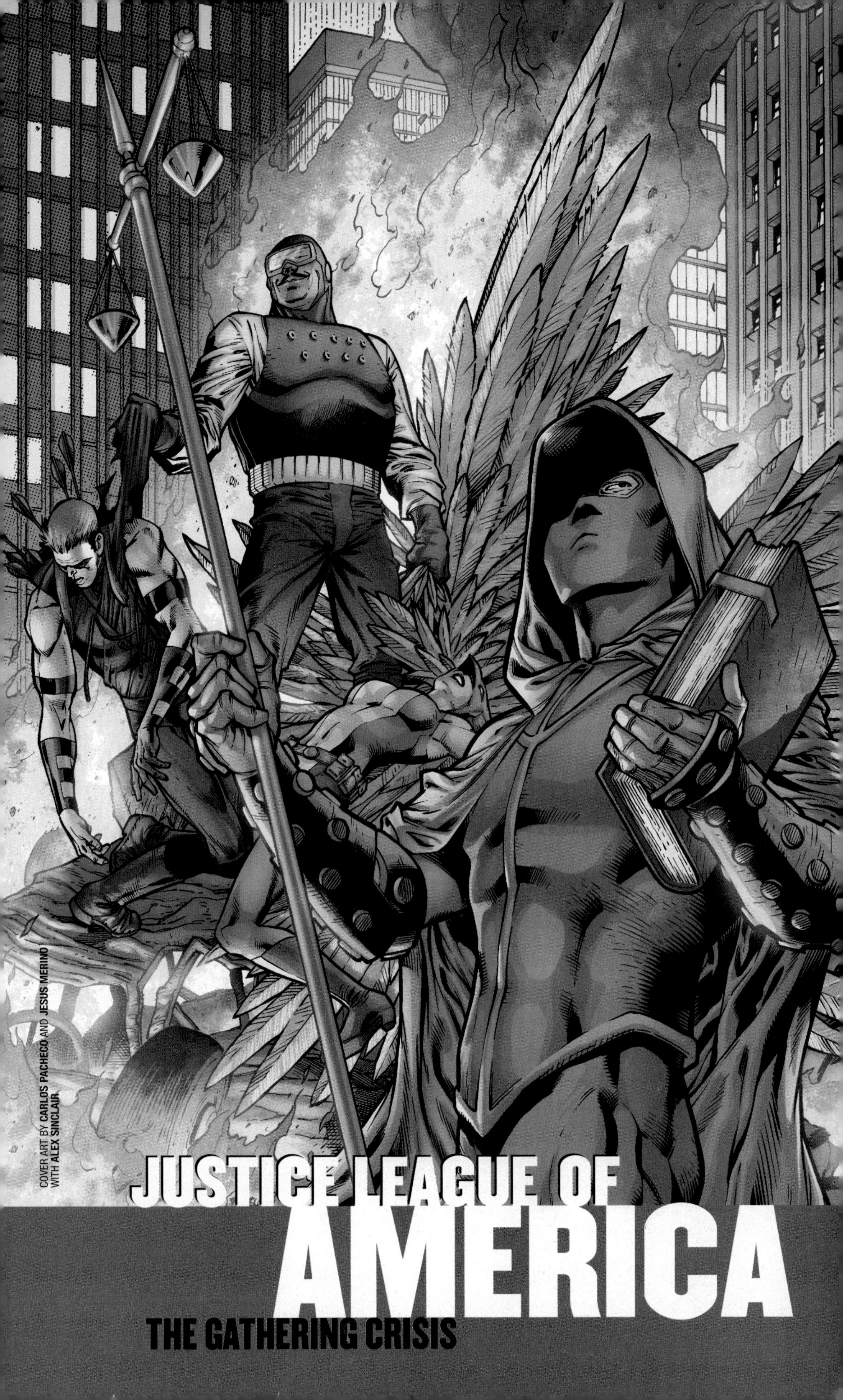

COVER ART BY CARLOS PACHECO AND JESUS MERINO
WITH ALEX SINCLAIR

JUSTICE LEAGUE OF AMERICA

THE GATHERING CRISIS

The Gathering Crisis

Dwayne McDuffie
Writer

Carlos Pacheco
Penciller

Jesus Merino
Inker

Rob Leigh
Letterer

Pete Pantazis
Colorist

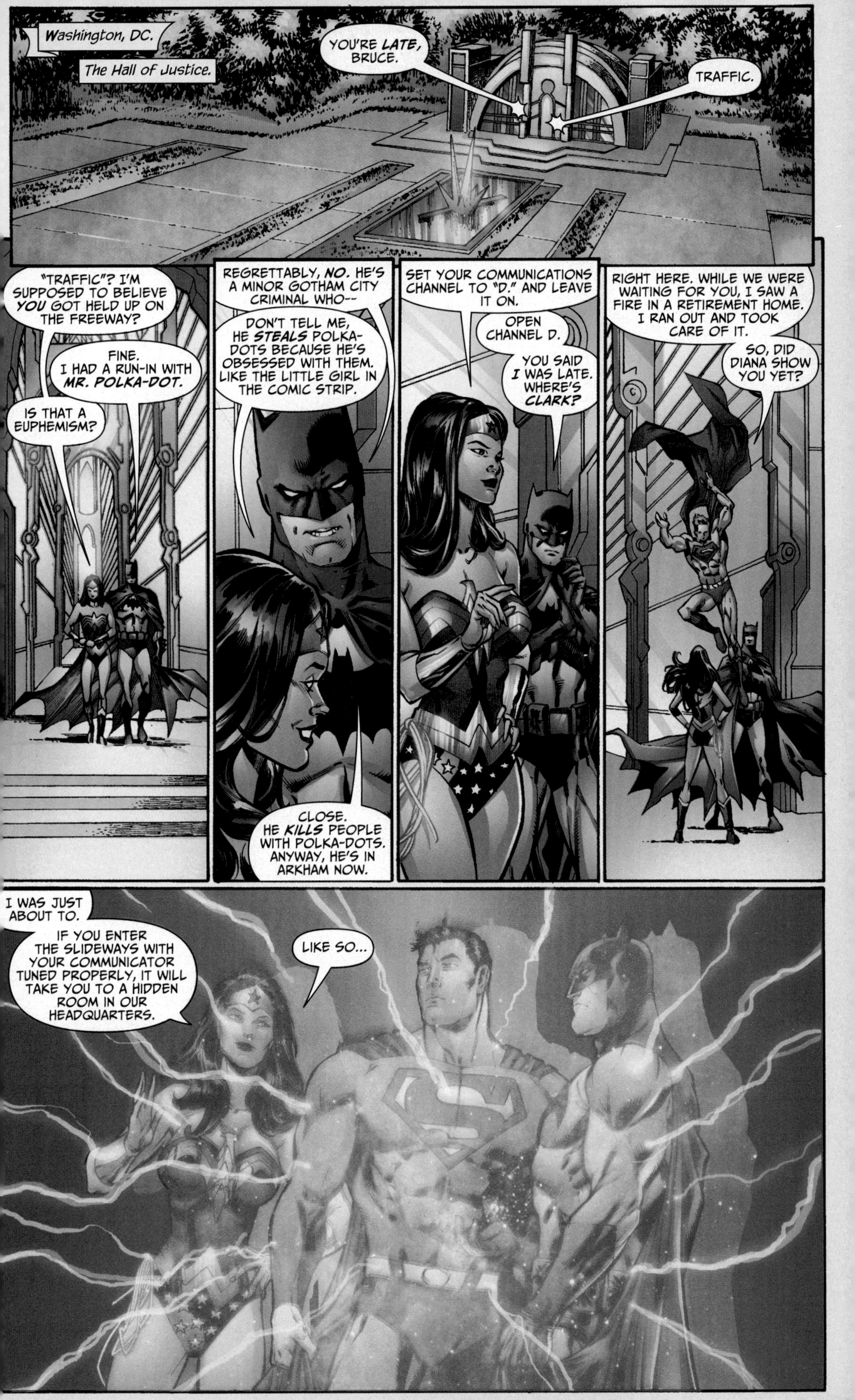

Washington, DC.
The Hall of Justice.
YOU'RE LATE, BRUCE.
TRAFFIC.
"TRAFFIC"? I'M SUPPOSED TO BELIEVE YOU GOT HELD UP ON THE FREEWAY?
FINE. I HAD A RUN-IN WITH MR. POLKA-DOT.
IS THAT A EUPHEMISM?
REGRETTABLY, NO. HE'S A MINOR GOTHAM CITY CRIMINAL WHO--
DON'T TELL ME, HE STEALS POLKA-DOTS BECAUSE HE'S OBSESSED WITH THEM. LIKE THE LITTLE GIRL IN THE COMIC STRIP.
CLOSE. HE KILLS PEOPLE WITH POLKA-DOTS. ANYWAY, HE'S IN ARKHAM NOW.
SET YOUR COMMUNICATIONS CHANNEL TO "D." AND LEAVE IT ON.
OPEN CHANNEL D.
YOU SAID I WAS LATE. WHERE'S CLARK?
RIGHT HERE. WHILE WE WERE WAITING FOR YOU, I SAW A FIRE IN A RETIREMENT HOME. I RAN OUT AND TOOK CARE OF IT.
SO, DID DIANA SHOW YOU YET?
I WAS JUST ABOUT TO.
IF YOU ENTER THE SLIDEWAYS WITH YOUR COMMUNICATOR TUNED PROPERLY, IT WILL TAKE YOU TO A HIDDEN ROOM IN OUR HEADQUARTERS.
LIKE SO...

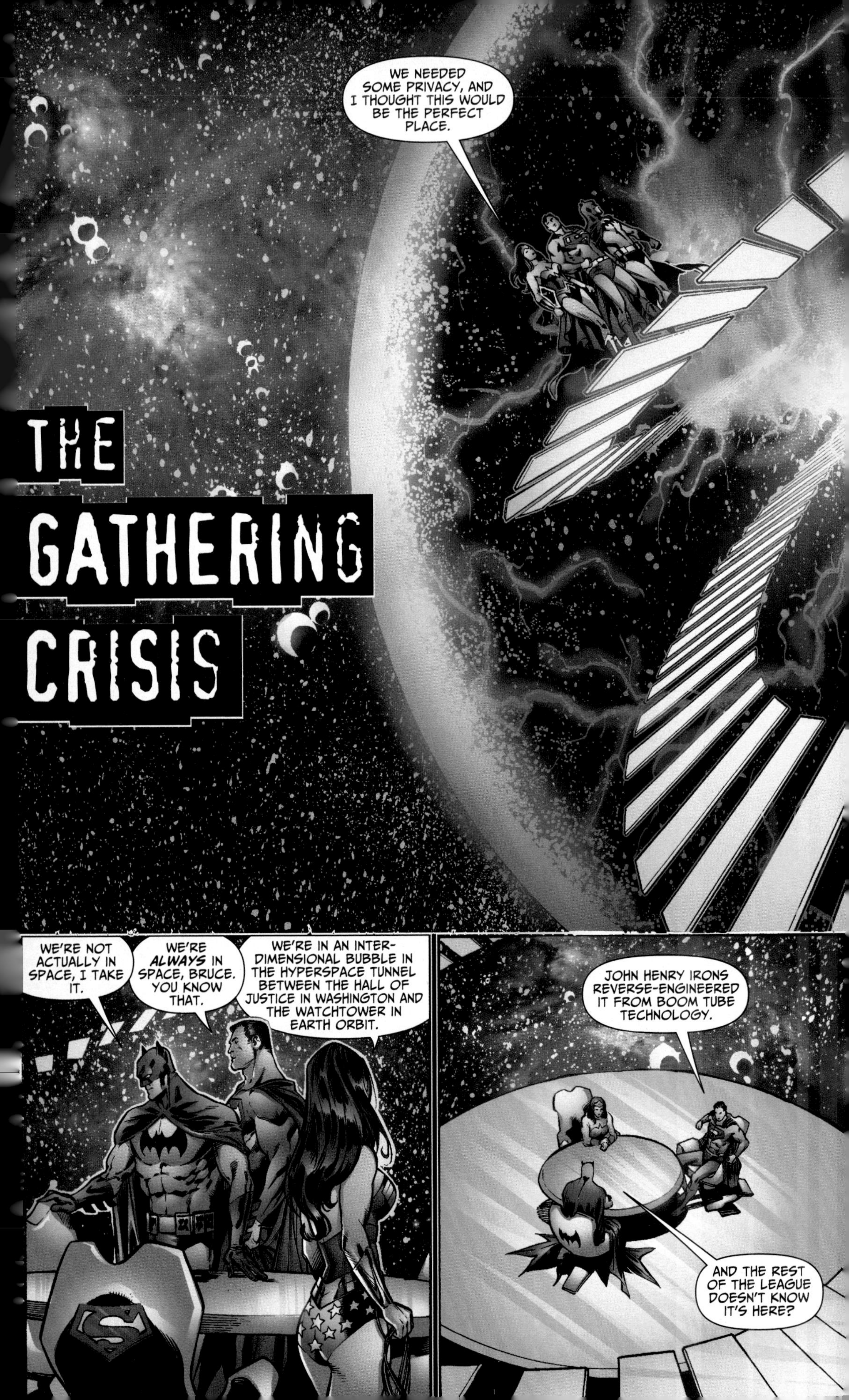
WE NEEDED SOME PRIVACY, AND I THOUGHT THIS WOULD BE THE PERFECT PLACE.
THE GATHERING CRISIS
WE'RE NOT ACTUALLY IN SPACE, I TAKE IT.
WE'RE ALWAYS IN SPACE, BRUCE. YOU KNOW THAT.
WE'RE IN AN INTER-DIMENSIONAL BUBBLE IN THE HYPERSPACE TUNNEL BETWEEN THE HALL OF JUSTICE IN WASHINGTON AND THE WATCHTOWER IN EARTH ORBIT.
JOHN HENRY IRONS REVERSE-ENGINEERED IT FROM BOOM TUBE TECHNOLOGY.
AND THE REST OF THE LEAGUE DOESN'T KNOW IT'S HERE?

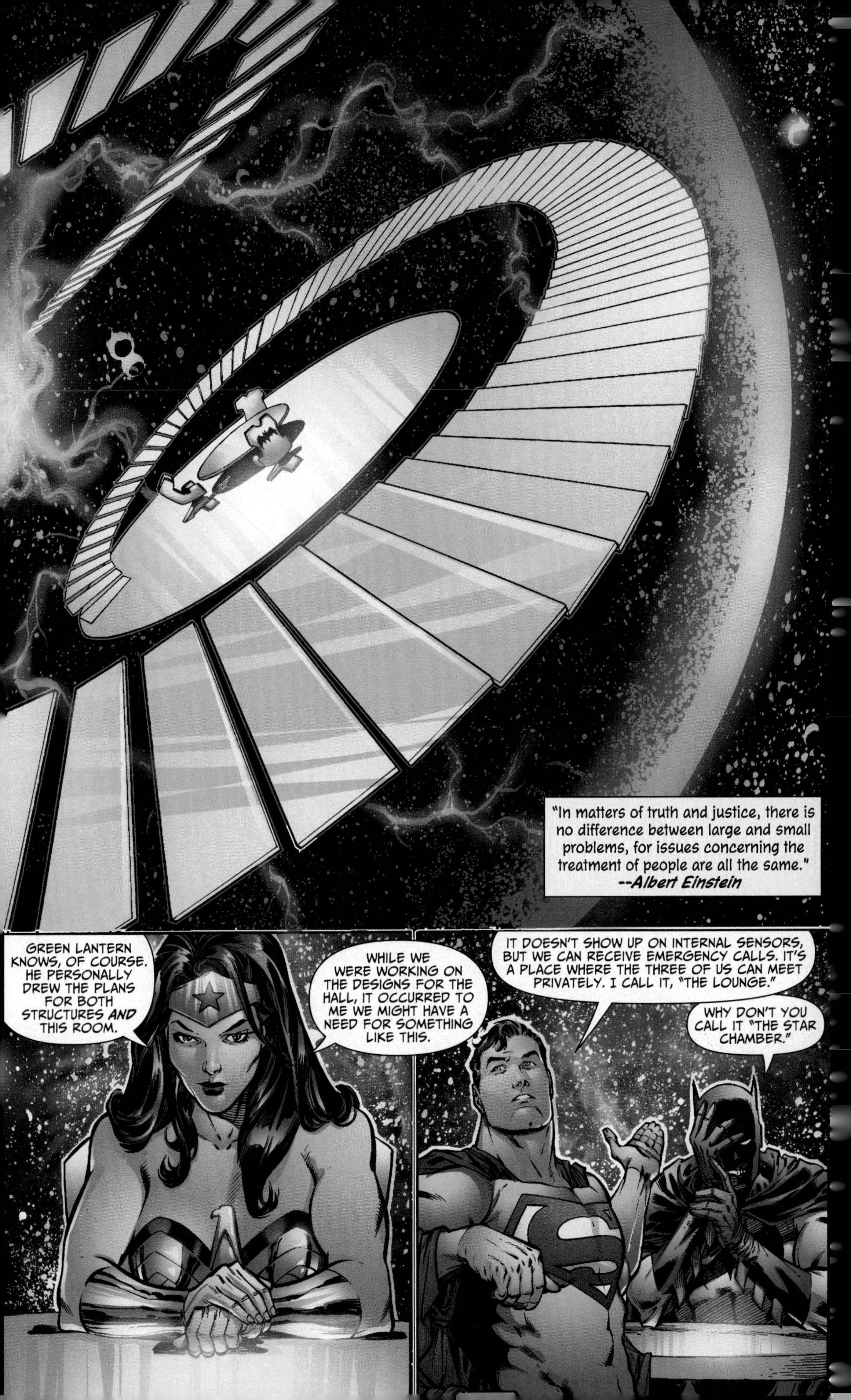
"In matters of truth and justice, there is no difference between large and small problems, for issues concerning the treatment of people are all the same."
--Albert Einstein
GREEN LANTERN KNOWS, OF COURSE. HE PERSONALLY DREW THE PLANS FOR BOTH STRUCTURES AND THIS ROOM.
WHILE WE WERE WORKING ON THE DESIGNS FOR THE HALL, IT OCCURRED TO ME WE MIGHT HAVE A NEED FOR SOMETHING LIKE THIS.
IT DOESN'T SHOW UP ON INTERNAL SENSORS, BUT WE CAN RECEIVE EMERGENCY CALLS. IT'S A PLACE WHERE THE THREE OF US CAN MEET PRIVATELY. I CALL IT, "THE LOUNGE."
WHY DON'T YOU CALL IT "THE STAR CHAMBER."

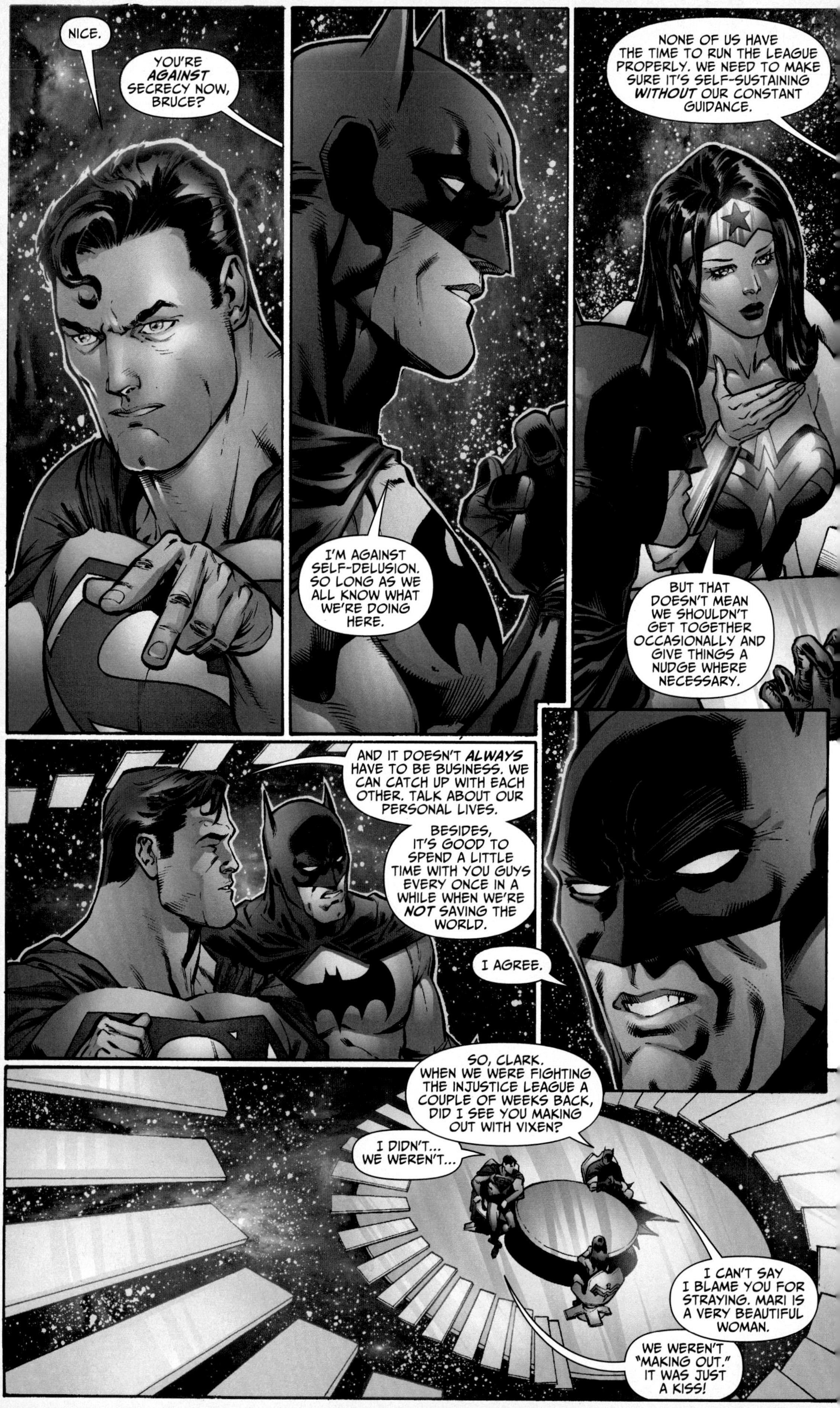
NICE.
YOU'RE AGAINST SECRECY NOW, BRUCE?
I'M AGAINST SELF-DELUSION. SO LONG AS WE ALL KNOW WHAT WE'RE DOING HERE.
NONE OF US HAVE THE TIME TO RUN THE LEAGUE PROPERLY. WE NEED TO MAKE SURE IT'S SELF-SUSTAINING WITHOUT OUR CONSTANT GUIDANCE.
BUT THAT DOESN'T MEAN WE SHOULDN'T GET TOGETHER OCCASIONALLY AND GIVE THINGS A NUDGE WHERE NECESSARY.
AND IT DOESN'T ALWAYS HAVE TO BE BUSINESS. WE CAN CATCH UP WITH EACH OTHER. TALK ABOUT OUR PERSONAL LIVES.
BESIDES, IT'S GOOD TO SPEND A LITTLE TIME WITH YOU GUYS EVERY ONCE IN A WHILE WHEN WE'RE NOT SAVING THE WORLD.
I AGREE.
SO, CLARK. WHEN WE WERE FIGHTING THE INJUSTICE LEAGUE A COUPLE OF WEEKS BACK, DID I SEE YOU MAKING OUT WITH VIXEN?
I DIDN'T... WE WEREN'T...
I CAN'T SAY I BLAME YOU FOR STRAYING. MARI IS A VERY BEAUTIFUL WOMAN.
WE WEREN'T "MAKING OUT." IT WAS JUST A KISS!

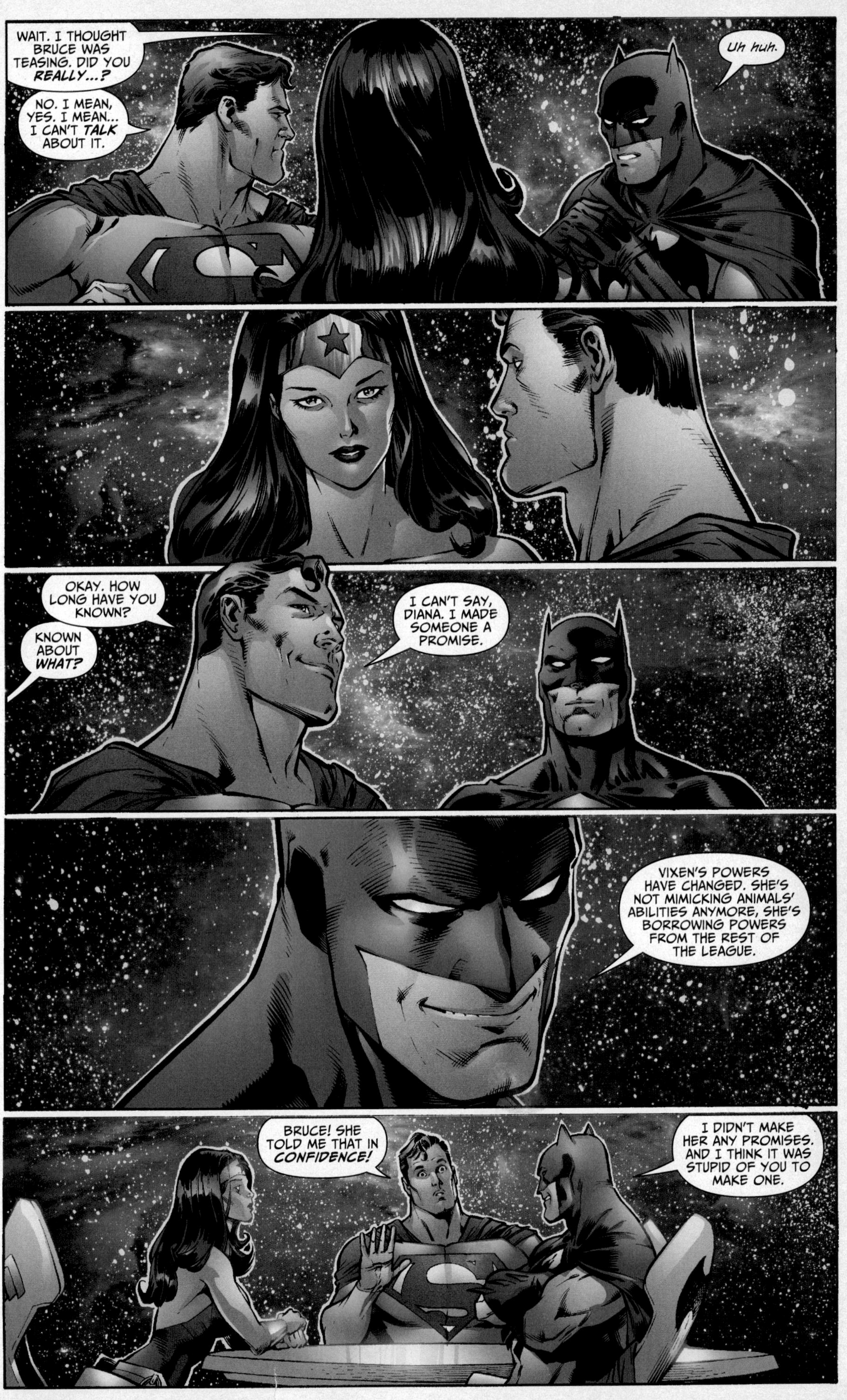
WAIT. I THOUGHT BRUCE WAS TEASING. DID YOU REALLY...?
Uh huh.
NO. I MEAN, YES. I MEAN... I CAN'T TALK ABOUT IT.
OKAY. HOW LONG HAVE YOU KNOWN?
KNOWN ABOUT WHAT?
I CAN'T SAY, DIANA. I MADE SOMEONE A PROMISE.
VIXEN'S POWERS HAVE CHANGED. SHE'S NOT MIMICKING ANIMALS' ABILITIES ANYMORE, SHE'S BORROWING POWERS FROM THE REST OF THE LEAGUE.
BRUCE! SHE TOLD ME THAT IN CONFIDENCE!
I DIDN'T MAKE HER ANY PROMISES. AND I THINK IT WAS STUPID OF YOU TO MAKE ONE.

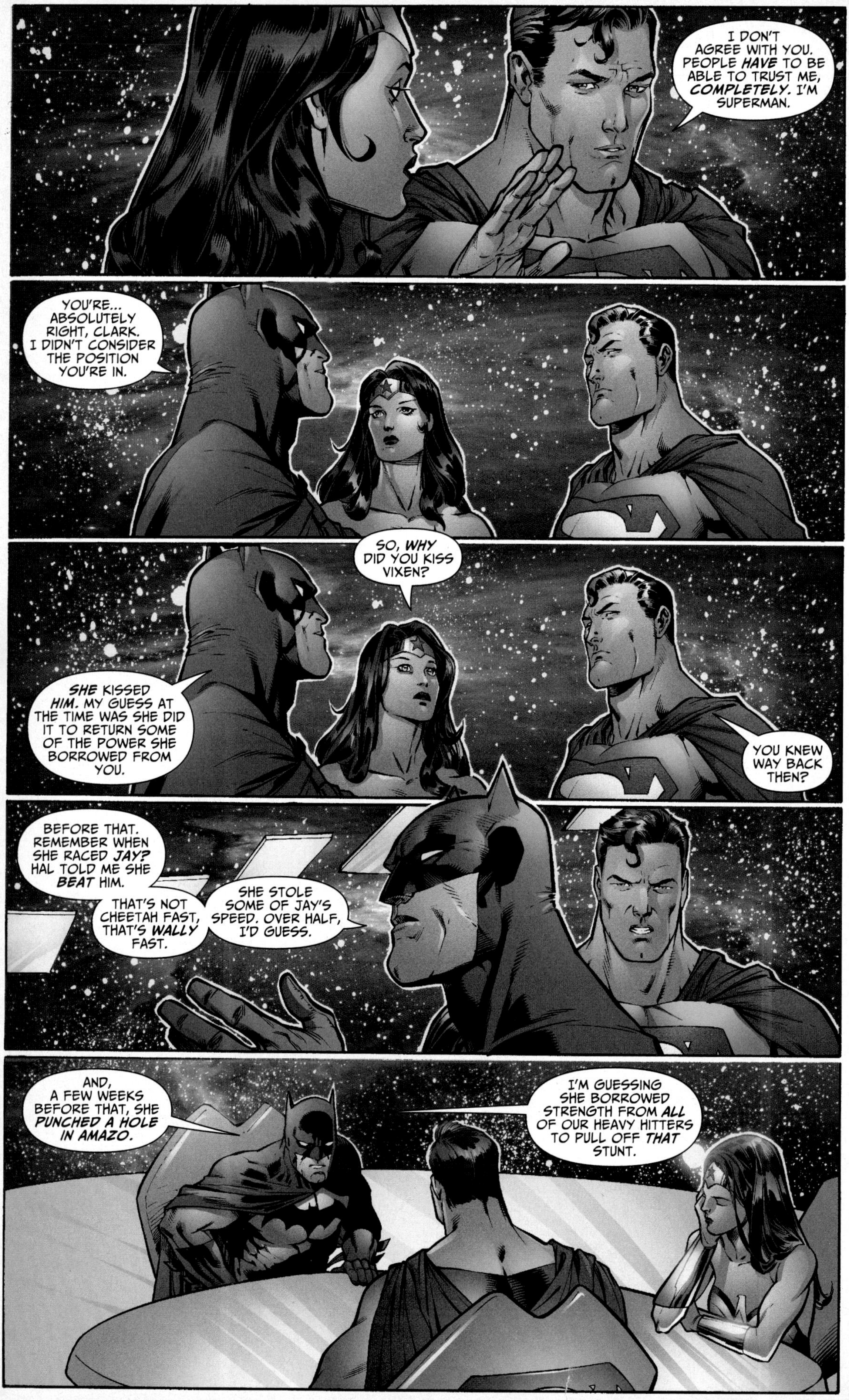
I DON'T AGREE WITH YOU. PEOPLE HAVE TO BE ABLE TO TRUST ME, COMPLETELY. I'M SUPERMAN.
YOU'RE... ABSOLUTELY RIGHT, CLARK. I DIDN'T CONSIDER THE POSITION YOU'RE IN.
SO, WHY DID YOU KISS VIXEN?
SHE KISSED HIM. MY GUESS AT THE TIME WAS SHE DID IT TO RETURN SOME OF THE POWER SHE BORROWED FROM YOU.
YOU KNEW WAY BACK THEN?
BEFORE THAT. REMEMBER WHEN SHE RACED JAY? HAL TOLD ME SHE BEAT HIM.
THAT'S NOT CHEETAH FAST, THAT'S WALLY FAST.
SHE STOLE SOME OF JAY'S SPEED. OVER HALF, I'D GUESS.
AND, A FEW WEEKS BEFORE THAT, SHE PUNCHED A HOLE IN AMAZO.
I'M GUESSING SHE BORROWED STRENGTH FROM ALL OF OUR HEAVY HITTERS TO PULL OFF THAT STUNT.

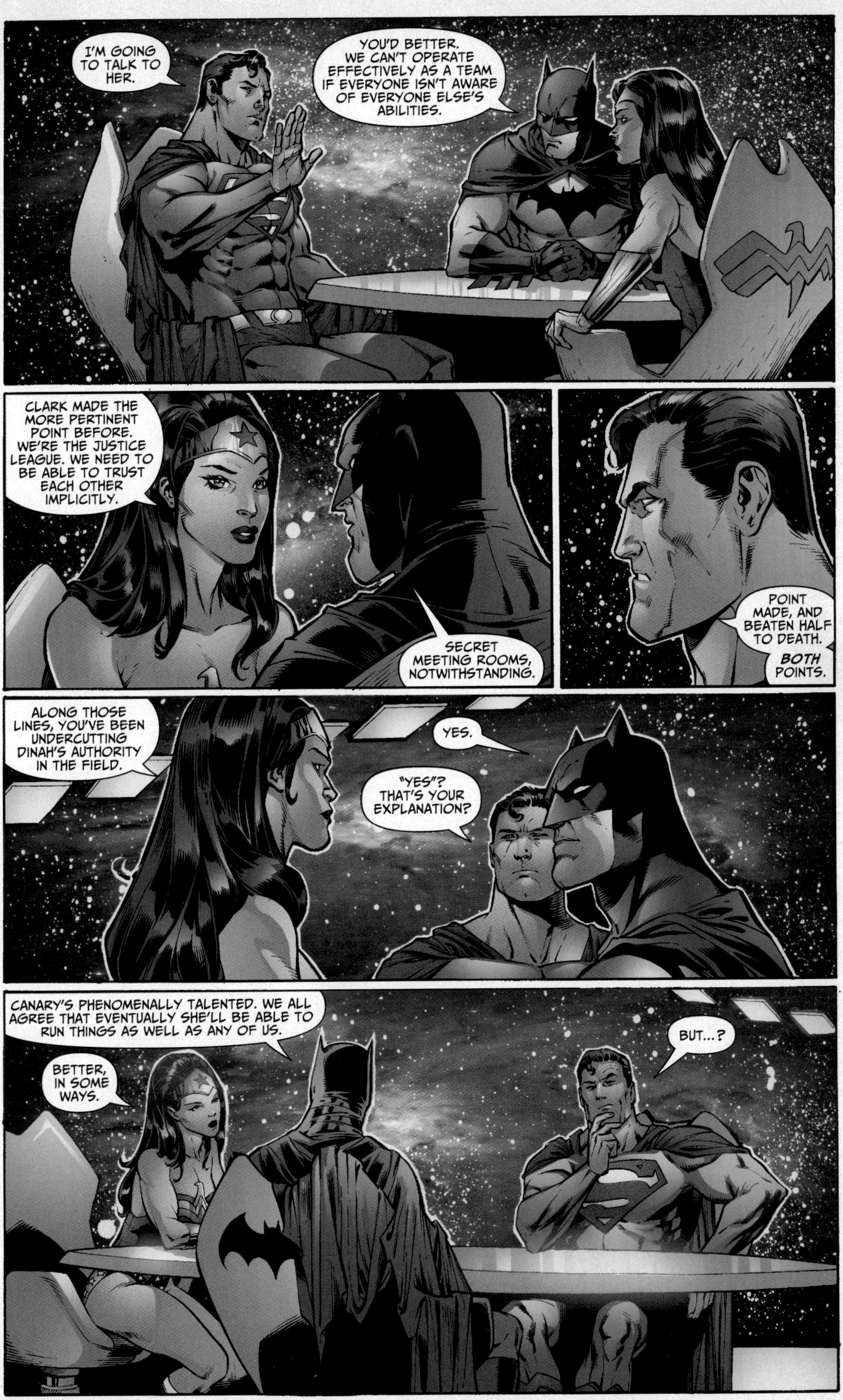
I'M GOING TO TALK TO HER.
YOU'D BETTER. WE CAN'T OPERATE EFFECTIVELY AS A TEAM IF EVERYONE ISN'T AWARE OF EVERYONE ELSE'S ABILITIES.
CLARK MADE THE MORE PERTINENT POINT BEFORE. WE'RE THE JUSTICE LEAGUE. WE NEED TO BE ABLE TO TRUST EACH OTHER IMPLICITLY.
SECRET MEETING ROOMS, NOTWITHSTANDING.
POINT MADE, AND BEATEN HALF TO DEATH. BOTH POINTS.
ALONG THOSE LINES, YOU'VE BEEN UNDERCUTTING DINAH'S AUTHORITY IN THE FIELD.
YES.
"YES"? THAT'S YOUR EXPLANATION?
CANARY'S PHENOMENALLY TALENTED. WE ALL AGREE THAT EVENTUALLY SHE'LL BE ABLE TO RUN THINGS AS WELL AS ANY OF US.
BETTER, IN SOME WAYS.
BUT...?

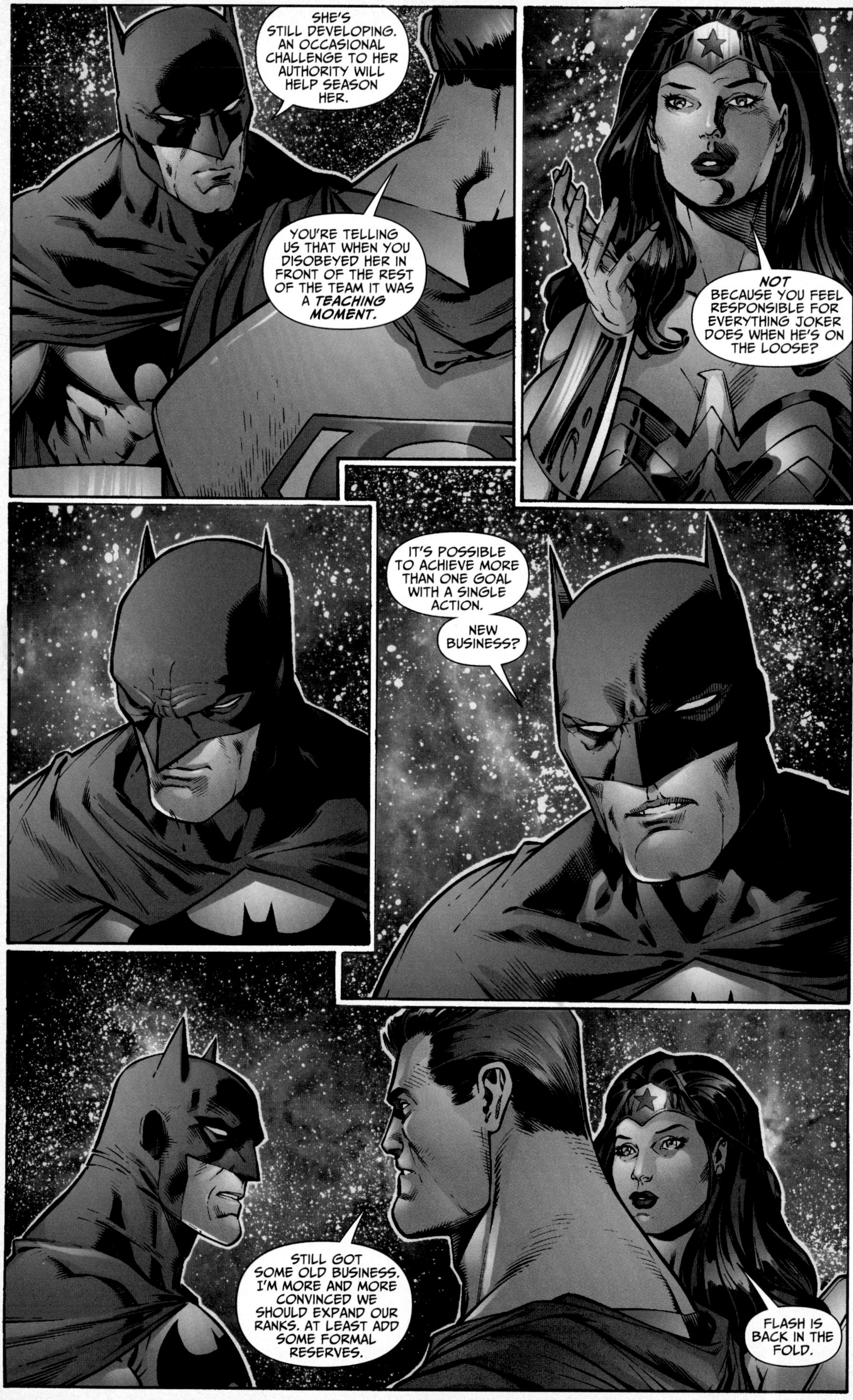
SHE'S STILL DEVELOPING. AN OCCASIONAL CHALLENGE TO HER AUTHORITY WILL HELP SEASON HER.
YOU'RE TELLING US THAT WHEN YOU DISOBEYED HER IN FRONT OF THE REST OF THE TEAM IT WAS A *TEACHING MOMENT.*
NOT BECAUSE YOU FEEL RESPONSIBLE FOR EVERYTHING JOKER DOES WHEN HE'S ON THE LOOSE?
IT'S POSSIBLE TO ACHIEVE MORE THAN ONE GOAL WITH A SINGLE ACTION.
NEW BUSINESS?
STILL GOT SOME OLD BUSINESS. I'M MORE AND MORE CONVINCED WE SHOULD EXPAND OUR RANKS. AT LEAST ADD SOME FORMAL RESERVES.
FLASH IS BACK IN THE FOLD.

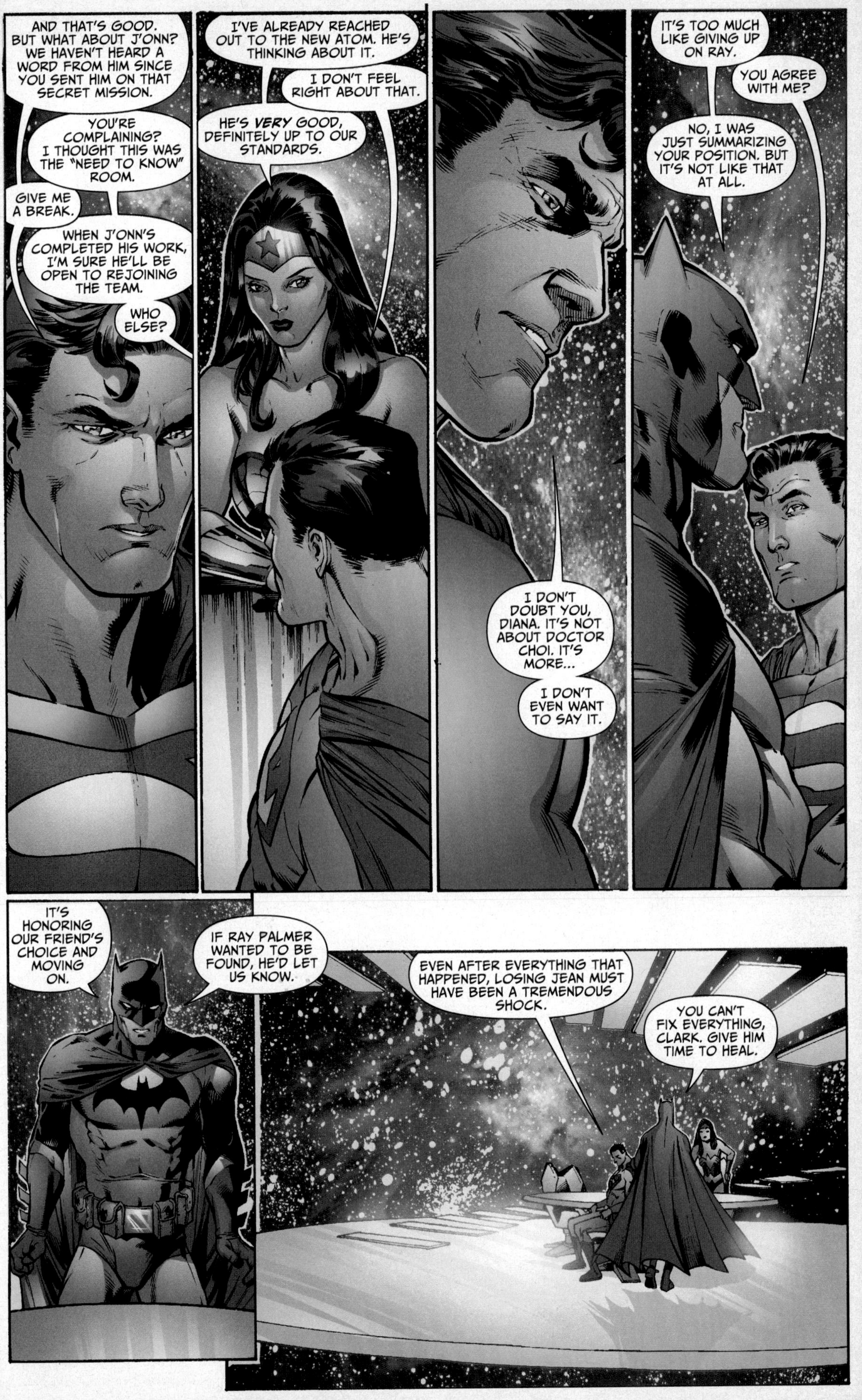
AND THAT'S GOOD. BUT WHAT ABOUT J'ONN? WE HAVEN'T HEARD A WORD FROM HIM SINCE YOU SENT HIM ON THAT SECRET MISSION.
YOU'RE COMPLAINING? I THOUGHT THIS WAS THE "NEED TO KNOW" ROOM.
GIVE ME A BREAK.
WHEN J'ONN'S COMPLETED HIS WORK, I'M SURE HE'LL BE OPEN TO REJOINING THE TEAM.
WHO ELSE?
I'VE ALREADY REACHED OUT TO THE NEW ATOM. HE'S THINKING ABOUT IT.
I DON'T FEEL RIGHT ABOUT THAT.
HE'S VERY GOOD, DEFINITELY UP TO OUR STANDARDS.
I DON'T DOUBT YOU, DIANA. IT'S NOT ABOUT DOCTOR CHOI. IT'S MORE...
I DON'T EVEN WANT TO SAY IT.
IT'S TOO MUCH LIKE GIVING UP ON RAY.
YOU AGREE WITH ME?
NO, I WAS JUST SUMMARIZING YOUR POSITION. BUT IT'S NOT LIKE THAT AT ALL.
IT'S HONORING OUR FRIEND'S CHOICE AND MOVING ON.
IF RAY PALMER WANTED TO BE FOUND, HE'D LET US KNOW.
EVEN AFTER EVERYTHING THAT HAPPENED, LOSING JEAN MUST HAVE BEEN A TREMENDOUS SHOCK.
YOU CAN'T FIX EVERYTHING, CLARK. GIVE HIM TIME TO HEAL.

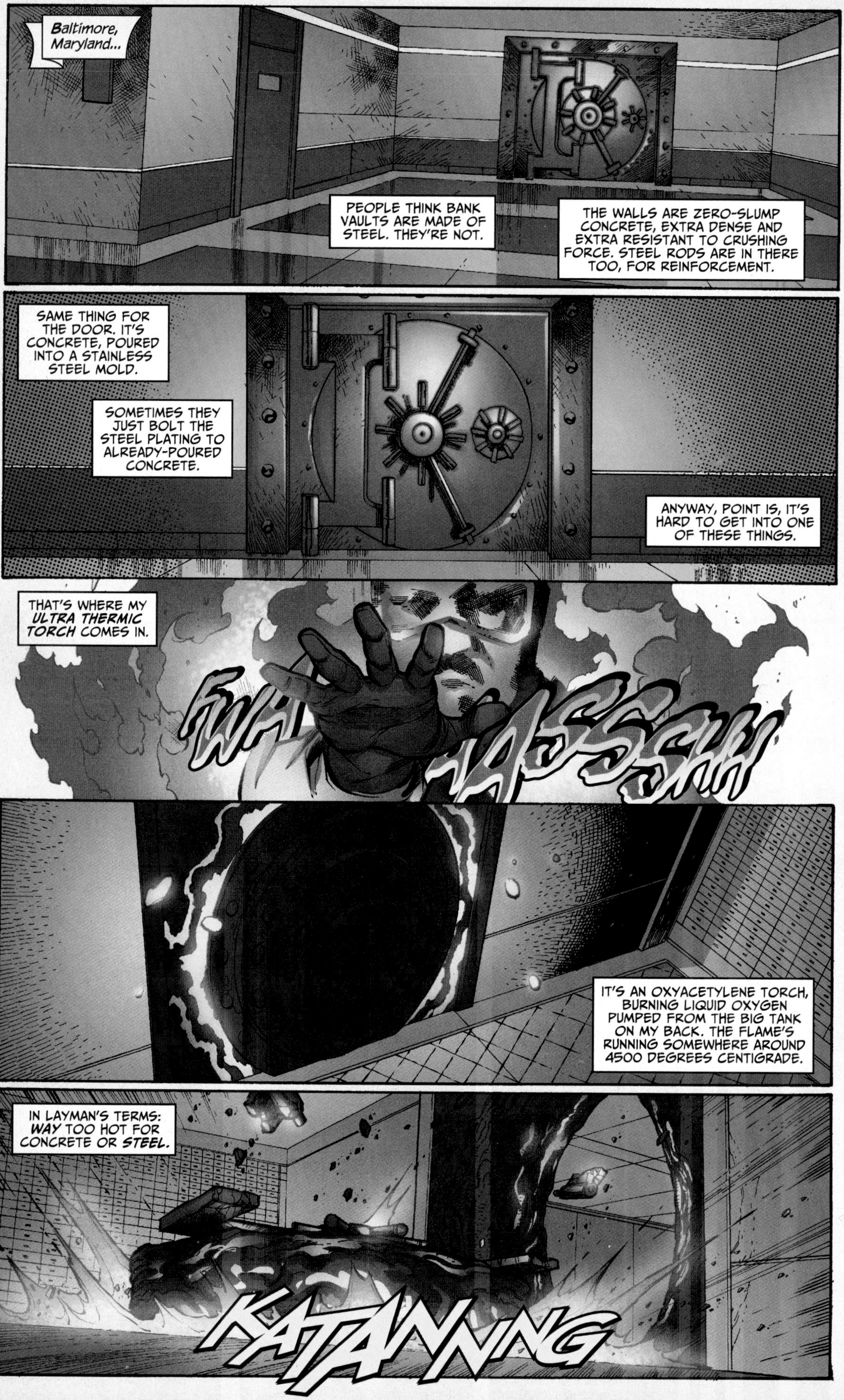
Baltimore, Maryland...
PEOPLE THINK BANK VAULTS ARE MADE OF STEEL. THEY'RE NOT.
THE WALLS ARE ZERO-SLUMP CONCRETE, EXTRA DENSE AND EXTRA RESISTANT TO CRUSHING FORCE. STEEL RODS ARE IN THERE TOO, FOR REINFORCEMENT.
SAME THING FOR THE DOOR. IT'S CONCRETE, POURED INTO A STAINLESS STEEL MOLD.
SOMETIMES THEY JUST BOLT THE STEEL PLATING TO ALREADY-POURED CONCRETE.
ANYWAY, POINT IS, IT'S HARD TO GET INTO ONE OF THESE THINGS.
THAT'S WHERE MY ULTRA THERMIC TORCH COMES IN.
IT'S AN OXYACETYLENE TORCH, BURNING LIQUID OXYGEN PUMPED FROM THE BIG TANK ON MY BACK. THE FLAME'S RUNNING SOMEWHERE AROUND 4500 DEGREES CENTIGRADE.
IN LAYMAN'S TERMS: WAY TOO HOT FOR CONCRETE OR STEEL.
KATANNNG

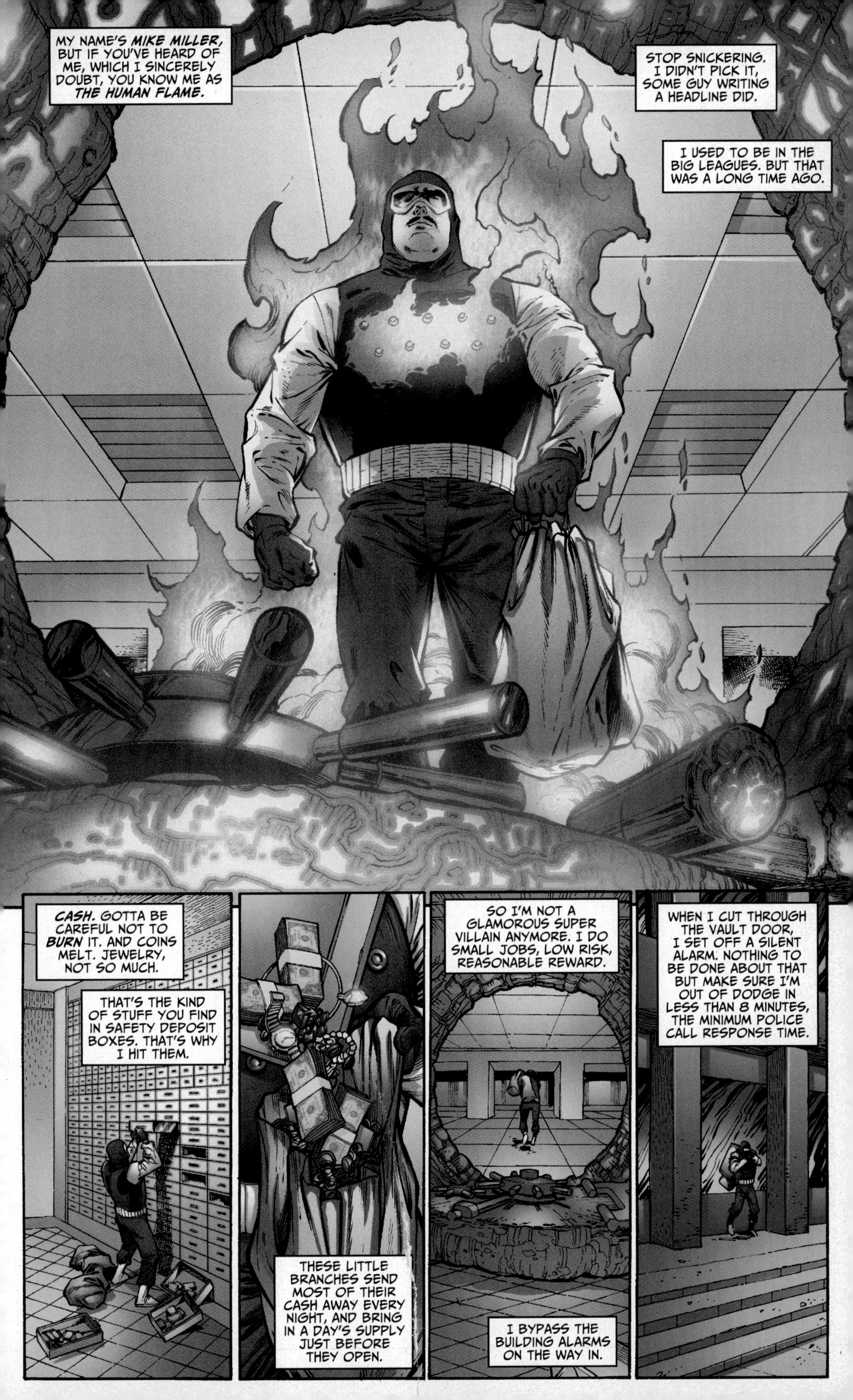
MY NAME'S MIKE MILLER, BUT IF YOU'VE HEARD OF ME, WHICH I SINCERELY DOUBT, YOU KNOW ME AS THE HUMAN FLAME.
STOP SNICKERING. I DIDN'T PICK IT, SOME GUY WRITING A HEADLINE DID.
I USED TO BE IN THE BIG LEAGUES. BUT THAT WAS A LONG TIME AGO.
CASH. GOTTA BE CAREFUL NOT TO BURN IT. AND COINS MELT. JEWELRY, NOT SO MUCH.
THAT'S THE KIND OF STUFF YOU FIND IN SAFETY DEPOSIT BOXES. THAT'S WHY I HIT THEM.
THESE LITTLE BRANCHES SEND MOST OF THEIR CASH AWAY EVERY NIGHT, AND BRING IN A DAY'S SUPPLY JUST BEFORE THEY OPEN.
SO I'M NOT A GLAMOROUS SUPER VILLAIN ANYMORE. I DO SMALL JOBS, LOW RISK, REASONABLE REWARD.
I BYPASS THE BUILDING ALARMS ON THE WAY IN.
WHEN I CUT THROUGH THE VAULT DOOR, I SET OFF A SILENT ALARM. NOTHING TO BE DONE ABOUT THAT BUT MAKE SURE I'M OUT OF DODGE IN LESS THAN 8 MINUTES, THE MINIMUM POLICE CALL RESPONSE TIME.

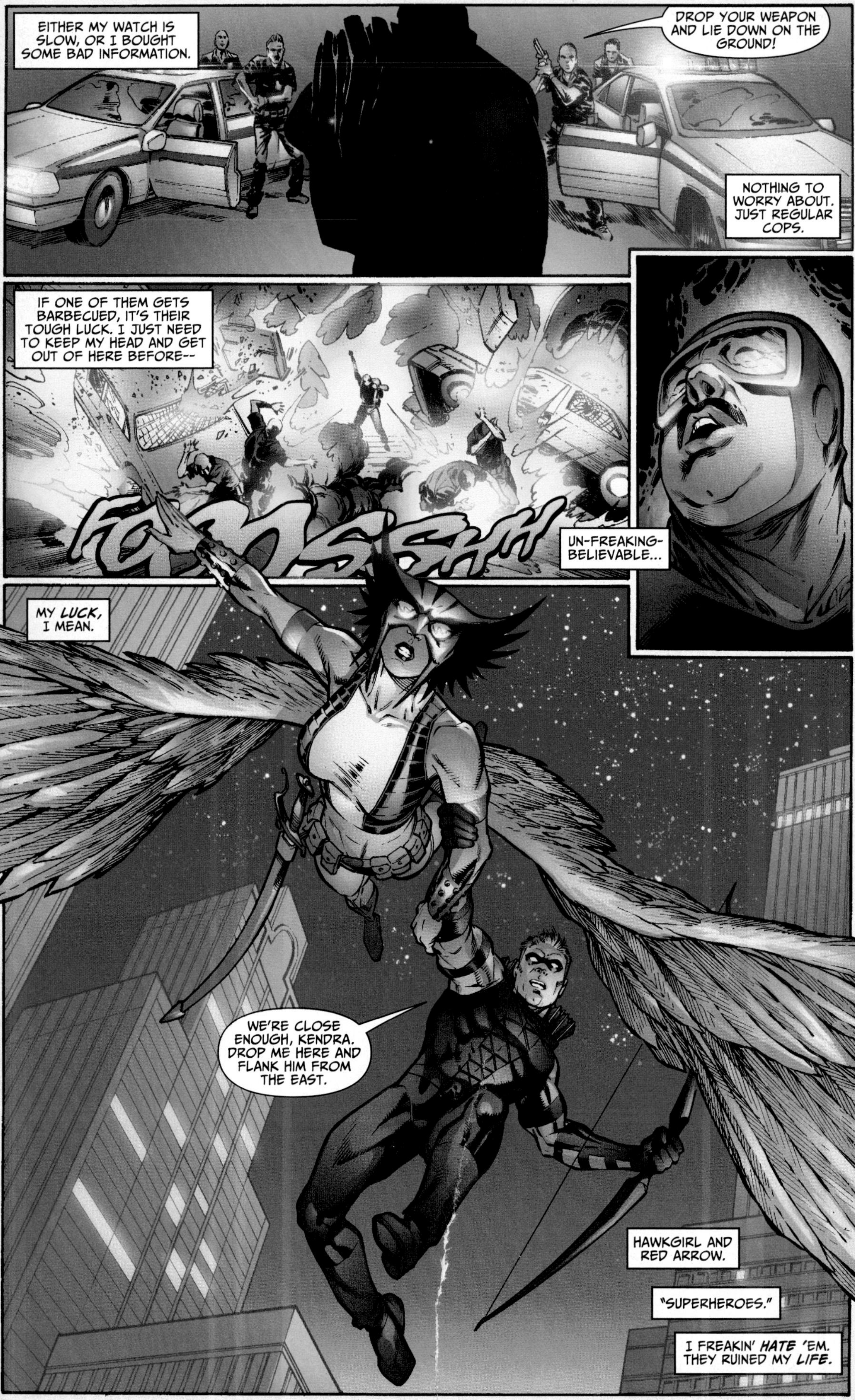
EITHER MY WATCH IS SLOW, OR I BOUGHT SOME BAD INFORMATION.
DROP YOUR WEAPON AND LIE DOWN ON THE GROUND!
NOTHING TO WORRY ABOUT. JUST REGULAR COPS.
IF ONE OF THEM GETS BARBECUED, IT'S THEIR TOUGH LUCK. I JUST NEED TO KEEP MY HEAD AND GET OUT OF HERE BEFORE--
FOOMSSHH
UN-FREAKING-BELIEVABLE...
MY *LUCK*, I MEAN.
WE'RE CLOSE ENOUGH, KENDRA. DROP ME HERE AND FLANK HIM FROM THE EAST.
HAWKGIRL AND RED ARROW.
"SUPERHEROES."
I FREAKIN' *HATE* 'EM. THEY RUINED MY *LIFE*.

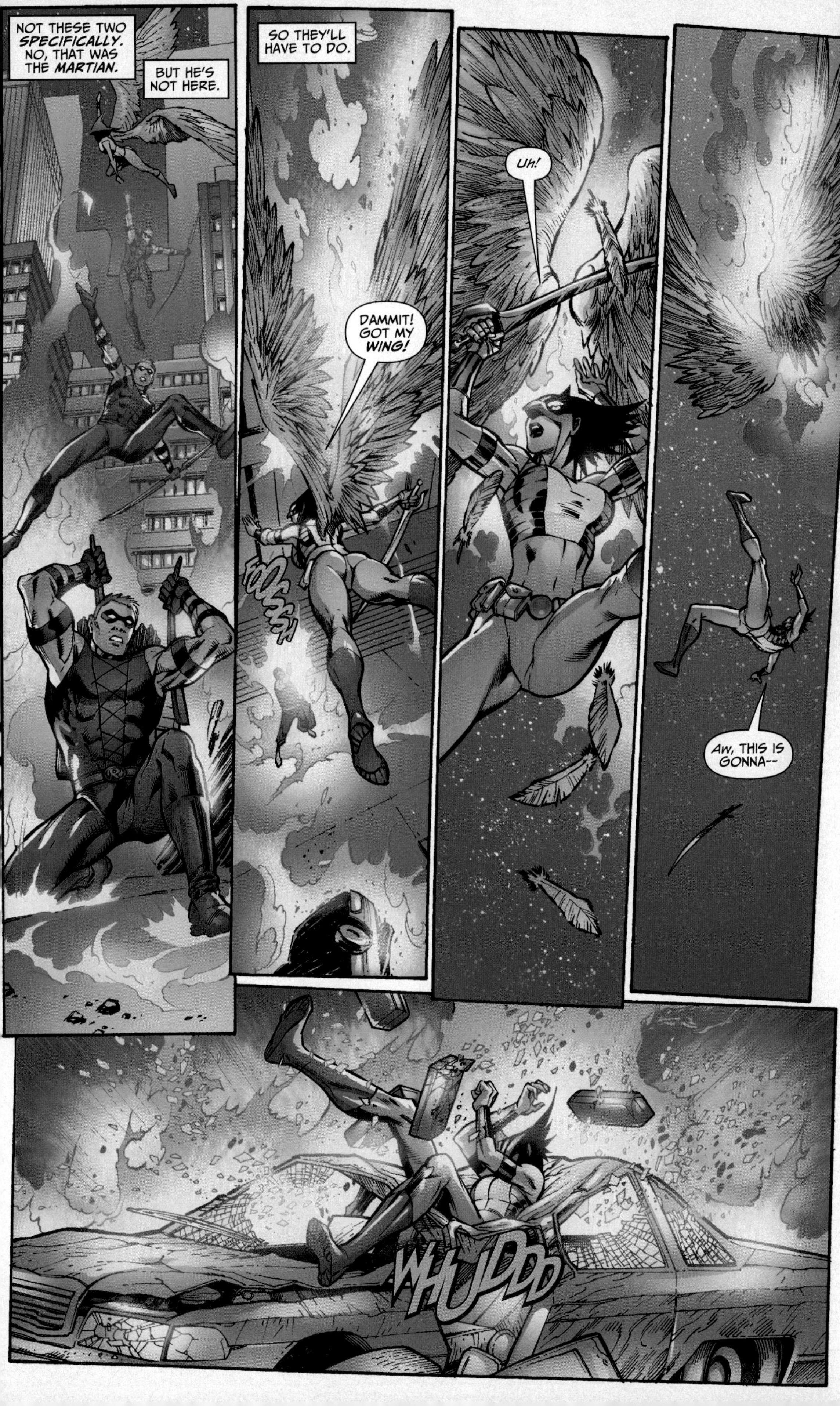
NOT THESE TWO SPECIFICALLY. NO, THAT WAS THE MARTIAN.
BUT HE'S NOT HERE.
SO THEY'LL HAVE TO DO.
DAMMIT! GOT MY WING!
FOOSSSH
Uh!
Aw, THIS IS GONNA--
WHUDDD

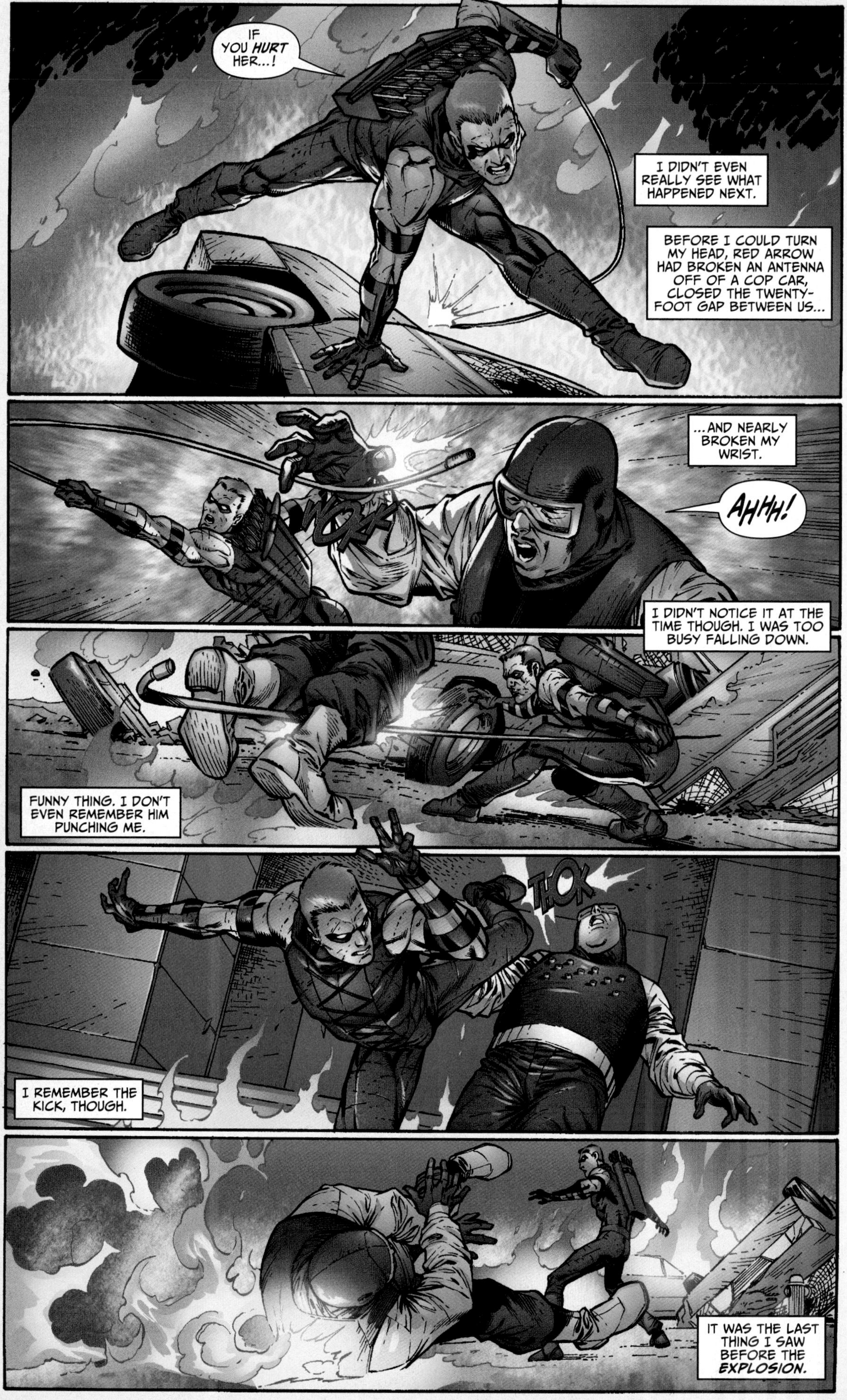
IF YOU HURT HER...!
I DIDN'T EVEN REALLY SEE WHAT HAPPENED NEXT.
BEFORE I COULD TURN MY HEAD, RED ARROW HAD BROKEN AN ANTENNA OFF OF A COP CAR, CLOSED THE TWENTY-FOOT GAP BETWEEN US...
...AND NEARLY BROKEN MY WRIST.
WOK
AHHH!
I DIDN'T NOTICE IT AT THE TIME THOUGH. I WAS TOO BUSY FALLING DOWN.
FUNNY THING. I DON'T EVEN REMEMBER HIM PUNCHING ME.
THOK
I REMEMBER THE KICK, THOUGH.
IT WAS THE LAST THING I SAW BEFORE THE EXPLOSION.

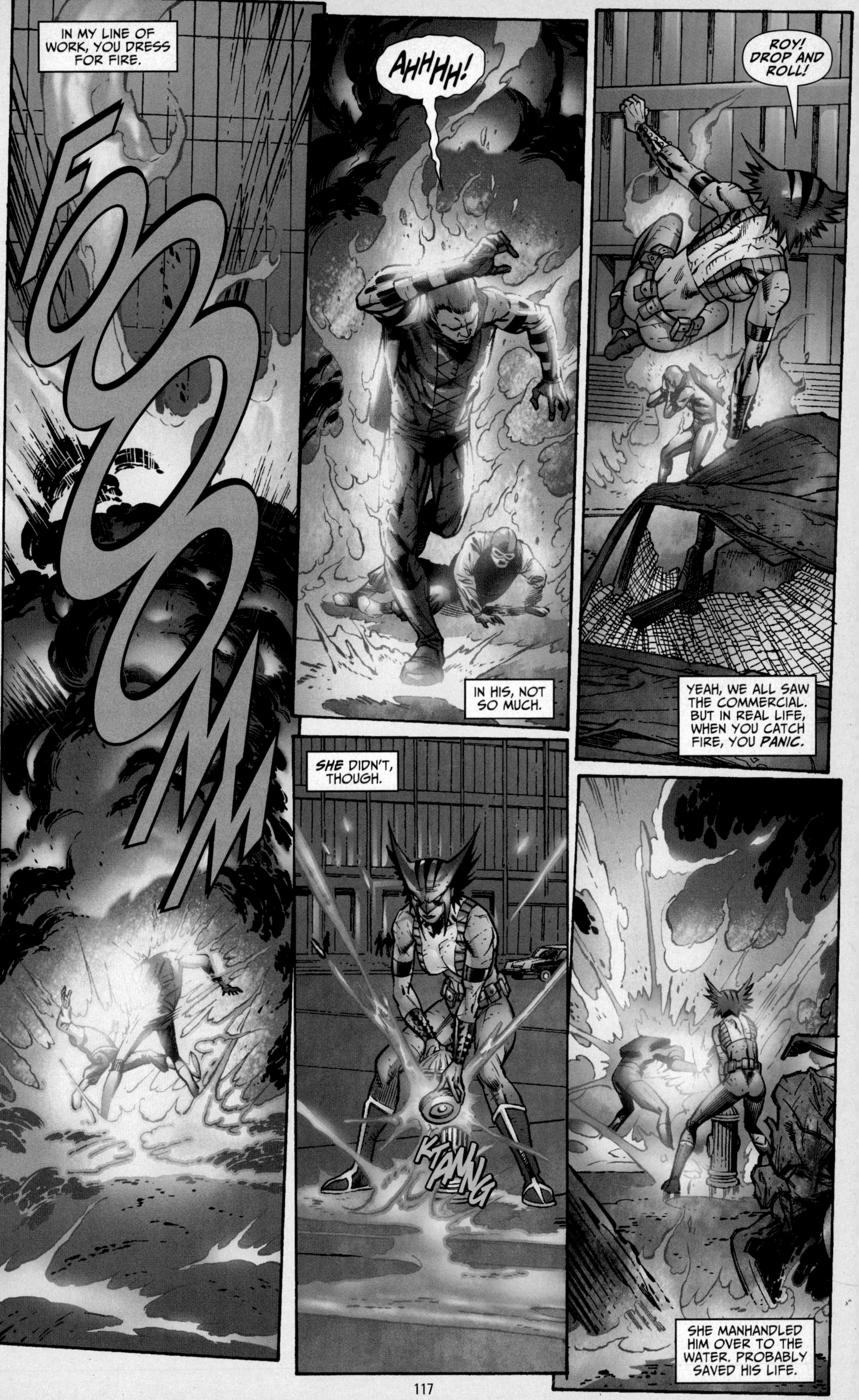
IN MY LINE OF WORK, YOU DRESS FOR FIRE.
FOOOOMM
AHHHH!
IN HIS, NOT SO MUCH.
ROY! DROP AND ROLL!
YEAH, WE ALL SAW THE COMMERCIAL. BUT IN REAL LIFE, WHEN YOU CATCH FIRE, YOU PANIC.
SHE DIDN'T, THOUGH.
KTANNG
SHE MANHANDLED HIM OVER TO THE WATER. PROBABLY SAVED HIS LIFE.

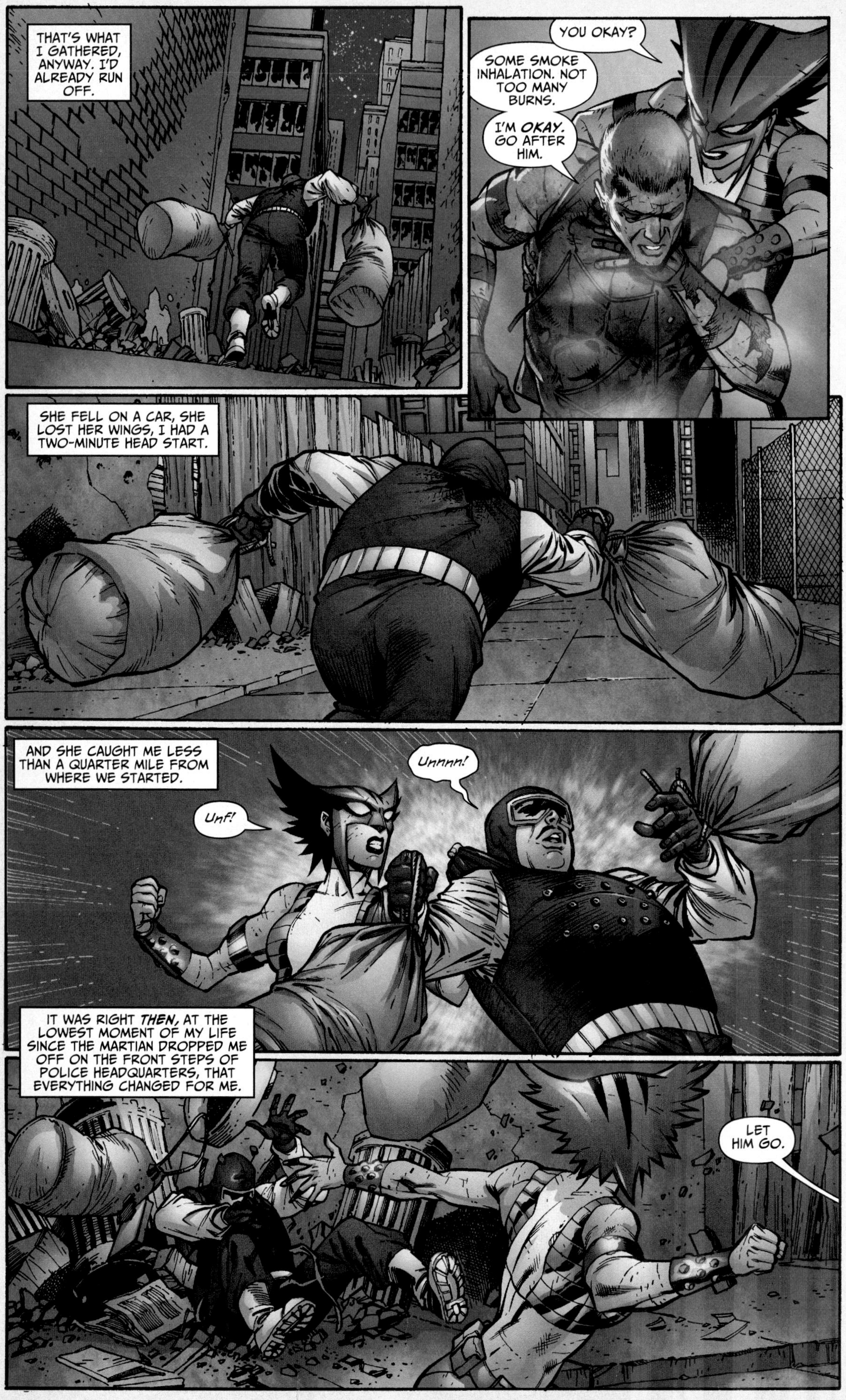

THAT'S WHAT I GATHERED, ANYWAY. I'D ALREADY RUN OFF.
YOU OKAY?
SOME SMOKE INHALATION. NOT TOO MANY BURNS.
I'M OKAY. GO AFTER HIM.
SHE FELL ON A CAR, SHE LOST HER WINGS, I HAD A TWO-MINUTE HEAD START.
AND SHE CAUGHT ME LESS THAN A QUARTER MILE FROM WHERE WE STARTED.
Unnnn!
Unf!
IT WAS RIGHT THEN, AT THE LOWEST MOMENT OF MY LIFE SINCE THE MARTIAN DROPPED ME OFF ON THE FRONT STEPS OF POLICE HEADQUARTERS, THAT EVERYTHING CHANGED FOR ME.
LET HIM GO.

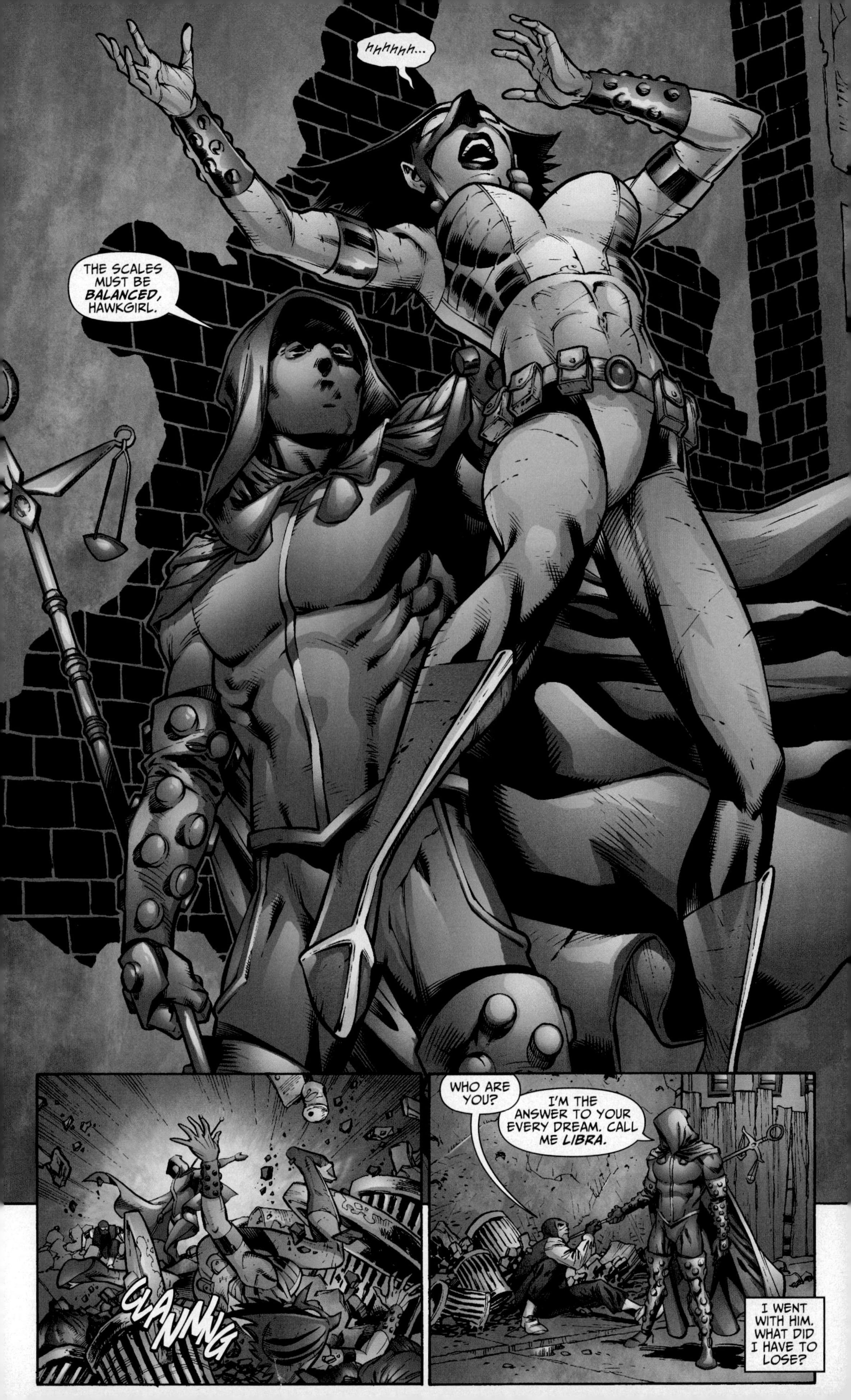
hhhhhh...
THE SCALES MUST BE ***BALANCED,*** HAWKGIRL.
CLANNNG
WHO ARE YOU?
I'M THE ANSWER TO YOUR EVERY DREAM. CALL ME ***LIBRA.***
I WENT WITH HIM. WHAT DID I HAVE TO LOSE?

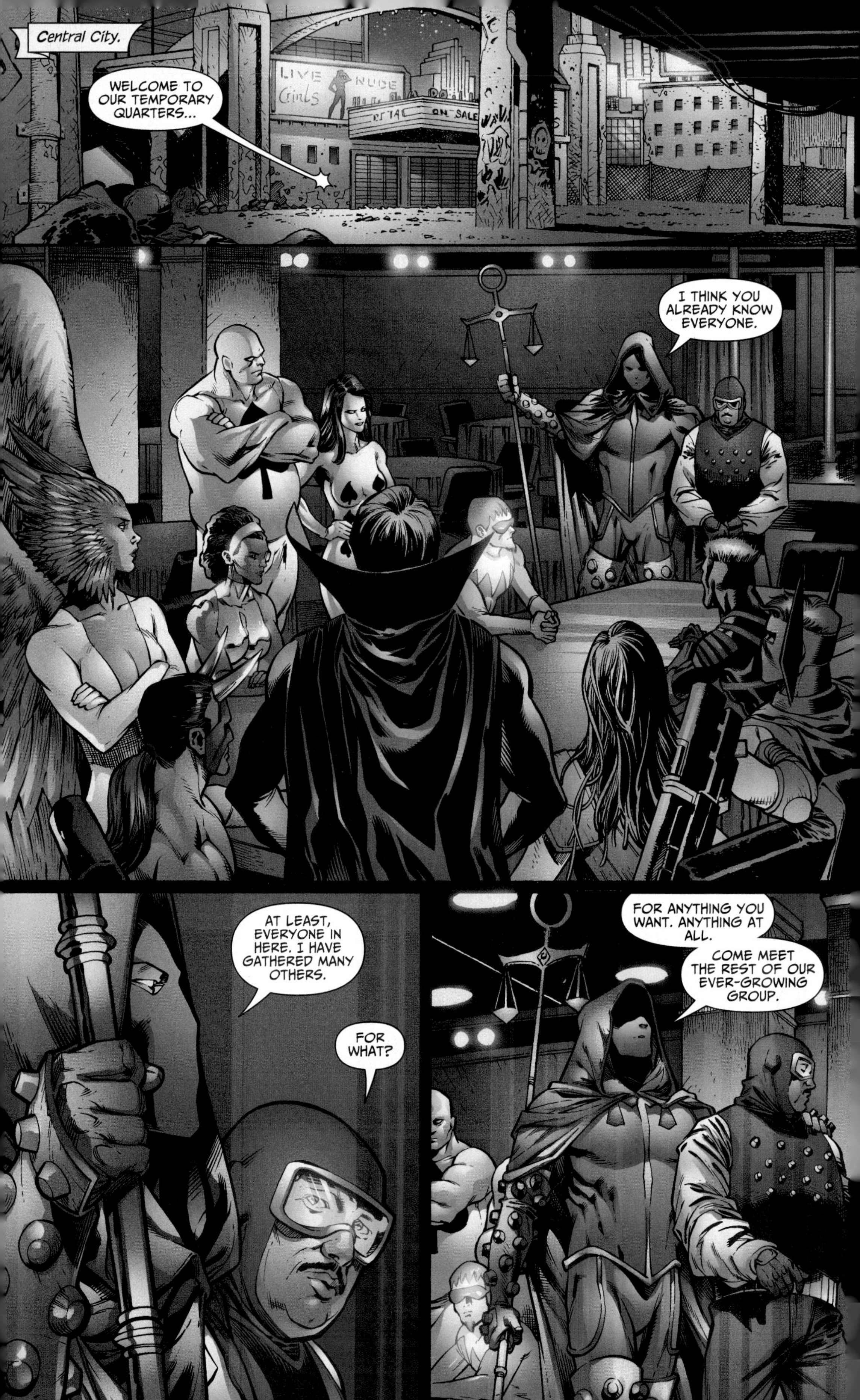

Central City.
WELCOME TO OUR TEMPORARY QUARTERS...
LIVE NUDE Girls
ON SALE
I THINK YOU ALREADY KNOW EVERYONE.
AT LEAST, EVERYONE IN HERE. I HAVE GATHERED MANY OTHERS.
FOR WHAT?
FOR ANYTHING YOU WANT. ANYTHING AT ALL.
COME MEET THE REST OF OUR EVER-GROWING GROUP.

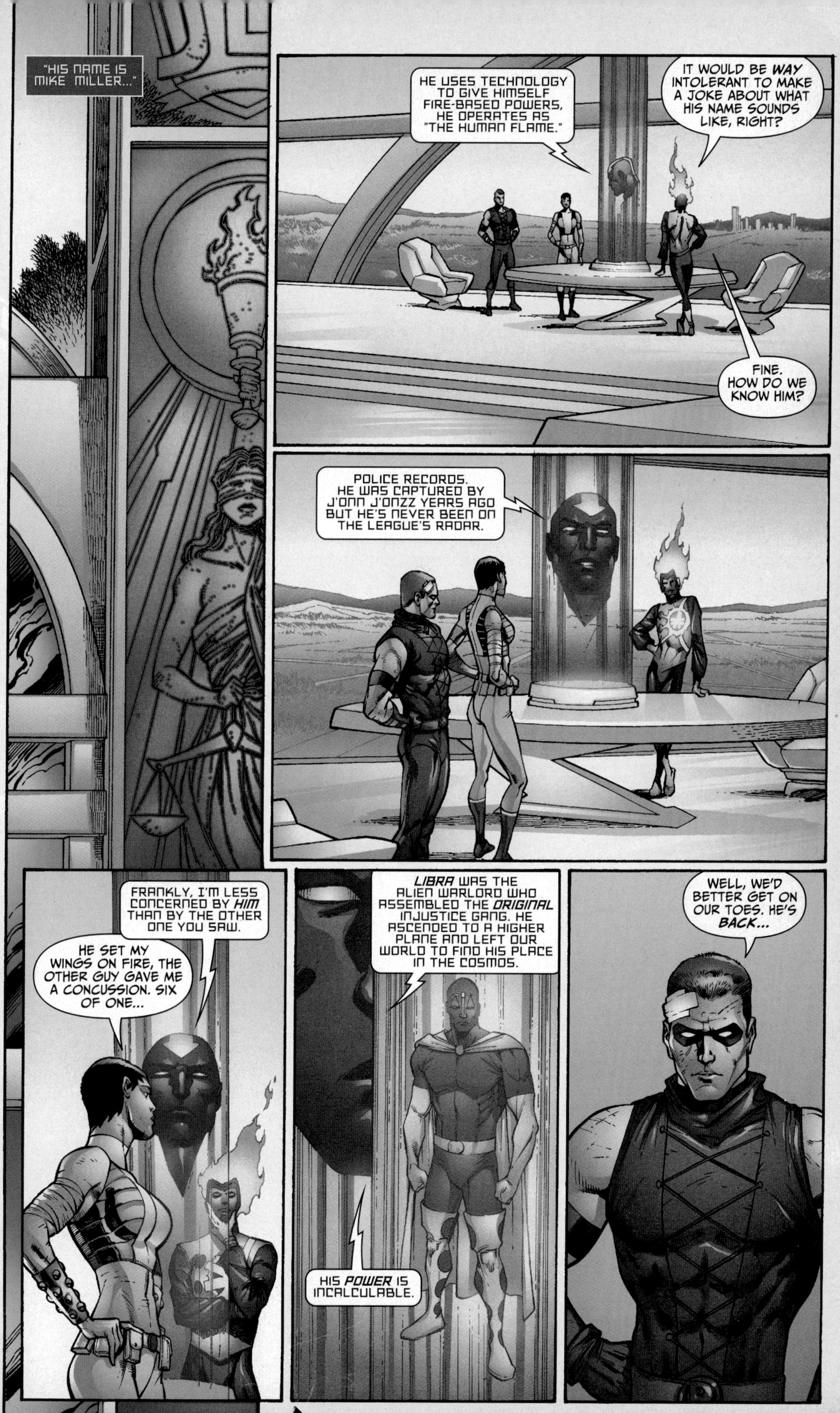
"HIS NAME IS MIKE MILLER..."
HE USES TECHNOLOGY TO GIVE HIMSELF FIRE-BASED POWERS, HE OPERATES AS "THE HUMAN FLAME."
IT WOULD BE WAY INTOLERANT TO MAKE A JOKE ABOUT WHAT HIS NAME SOUNDS LIKE, RIGHT?
FINE. HOW DO WE KNOW HIM?
POLICE RECORDS. HE WAS CAPTURED BY J'ONN J'ONZZ YEARS AGO BUT HE'S NEVER BEEN ON THE LEAGUE'S RADAR.
FRANKLY, I'M LESS CONCERNED BY HIM THAN BY THE OTHER ONE YOU SAW.
HE SET MY WINGS ON FIRE, THE OTHER GUY GAVE ME A CONCUSSION. SIX OF ONE...
LIBRA WAS THE ALIEN WARLORD WHO ASSEMBLED THE ORIGINAL INJUSTICE GANG. HE ASCENDED TO A HIGHER PLANE AND LEFT OUR WORLD TO FIND HIS PLACE IN THE COSMOS.
HIS POWER IS INCALCULABLE.
WELL, WE'D BETTER GET ON OUR TOES. HE'S BACK...

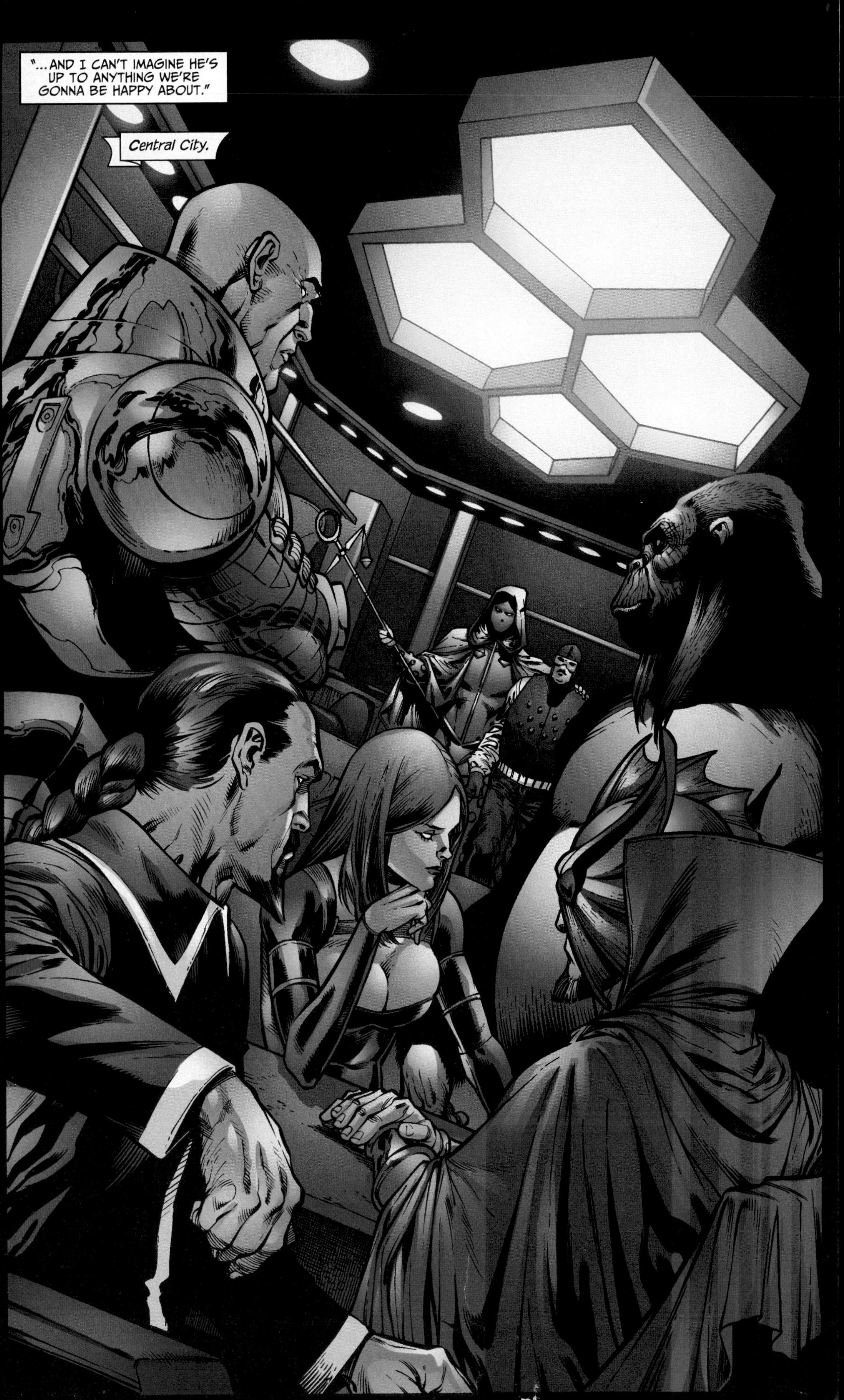
"...AND I CAN'T IMAGINE HE'S UP TO ANYTHING WE'RE GONNA BE HAPPY ABOUT."
Central City.

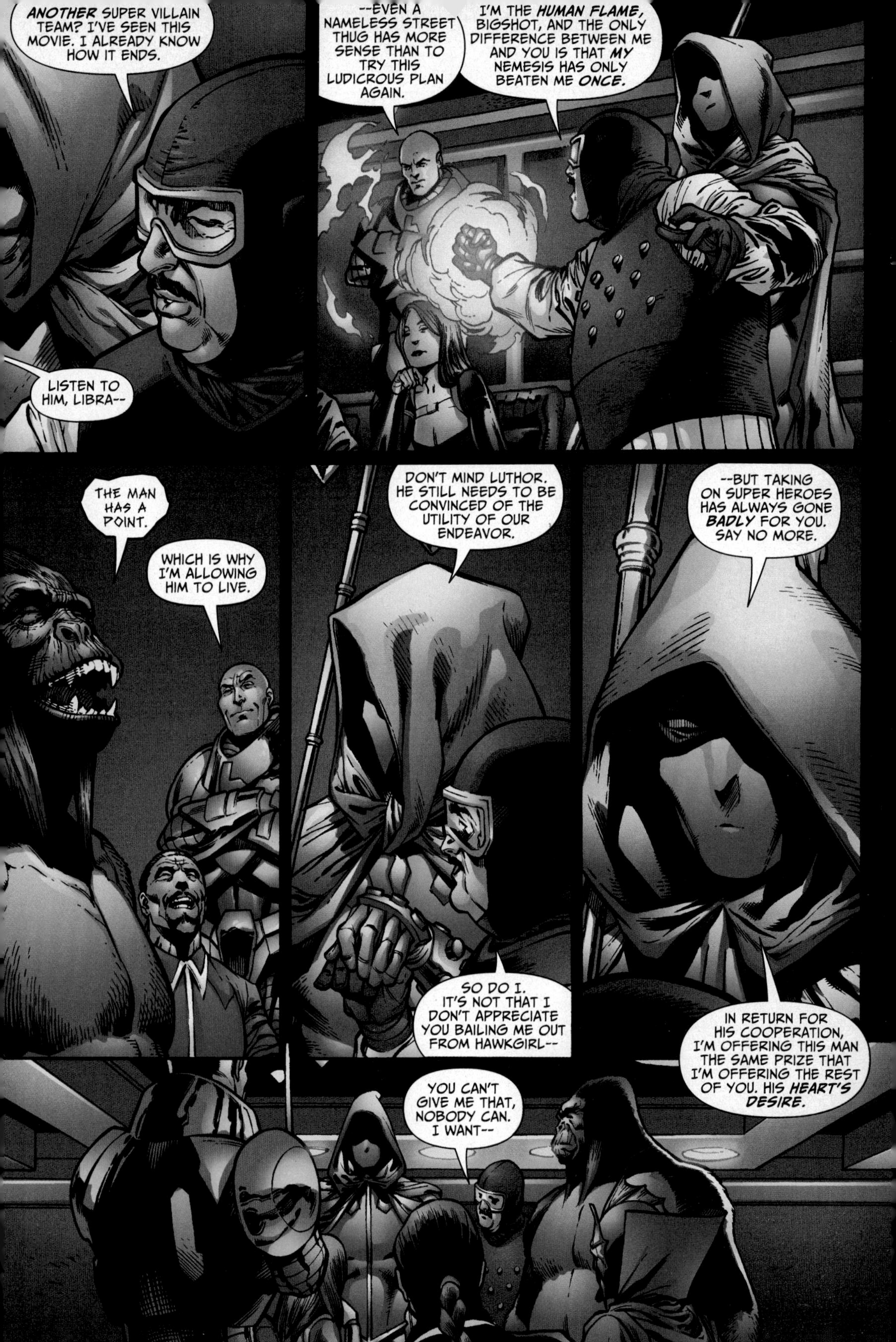
ANOTHER SUPER VILLAIN TEAM? I'VE SEEN THIS MOVIE. I ALREADY KNOW HOW IT ENDS.
LISTEN TO HIM, LIBRA--
--EVEN A NAMELESS STREET THUG HAS MORE SENSE THAN TO TRY THIS LUDICROUS PLAN AGAIN.
I'M THE HUMAN FLAME, BIGSHOT, AND THE ONLY DIFFERENCE BETWEEN ME AND YOU IS THAT MY NEMESIS HAS ONLY BEATEN ME ONCE.
THE MAN HAS A POINT.
WHICH IS WHY I'M ALLOWING HIM TO LIVE.
DON'T MIND LUTHOR. HE STILL NEEDS TO BE CONVINCED OF THE UTILITY OF OUR ENDEAVOR.
SO DO I. IT'S NOT THAT I DON'T APPRECIATE YOU BAILING ME OUT FROM HAWKGIRL--
--BUT TAKING ON SUPER HEROES HAS ALWAYS GONE BADLY FOR YOU. SAY NO MORE.
IN RETURN FOR HIS COOPERATION, I'M OFFERING THIS MAN THE SAME PRIZE THAT I'M OFFERING THE REST OF YOU. HIS HEART'S DESIRE.
YOU CAN'T GIVE ME THAT, NOBODY CAN. I WANT--

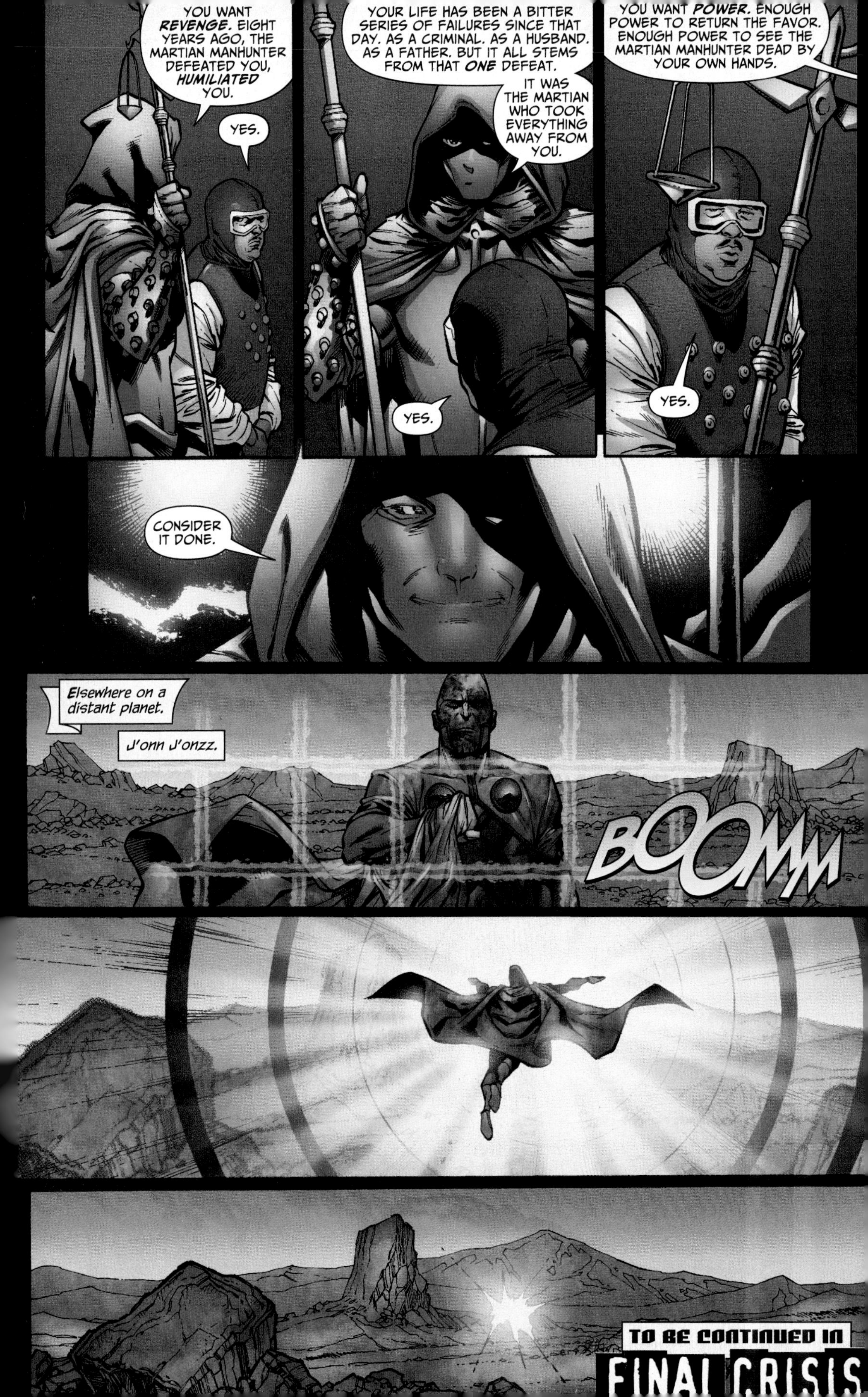
YOU WANT *REVENGE.* EIGHT YEARS AGO, THE MARTIAN MANHUNTER DEFEATED YOU, *HUMILIATED* YOU.
YES.
YOUR LIFE HAS BEEN A BITTER SERIES OF FAILURES SINCE THAT DAY. AS A CRIMINAL. AS A HUSBAND. AS A FATHER. BUT IT ALL STEMS FROM THAT *ONE* DEFEAT.
IT WAS THE MARTIAN WHO TOOK EVERYTHING AWAY FROM YOU.
YES.
YOU WANT *POWER.* ENOUGH POWER TO RETURN THE FAVOR. ENOUGH POWER TO SEE THE MARTIAN MANHUNTER DEAD BY YOUR OWN HANDS.
YES.
CONSIDER IT DONE.
Elsewhere on a distant planet.
J'onn J'onzz.
BOOMM
TO BE CONTINUED IN
FINAL CRISIS

JUSTICE LEAGUE of AMERICA

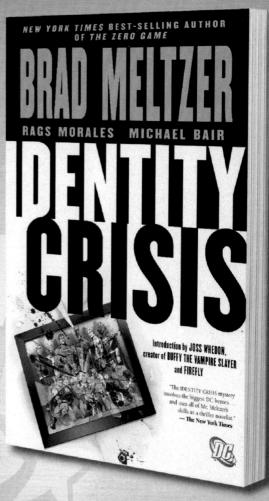